Unconditional
Education

UNCONDITIONAL EDUCATION SUPPORTING SCHOOLS TO SERVE ALL STUDENTS

Robin Detterman
Jenny Ventura
Lihi Rosenthal
with
Ken Berrick

OXFORD
UNIVERSITY PRESS

Oxford University Press is a department of the University of Oxford. It furthers
the University's objective of excellence in research, scholarship, and education
by publishing worldwide. Oxford is a registered trade mark of Oxford University
Press in the UK and certain other countries.

Published in the United States of America by Oxford University Press
198 Madison Avenue, New York, NY 10016, United States of America.

© Oxford University Press 2019

Library of Congress Cataloging-in-Publication Data
Names: Detterman, Robin (Robin L.), author. | Ventura, Jenny (Jenny A.), author. |
Rosenthal, Lihi (Lihi L.), author. | Berrick, Ken, author.
Title: Unconditional education : supporting schools to serve all students /
Robin Detterman, Jenny Ventura, Lihi Rosenthal, and Ken Berrick.
Description: New York, NY : Oxford University Press, [2019] |
Includes bibliographical references and index.
Identifiers: LCCN 2018039361 (print) | LCCN 2018050438 (ebook) |
ISBN 9780190886523 (updf) | ISBN 9780190886530 (epub) |
ISBN 9780190886516 (pbk. : alk. paper)
Subjects: LCSH: Inclusive education. | Mainstreaming in education.
Classification: LCC LC1200 (ebook) | LCC LC1200 .D47 2019 (print) | DDC 371.9/046—dc23
LC record available at https://lccn.loc.gov/2018039361

9 8 7 6 5 4 3 2

Printed by Sheridan Books, Inc., United States of America

To Joseph Starr and all of the students who have served as our teachers.

Contents

Foreword

In picking up this book, you will soon get to know someone I hold dear to my heart, a very real student with a very cheesy pseudonym: Joseph Starr. His story provides a case study throughout the chapters of this book, but before he became that he was my baby, a student at my school. I first met him as a fourth-grader in my third year as principal of a high-needs public charter school in Oakland, California. We were already halfway through the fall semester on Joseph's first day. Within 10 minutes of the bell, he had walked up to a student and punched him in the nose, unprovoked by all accounts, and was in my office. Well, he was likely in the office about 30 minutes after the bell, as it took about 15 minutes to get him out of class, through the school courtyard, down the hallway, and into my office—15 minutes that felt like forever.

A first impression quickly stamped on my mind, and Joseph soon gave me the opportunity for a second and third impression as well—he wasted no time with pretense or the traditional honeymoon stage of a new student. Day 1's episode was followed by him cursing out the teacher on day 2, throwing balls after recess at another on day 3, and other examples of unsafe and outright defiant behaviors on days 4 through, seemingly again, forever. Within the first few months of his joining our school community, we held five team meetings on his behalf, submitted paperwork for special education testing, and sent him home at least 15 times (mostly unofficially, as is too often the case). His teacher banned him from the classroom on numerous occasions and he had exhausted all grace other teachers could offer when he was sent to their rooms through our buddy class system.

I said that I met Joseph Starr in my third year as principal. But the truth is that I had met Joseph Starr countless times before in my career as an urban educator. I entered the field as a classroom teacher determined to disrupt narratives for the most vulnerable of communities. As such, I sought school settings in communities characterized by a high incidence of trauma and various forms of modern-day apartheid; I served student populations that were far below academic proficiency targets, representative of ethnically, linguistically, and socioeconomically disenfranchised groups, and at otherwise "very urban" and high-needs schools. My career—more appropriately, my passion and calling—was about transforming the educational system and teaching to transgress, promoting social justice, and working toward a more equitable education for all, most notably for students like Joseph Starr.

Joseph went by Caron in my third-grade classroom, always hitting people, yelling out in class, and throwing objects when he was angry. His name was Shaneese my first year as an elementary school principal, refusing to go to class and sitting under the table in my office for hours, throwing crying tantrums. He was called Carlos, the kid who would display oversexualized behaviors and leave campus without warning. Sometimes he went by Dialo, stealing things, eloping from campus, and otherwise epitomizing all things defiant. I had met him too many times before and under too many different pseudonyms, but like all of the students I worked with, I just called him "my baby"—so was my desire to see him succeed and, through him, to know that others could too.

I was accustomed to Joseph Starr and babies like him. Over time, I had grown quite proficient at managing these students and their behaviors. But, as I would soon learn, somewhere along the way I excused myself from truly trying to serve them well.

Back then, I would have never said that I was not serving the Joseph Starrs. On the contrary, I would have argued that my team and I were among the small number of educators who could serve them. I patted myself on the back for keeping Joseph Starr in school, maintaining low suspension and expulsion rates for the school as a whole and having relationships that helped him listen to me and a select few others (though really, almost no one else). A quiet arrogance clouded my view as I prided myself for my high tolerance for these students. Surely I was going above and beyond, as Joseph Starr and others like him would have definitely been kicked out of other schools by now.

The truth is, though, that I was good at dealing with the kids. But I had no idea how to serve them well. They were not learning. They were not developing prosocial skills. They were in no way being held in the ways that they needed. They were being managed, kept, and maintained. Our school's systems were not set up to do anything more than that. Our system was not capable of responding to and meeting these babies' needs. The result was hours of my day being spent managing these students and making altogether too many phone calls to families—both those of the high fliers, who were upset that I was calling again, and those of the other students, who wanted me to explain how and why I was prioritizing the "bad kids" over the safety of all of the others.

My staff were frustrated. Morale suffered as my teachers, every one of them equity driven and well intentioned, grew angry that "these kids" were running the school. Tensions developed between teachers and the office team, too, separating those who almost by default built positive relationships with the Joseph Starrs because the office is where they spent most of their school day and the classroom teachers who all too readily sent students to the office in the first place, only to complain that they did not agree with what was being done there for them. Inevitably, when the adults grew tired of blaming one another, they targeted and blamed the kids. Everyone was exhausted.

A funny thing is true of urban education, though. Despite everything that played out, the school was considered remarkably successful by many accounts and was increasingly sought after as a potential model for school turnaround. Like many schools that fit these criteria, we showed significant decrease in suspensions and referrals amid increases in attendance and proficiency. Still, we were far from becoming the school our students deserved. Keeping us otherwise occupied was a small percent of the student population that was dominating a large percent of our time.

In my tenure as an urban educator, I have worked in and with a variety of schools, both traditional public and public charter schools. In most every experience, the organization's motto highlighted equity, the whole child, student-centered approaches, and the notion that all means all. And in every experience, regardless of my role, I found a grave disconnect between the priorities, practices, and philosophies that represented these education institutions on paper and what they demonstrated in practice. As a member of each of these organizations, I am confident that the majority of individuals doing the work indeed sought to put children first, use education as tool for social justice, and right some fundamental wrongs in our society. But the structures and systems were at odds with those ends and, in many cases, prevented us from fully embracing and fulfilling that vision.

I have served in a number of capacities since my first classroom—principal of large urban elementary schools, chief of schools for a K-8 network, professor of urban education and, now assistant superintendent of one of California's largest urban school districts. As such, I have come to understand that the opportunity gaps that exist in education are not solely the result of individuals in the classroom or in the principal's office or even in the illusive central office. It is easy to assume that it's the adults who are failing students facing these kinds of challenges. My experience and my relationships with other school professionals insist that it's not so simple. It is the system that is failing everyone.

Regardless of who owned the failure, my former school team and I were feeling it daily with regard to Joseph Starr. There was only one difference I could point to: we had recently signed on to partner with an esteemed local nonprofit, Seneca Family of Agencies. Seneca's arrival signaled an increased capacity to meet Joseph's needs. Far from being overwhelmed, these staff Seneca staff had experienced success with even more challenging students. Seneca had long operated a series of high-end residential and day treatment programs for youth with significant behavioral needs. For every Joseph Starr I knew, they knew one too, and had followed the trajectory of these students long after they had been removed from public school campuses like mine.

Seneca's approach, unconditional education, insisted that we reimagine an entire school system—seeking to address fundamental flaws in the structural design of schools out of a belief that these flaws in turn caused the school climate issues and funding shortfalls that contributed to the school-to-prison pipeline. As you'll come to read in these pages, Seneca's approach was different from any I had experienced before and, in time, changed the trajectory for Joseph and babies just like him. As the school's principal, many of my days now began with a 10-minute check-in with Joseph Starr's classroom teacher and his wider team every morning, but after that, most of the direct interventions were done in the classroom and not in my office. It was a strange feeling, and my messiah complex took a bit of a beating as I saw others do the work I had prided myself on doing alone before. To distract from the discomfort that realization left me with, I began searching for other things to oc-cupy my time. I spent more time observing instruction in classrooms and designing solutions to parents' concerns. I planned coaching conversations and evaluations before teachers physically showed up in my office! I even made time to read about best practices and plan on how to incorporate them within our existing systems. I worked just as hard as I ever had, but now I was putting my energy into those tasks only I could hold as the principal, rather than making up for a system deficiency by spending my day plugging a hole.

Seneca's unconditional education model brought to the team a host of "experts" and perspectives that truly helped our school identify root causes, differentiate them, and develop comprehensive responses. It also spurred a complete transforma-tion of how we did school and moved us from a reactive to proactive stance. In the schools I work in today, I still recognize the Joseph Starr babies. They are the ones wrapped in the most love, because that's what they need to succeed as individuals, AND because it's what their schools need in order to work for all of their students.

Happy reading!

Enikia Ford Morthel
Assistant Superintendent,
San Francisco Unified School District

Preface

After 30 years of working with children and families in the deep end of the child welfare, mental health, and education system, I have learned a considerable number of hard lessons. The most profound have come from witnessing the harm enacted when these systems refuse to work together. Too often, we see mental health professionals ignore children's educational needs and educators ignore children's mental health needs. Professionals from these realms work in silos as though learning disabilities do not impact a child's emotional life or a child's emotional responses to disruption or trauma somehow do not impact a student's learning. A child's mental health and their intellect are not separate; they are simply and obviously one. And when the systems designed to support a child's well-being insert arbitrary divisions, the result is both frustrating and absurd. For many years, we observed from the periphery as schools failed those students who experienced the most profound behavioral and mental health struggles. We ourselves operated from within the strict confines of the mental health and child welfare systems and, consequently, continued to fail children who were struggling in the general education setting as a result of their emotional experiences.

The journey toward an integrated approach in schools extends all the way back to our founding work in residential treatment for children who had been failed by a series of placements that led them to the most restrictive, institutionalized settings. We witnessed the negative impacts that a lack of systems integration had on the lives of these children. Interventions occurred so late in a child's development that they were primarily undoing the negative impact of neglect, rather than proactively facilitating a child's growth. Acutely aware of our role in the expanding sea of residential placement options and feeling deeply committed to returning youth to their families, Seneca co-authored SB2234, the legislation that resulted in intensive treatment foster care (ITFC). The implementation of ITFC allowed counties to use a "stepped" approach to moving children from residential care to family-like settings. Instead of making the very significant step from residential care to a permanent, family placement, youth could now step from residential care down to highly trained and committed foster parents who could mimic the intensity of the support the youth received in residential care, while offering ongoing assistance to the permanent families the youth would transition to later. Now a foundational component of the foster care continuum in California, ITFC has been seminal in the development of the Continuum of Care Reform legislation (AB403), implemented January 2017.

In the early to mid-1990s, Seneca began to notice yet another concerning trend: the lack of available resources to prevent youth from being placed in residential care. Important questions began to arise that would shape the next step in our evolution: What would it take to prevent a youth from going into residential care to begin with? Or rather, What could we accomplish if we took the funding allocated for residential care and flexibly used that to prevent a child's placement altogether? These questions led Seneca to author an initial bill in 1995 to create a flexible funding source for this purpose, which became SB163. With bipartisan support and approval by the state legislature, Wraparound was born in California. Fully prepared to implement, Seneca was named one of four initial agencies to pilot this new and innovative service.

Once we made the leap to these integrated approaches across child welfare and mental health that favored prevention over failure, we began to wonder how similar methods could be extended to education. We came to realize we could no longer continue to address children's educational needs in a separate and uncoordinated way, and began the journey of partnering with public schools to develop the unconditional education model. And while the approach is designed for students with the most profound and complex needs, what has ultimately transpired is a set of systems and practices better suited to support all children. This book seeks to demonstrate what is possible when we overcome the dictates of siloed funding streams and service systems and begin to intentionally integrate the wisdom and expertise that these systems bring to the table. On the following pages, we share our journey of intervening in ways that connect school climate and school culture, students' emotional well-being, and students' learning and, in doing so, change the very fiber and texture of schools.

Our experience in this work has confirmed time and again that an integrated approach is transformative both for whole systems and for students' individual experiences. The silos within and between mental health, child welfare, and education have profound implications for the children and families they are designated to serve. Through the development of an integrated approach, we can create change for our most marginalized students—those we have traditionally channeled to progressively more segregated settings, resulting in experiences of profound isolation and poor life outcomes. As a counter-response to this unacceptable reality, the unconditional education model presented in this book seeks to help schools create truly inclusive learning environments where all students and families are able to thrive.

Ken Berrick

Founder and President,

Seneca Family of Agencies

Acknowledgments

Unconditional education as it has developed is not ours alone, but has grown out of deep partnerships with a host of educators and leaders we have been honored to learn alongside. Most notably, the work would not have been born without Hae-Sin Thomas and Enikia Ford-Morthel, whose unwavering commitment continues to push the boundaries of what is possible for our most vulnerable children.

The journey from its inception to its current form would not have taken shape without the many principals, district leaders, and staff who have helped to translate these broad ideas into a reality in their schools. Theirs are the learnings and stories you will read throughout this book. In particular, we thank the SOAR Academy Board of Directors, along with leaders Leo Fuchs, Morgan Alconcher, Kevin King, Daniel McLaughlin, Antonio Tapia, Emily Bobel Kilduff, Jenna Stauffer, and Steve Sexton for their trust and collaboration along this journey.

Likewise, Steve Collins and Elizabeth Carmody of West Contra Costa Unified School District, Thomas Graven of San Francisco Unified, Wyeth Jessee of Seattle Public Schools, along with behavioral health leaders Vern Wallace and Helen Kearns of Contra Costa County, Alex Briscoe and Jeff Rackmil of Alameda County, Ken Epstein and Max Rocha of San Francisco, and the entire teams of the El Dorado County Charter SELPA and the Washington State Charter Schools Association have all distinguished themselves as innovative thinkers and valued partners in the implementation of integrated systems. The generous support our foundation partners, in particular the Thomas J. Long and Bill and Melinda Gates Foundations, has been instrumental in fostering validation of the innovations and ideas presented throughout this book.

Our Unconditional Education Advisory Board, which includes Dr. Rob Horner, Dr. John Shindler, Dr. Susan Stone, Gloria Lee, Gina Plate, and Dr. Jose Blackorby, has provided explicit guidance in shaping the direction of this work and the ideas presented here. In addition to Jose, Carl Sumi and Jennifer Yu of SRI have been instrumental in advancing our learning about what works through their evaluation of the practice. Neil Gilbert, Seneca's Board Chair, has been immensely helpful in facilitating the publication process.

The work as it is described must undoubtedly be credited to a remarkable team of Seneca staff that have approached this journey with courage and curiosity, and embody the spirit and values of unconditional education. In this formidable work, we are endlessly inspired by the persistence, hope, and joy they bring to their students, families, and schools each and every day. Several members of our team have made particular contributions to the content of this book. Robyn Ganeles and Moses Santos have provided a foundation for its conceptualization, Sean Murphy has consistently reviewed drafts and helped to shape the formulation of its ideas, and MK Morrison has contributed to its visual design. Through his authorship and careful articulation of *Unconditional Care*, John Sprinson has provided inspiration and been instrumental in grounding both this book and the practice it represents within a strong theoretical framework.

Finally, in the journey of this work we are indebted to our families. Jill, Sierra, Eli, Garth, Ruby, Rezene, Amit, Jonah, Elan, and Uri have provided love and encouragement at every turn. With them we celebrate Odin and Soliana who have come into the world amidst this project and bid farewell in loving memory to Shira Cohen Rosenthal. Together, they have all taught us a great deal about unconditional care.

Unconditional
Education

1 Introduction

Unconditional education (UE) is driven by the belief that public schools are responsible for all students. This may seem a foregone conclusion: national trends in education never seem weary of exclaiming that no child shall be left behind, that all children in this nation will have the opportunity to attain an excellent education or, more recently, that every student shall succeed. The concept of unconditional education is not new. However, public schools have yet to fully deliver on its promise, failing to build truly inclusive systems of care capable of serving students with the most exceptional needs.

The UE model, as presented in this book, serves as an organizing framework for education leaders who are looking to reshape their schools in order to better meet the broad range of needs of their students, families, and staff. This book may appear to focus only on students with the most exceptional needs. That focus, however, is not limited. UE is founded on the belief that improving the educational experience of our most vulnerable children, in the end, benefits all children. Its aim is to create learning environments where students receive the support they need when they need it, not only after they have reached a certain, designated threshold of failure. UE seeks to build truly engaging and exhaustively positive environments where all students, their families, and the school's staff feel safe and deeply connected to the community, laying the foundation necessary for academic success.

This is a book about transformational change in schools. Such change, by its very definition, requires a fundamental shift in the way schools do business. To be even more clear: this is a book that seeks to disrupt the well-established ways in which schools operate, from the daily experiences of students, families, and staff to the organizing structures that influence them, such as schedules, discipline practices, working conditions, service delivery, and physical space. This is a book about how to create actual changes within actual schools. Not surprisingly, the book offers no magic answers or quick fixes but aims to serve as a case study of what is possible in the noble but arduous task of transforming public education.

This is a book for school teams and leaders, including stakeholders in both mental health and education—school social workers, teachers, school administrators, and district-level leaders. These are the professionals whose collaborative efforts can create unconditional educational opportunity for students facing some of the most extraordinary challenges to academic achievement. For such readers, we hope to provide both a theoretical foundation as well as a concrete conceptualization for a system of responsive school supports. This book aims to inspire experienced as well as future professionals who serve as advocates for students like our very own Joseph Starr.

MEET JOSEPH STARR

Joseph Starr's story is a test of the principles outlined in this book and the extent of one school's commitment to youth and families. The UE story is, in many ways, the story of Joseph Starr and the myriad students he represents.

We met Joseph Starr[1] at the start of Seneca's partnership with our first UE school—a large, public elementary school in Oakland, California, which we will call Ford Elementary. Located in a diverse neighborhood highly impacted by poverty and community violence, the school contained its fair share of students struggling both academically and behaviorally. Still, it stood bright and lively, a beacon within the community. Every afternoon, its halls transformed into a parking lot for strollers as family members, young and old, filed in to collect their children. Families were likely to stick around to share a tray of home-cooked food with others, stop by the office to say hello to the charismatic principal, check out the community garden, or watch as their children climbed over the huge play structure out back.

Joseph was a new student at school, having enrolled mid-year. He was a handsome and charming fourth-grader; a child whose eyes lit up when he smiled and that revealed, in more serious moments, a wisdom beyond his years. Joseph shone in his first few days at school, captivating students with his humor, energy, and lack of inhibition. He also struggled from very early on—from a suspension for forwardly touching a female student on her inner thigh, to an incident in which he injured a staff member who was trying to put away supplies from recess, including the ball that Joseph was playing with, alone on the playground, long after his classmates had returned to their studies.

The pieces soon began to fall into place. Although his mother had not shared this information with the school upon his enrollment, we learned that Joseph had previously qualified for special education as a student with an emotional disability. We learned that he had been retained in a previous grade, suspended numerous times, and had been considered for expulsion more than once. We learned that Joseph had been enrolled in an intensive specialized classroom for students with challenging behaviors. And, we learned that the team there had recommended a placement in an even more restrictive setting, a plan his mother had rejected. Instead, she chose to enroll him at the family's neighborhood school, Ford Elementary.

The specialized school to which Joseph was recommended, but ultimately didn't attend, was one of the most restrictive settings available for students in special education. This placement was located on a segregated school campus, referred to

---

[1] All names used throughout this book are pseudonyms.

in California as a non-public school (NPS). NPSs offer highly structured learning environments for students whose social emotional needs significantly hinder their ability to access educational content in a general school setting. Such schools are richly staffed with special education teachers whose work is supported by a large number of behavioral interventionists and mental health clinicians.

Joseph's arrival at Ford Elementary coincided with the school's shift to a new approach for addressing the needs of students: a UE model committed to the idea that all students deserve to experience success in their community school. UE operates on the belief that students with disabilities are best served alongside their non-disabled peers. Joseph's mother's desire for him to be served at his local school felt like an obvious point of alignment. However, it soon became clear that engaging her would be no easy feat. Early attempts by school staff to gather more information were largely unsuccessful. The school's halls—inviting to so many families—were not so for Joseph's mother. When school staff attempted to connect with her in the hallways in the afternoons, she began to wait for Joseph outside in her car, the engine running. When staff tried to meet her outside, she stopped coming onto the block at all, parking instead at a local community center and instructing Joseph to meet her there.

Joseph's behavioral problems continued to escalate in those early weeks. School staff became agitated. His classroom teacher, an exceptional educator, worried that she did not have the training she needed to support him, let alone keep her 25 other students safe. Even the special educator, who had extensive experience working with students with emotional and behavioral disabilities, was mystified. In 3 weeks of one-on-one work, Joseph had refused to commit even a single sentence to paper. Nothing like this had ever happened to this teacher, who was an undisputed favorite among the school's students.

Murmurs around campus questioned the sanity of the school's new commitment to "this unconditional education business." It sounded great in theory—the idea that schools belonged to their students, *all of them*, and that not continuing to welcome a child, *any child*, was simply not an option. But in practice? Did the school have the resources needed to make this a reality? Behind closed doors, everyone involved, from the principal to the implementers of UE, started to ask the same questions.

The team always ended up exactly where it began. Joseph's mother would not agree to a more restrictive special education setting; if they were to insist, she would most likely pull Joseph again and place him at yet another public school. If the pattern of rejection and failure that we believed fueled his behavioral outbursts was going to change, it had to be here, at this school, and soon. So, despite waking up in the morning to see the image of Joseph's face swimming in her cereal bowl and going to bed at night with his troubles still on her mind, the school's principal stood strong in messaging to staff that "All means All." She was adamant that there could be no exception.

And so it happened that 10-year-old Joseph Starr brought a school community together to design an entirely new and individualized program within the mainstream environment. The school's newly inaugurated coordination of services team (COST), a UE model staple, met to examine the data they had collected on Joseph and came up with a truly comprehensive plan. A counselor with over 20 years of mental health experience was assigned to be Joseph's behavior coach and, initially, spent every moment of the school day with Joseph to assess his needs and design interventions. Gradually, the counselor shifted his energies toward training other staff members to implement the interventions now proven successful. A therapist began seeing Joseph for weekly therapy sessions, once individually and once with the behavior coach, with an open invitation to his parents to attend, should they so wish.

Until the family felt comfortable approaching the school and joining sessions, Joseph's new behavior coach initiated a connection with his mother by walking Joseph to the community center where she picked him up in order to avoid the school. It took several days before they even exchanged a verbal hello. It would have been easy to see Joseph's parents as difficult and to blame them for the challenges Joseph and his teachers faced. Instead, the team stretched themselves to understand the parents' mistrust as a legitimate result of harmful past experiences with the education system.

Meanwhile, the therapist provided the classroom teacher with weekly coaching sessions to support her in understanding Joseph's behaviors and in processing her own reactions to them. The special educator continued to forge a relationship with Joseph, who soon wrote more sentences in ten minutes than in all of those notorious first few weeks. She also designed a boys' leadership group, in which fourth- and fifth-grade boys, including Joseph, learned and practiced new games together, then taught these to kindergarten students during recess. The school principal instituted a daily chat with Joseph, where he came to her office to check in, and where she discovered his passion for rap music and any other art form that put him in front of a microphone, a discovery she soon parlayed into a distinguished role at the school's assemblies.

There were ups and there were downs, but by the spring awards ceremony—which Joseph emceed with his mother in the front row—he received awards for attendance, academic improvement, and citizenship. As the school year drew to a close, the fifth-grade teaching team began expressing interest in having Joseph in their classes the following year. They had, after all, spent most of the year hearing his fourth-grade teacher gush about her conferences with the therapist and the supportive role the behavior coach played in her classroom. His mother not only began driving him to the school again but invited the behavior coach and therapist in to see him over the summer break.

Oversimplified as it is in the telling Joseph's story is inspiring. Supporting students like Joseph is unavoidably messy and exhausting (as will be addressed in more depth in coming chapters), but it highlights a foundational tenet of UE—to protect the rights of those students who are most readily disenfranchised by the existing education system. Many efforts at school transformation aimed at building success for all have been heralded triumphant when they achieve success for some, many, or most. Without diminishing the gains achieved through these reforms, it is vital that we recognize that they are not enough. In resource-strapped environments, it is only by first considering the needs of our most vulnerable students that we will be prompted to build a system of education that is effective for all.

Joseph represents the hundreds of children and youth who have served as our teachers. The tough lesson they have taught us is that our education system is, in fact, failing in its promise to support *all* students' success. UE was founded on the belief that when youth find themselves struggling to the extent that Joseph struggled, the failure lies not in the youth but, rather, within the very systems that were designed to serve them. Those lessons have influenced our agency's partnership with the public education system and have led us—a group of social workers and educators—to write a book about sweeping educational reform.

MEET SENECA FAMILY OF AGENCIES

Seneca was founded in 1985, based on the belief that all youth are capable of success when their unique needs and experiences are responded to. By the mid-1980s, Oakland, California, was a notoriously difficult place for many of its young people. Seneca's founder was working at a local residential facility for youth whose severe emotional and behavioral challenges had resulted in removal from their family or foster homes. When this facility contemplated shutting its doors in response to increasingly disruptive behaviors, he banded together with a small group of like-minded individuals to develop a new option. Rather than entertain the idea that these youth would experience yet another displacement that would keep them further isolated from their families, peers, and communities, the group established a small residential program into which the youth were welcomed regardless of the behaviors that had made their previous placement untenable.

Recognizing the failure of public systems to provide adequately for the needs of young people who have experienced profound trauma and loss, Seneca's founders made a commitment that many of them had never experienced before: unconditional care. Unconditional care is the promise that a child would never be rejected or expelled from a Seneca program for the behaviors that brought them there. This founding commitment of unconditional care—persisting to support a young person's' success even when doing so was immensely difficult—drove the agency's early efforts and stands at the core of our work to this day.

Two things followed. First, disruptive behaviors, including the extreme violence and dangerous self-injury that Seneca's founders had experienced in youth with similar histories of trauma, did not magically go away. The second result was less expected. In a program built around unconditional care, where the option to reject a young person was forever off the table, the creativity of adults blossomed. It was not always easy, and it was not always fast. But behaviors did begin to change as the youth realized that, even through their hardest moments, the adults in their lives would stand by them, with boundless new tools or strategies to help them heal and thrive.

These early successes soon gave way to an unpleasant reality: no matter how much progress young people made while in Seneca's care, the agency was not able to assure similar success once they left the program. Providing support at a single point in the trajectory of their lives and that of their families simply proved insufficient. That sobering realization prompted the founding staff to envision seamless services delivered across time and place, so that young people and their families could receive ongoing support regardless of fluctuations in their level of need. This continuum of care—where a broad range of cross-sector services is made available in different settings at all levels of need—made transition out of higher-level services easier while simultaneously preventing the future need for those services. From this foundation, Seneca worked to partner with the mental health, education, social welfare, and juvenile justice systems to provide a continuum of community- and school-based services that challenge the existing narrative of what is possible for vulnerable youth.

Over the years, Seneca has tested and refined the agency's core beliefs about how to intervene with youth and families in need. These beliefs have since been developed into the highly articulated treatment approach presented in Sprinson and Berrick's (2010) *Unconditional Care: Relationship-Based Behavioral Intervention for Vulnerable Children and Families*. As a treatment model, unconditional care integrates attachment, learning, and systems theories to provide tools to assess and address youths' complex relational, behavioral, and ecological needs. What is unique about the approach is that it rests not only on operationalizing these three theories but also on capitalizing on their intersection. Unconditional care conveys an implicit set of beliefs that youth whose experiences are shaped by chronic stress and trauma are capable of healing when they (1) experience secure relationships that promote a sense of safety and belonging; (2) are systematically taught new skills and mindsets; and (3) are surrounded by a strong network of supports embedded in their natural environments.

FROM UNCONDITIONAL CARE TO UNCONDITIONAL EDUCATION

Students like Joseph Starr inspired the translation of the tenets of unconditional care into unconditional education—a public school model that has the potential to provide students with the supports they need within their community school. The desire to prevent a trajectory toward more restrictive and institutional education placements actually stems from Seneca's experience running those very types of programs. The telling of Joseph Starr's story glossed over the fact that the NPS that Joseph was recommended for was, in fact, a school run by Seneca. Within this intensive mental health setting Seneca had spent decades applying the principles of unconditional care.

The UE model was not created because NPSs are unsuccessful; on the contrary, they work exceptionally well. Once students arrive at Seneca's NPSs many flourish: schools are well organized; routines are structured; expectations are clear and consistent; staff are well trained in trauma-informed practices and in Seneca's unconditional care model. But the supports and strategies developed in the NPS setting can be enacted much sooner in students' school trajectories, well before they are forced to internalize a sense of personal failure and endure the stigma that accompanies it. Put simply, the things that work for vulnerable children in specialized settings work for vulnerable children in generalized ones too, and far more efficiently.

Our nation's failure to create inclusive and restorative school communities particularly affects poor students of color. A substantial body of research indicates that students from culturally and linguistically diverse backgrounds experience higher rates of suspensions, expulsions, and office disciplinary referrals, and that these students are more likely to be referred to special education and the criminal justice system (Simmons-Reed & Cartledge, 2014). With this in mind, it is important to acknowledge the fact that Joseph Starr's mother had good reason to reject sending her child to an NPS. Beyond being a student diagnosed with a disability, Joseph was an African American boy. Joseph's mother likely understood an unspoken reality: students who looked like her son are being pushed out of schools at alarming rates. The trajectory is uncomfortably common: boys of color experience disproportionate rates of disciplinary action for subjective offenses such as "disrespect" and "defiance" and disproportionate diagnosis for two of the most subjective special education categories, "emotional disturbances" and "specific learning disabilities" (Noltemeyer & McLoughlin, 2012). These experiences often result in either a disciplinary hearing or a placement in an NPS, both of which signal the beginning of a pipeline that quite often leads to prison (Osher, Woodruff, & Sims, 2002).

Students placed in NPS settings, while small in number, are an incredibly diverse group of young people, with unique life circumstances, mental health challenges, and academic needs. Yet, the common denominator for these students is a history of attending schools unequipped to meet their highly individualized needs. Indeed, prior to ever being referred to an NPS, a young person must first qualify for special education, which in and of itself indicates that they have struggled in school for some time. Those students whose eligibility for special education includes an emotional disability will most likely have received counseling support and individualized instruction within their public, general education setting. If they continue to struggle academically and behaviorally, a specialized classroom within a public school—often located on a different campus than the one they currently attend—may be recommended. Only if the student continues to struggle intensely within this structured setting, as was the case with Joseph Starr, will a placement like a Seneca NPS be considered.

The aim of unconditional education is to transfer the principles and practices of unconditional care to the public school setting in order to prevent this pattern of placement into more and more restrictive school settings. This preventative approach is becoming more critical as schools find themselves serving an increasing number of students who experience a variety of barriers to learning. While the overall intensity of Joseph Starr's struggles would be considered extraordinary, his story is not unusual. Schools across the nation are looking for ways to better equip themselves to meet the multifaceted needs of their students, needs that often stem from the nuanced interplay of poverty, trauma, and academic struggles.

Across the nation, 20% of school-aged children have a diagnosable mental health condition, yet only a fraction of them receive sufficient mental health services (Merikangas et al., 2010; Power, Eiraldi, Clarke, Mazzuca, & Krain, 2005). For those students coming from low-income backgrounds, of which 85% are Black or Latino, the prevalence of mental health challenges is even greater (Orfield, Kucsera, & Siegal-Hawly, 2012). Children raised in poverty experience greater exposure to risk factors, since they are more likely to live in communities affected by compounding and intersecting challenges such as community and domestic violence, lack of resources, substance abuse, police brutality, multigenerational incarceration, high unemployment, and instability due to homelessness and/or immigration status (American Psychological Association, 2008; Stevens, 2013). Childhood exposure to traumatic events or situations, often measured through the presence of adverse childhood experiences (ACEs), is directly correlated with poor school outcomes (Blodgett & Harrington, 2012). Students with high ACE scores face overwhelming obstacles when they enter the classroom, falling behind in schools that fail to meet their specialized needs while finding themselves disproportionately subjected to exclusionary practices.

These alarming trends influence disparities in achievement for some of our most vulnerable student groups. UE seeks to disrupt the cycle of poor achievement and exclusion experienced by students like Joseph Starr by implementing the tenets of unconditional care to transform schools into communities in which all students are welcomed and can thrive.

INTRODUCING UNCONDITIONAL EDUCATION

UE is a holistic, multi-tiered system of supports (MTSS) that pairs evidence-based academic, behavioral, and social-emotional interventions with an intentional focus on overall culture and climate. The model promotes systematic coordination and integration of general education, special education, and mental health funding and services. This strategic collaboration between traditionally siloed systems promotes efficient allocation of available resources so that gaps in service are identified and redundancies eliminated. The emphasis in UE is on early intervention. By utilizing data to identify student needs and then providing services to address those needs *before* students fail, schools can reduce more intensive and costly remediation in the future.

UE exists, in the simplest terms, because we believe in the promise of public education in this country. Our schools have the potential to prepare future citizens to coexist in harmony despite their differences, but this potential is lost if we create an education system that sorts and segregates students along the lines of race, class, family experience, and ability. When talking of UE's primary goal—to increase the academic performance and the social-emotional well-being of the most struggling students—we mean specifically those students who, owing to circumstances outside of their control, face additional barriers to accessing a quality education. These include the following:

- *Students in poverty:* By age 2, low-income children—regardless of race—are already 6 months behind their higher-income peers in language development, and by age 5 they are more than 2 years behind (The Education Trust–West, 2015).
- *Students who experience chronic stress and trauma*: Children who experience complex trauma are three times more likely to drop out of school than their peers and have a greater tendency to be misclassified with developmental delays or referred for special education services (National Child Traumatic Stress Network, 2014).
- *Black students*: Black students in California are most likely to be suspended or expelled, taught by ineffective teachers, identified for special education, and to take remedial, non-credit-bearing coursework as college students (The Education Trust–West, 2015).
- *Foster youth*: Youth in foster care graduate at relatively low rates and are less likely to complete high school than their non–foster care peers. For example, in California during the 2009–2010 school year, the graduation rate for high school students statewide was 84%, but for students in foster care it was just 58%—the lowest rate among the at-risk student groups (Barrat & Berliner, 2013).
- *English-language learners:* As of the 2013–14 school year, only 62.6% of students classified with limited English proficiency graduated from high school. This is a trend that has become increasingly alarming, given that English-language learners are the fastest growing subgroup in American schools (National Center for Education Statistics, 2015).
- *Students with disabilities*: Across the country, 37% of children with disabilities do not graduate from high school. This is over twice the rate of students without disabilities (National Center for Education Statistics, 2015).
- *Students who are already behind:* Students who do not read proficiently by third grade are four times more likely to leave school without a diploma when compared to proficient readers. This number rises when those children's families live in poverty (Hernandez, 2012).

Attempts to improve outcomes for our nation's most struggling youth have often been piecemeal and uncoordinated, leading to a system that is full of inefficiencies and produces limited results (Masten, 2003). This reality leads us to UE's second goal—to increase the efficiency of schools in delivering effective interventions to all students through implementation of a transdisciplinary, multi-tiered framework. UE's first goal is to provide immediate supports to students like Joseph Starr. The second, addresses the capacity of our public systems to intervene with future high-needs students.

WHY NOW?

This time in our history is marked by a collective awakening among parents, educators, researchers, and policymakers to the realization that focusing strictly on academic achievement and high-stakes, standardized testing has not been enough to eliminate the persistent achievement gaps in our education system. This understanding has resulted in a shift in the national policy landscape, one that is encouraging educators to think more holistically about their obligation to support student success.

It is within this context that schoolwide, evidence-based models like UE become a valuable illustration of what is possible. The UE approach aligns with many of the best practices proposed within recent education policy, three of which are described in detail next: (1) expanding the purview of education to include more explicit responsibility for the social-emotional development of students; (2) creating alternatives to exclusionary discipline practices and dedicating resources to improving school climate; and (3) increasing expectations for the scope of school-based mental health services in schools.

Policy Focus on Holistic Standards and Accountability

Woven throughout the new national educational standards for teaching and learning, referred to as the Common Core State Standards Initiative, is the expectation that students will build their capacity for problem-solving, collaboration, and communication. These skills fall outside the strict boundaries of cognition and require that schools pay explicit attention to the social-emotional development of their students. Within this new landscape, those who struggle behaviorally, socially, or both will find it harder and harder to succeed, and unless schools make it a priority to provide support in these areas, the achievement gap will continue to grow.

The passage of the Every Student Succeeds Act (ESSA), the latest reauthorization of the 1965 Elementary and Secondary Education Act, ensures that these more holistic expectations of students are accompanied by more holistic expectations of how districts and schools create educational environments that promote overall student health and well-being. ESSA marks a clear shift from its predecessor, No Child Left Behind (NCLB). Unlike NCLB's emphasis on high-stakes testing, ESSA expands its focus and encourages schools to develop positive learning environments, requiring states to report on at least one indicator of school climate and safety.

This new authorization also lends itself to increased local control among states and districts. For example, rather than requiring the federal government to intervene in low-performing schools, it requires these schools to collaborate with parents and staff to adopt evidence-based, schoolwide programs that explicitly address the needs of historically underserved students. Suggested strategies include the implementation of schoolwide, tiered models that prevent and address behavioral, social-emotional, and academic needs, a strategy within which UE clearly belongs.

While states across the nation are developing accountability indicators that align with ESSA, California provides a clear example of state legislation that has been designed to focus on student engagement and climate. Through the Local Control Funding Formula, public schools in California are now held accountable for developing, implementing, and monitoring services and supports that have an impact on school climate, including safety and student and parent engagement. For our partnering schools in the Bay Area of California, the UE model, with its explicit focus on measuring and improving school culture and climate, supports this statewide expectation.

A Call to Improve Discipline Practices

The US Department of Education and Department of Justice joined forces in 2014 to release the School Discipline Guidance Package aimed at improving school discipline policies and practices. This effort recognized the grave disparities that exist in school discipline rates across the nation and challenged schools and districts to reduce the use of punitive, exclusionary practices such as suspension and expulsion. Guidance on how to do so includes recommendations to (1) make deliberate efforts to create a positive and safe school climate; (2) use evidence-based prevention strategies, such as tiered supports, to promote positive student behavior; (3) integrate schoolwide social-emotional learning curricula; and (4) partner with local mental health agencies to align resources and provide supports. The UE model with its emphasis on providing tiered behavioral and social-emotional supports addresses all four of these recommendations for creating more positive and restorative discipline practices.

Expectations of School-Based Mental Health Services

The Final Report for the President's New Freedom Commission on Mental Health, published in 2003, provided a series of recommendations aimed at the Commission's ultimate vision:

We envision a future when everyone with a mental illness will recover, a future when mental illnesses can be prevented or cured, a future when mental illnesses are detected early, and a future when everyone with a mental illness at any stage of life has access to effective treatment and supports—essentials for living, working, learning, and participating fully in the community. (Center of Mental Health in schools, 2003, p. 1)

These recommendations included improved access to mental health services, such as early mental health screening, assessment, and referral. To that end, for children and youth, the Commission urged an improvement and expansion of school mental health programs.

Since publication of the report, some progress has been made in co-locating mental health services on school campuses. However, there is also an increasing awareness of limitations, including the fact that most clinicians rely on an outpatient model through which only a handful of students, most often those in special education, receive intensive individual therapy that is not formally integrated into their daily education program (Weist, Ambrose, & Lewis, 2006). It is within this context that schools around the country are joining forces with community mental health systems, families, and community stakeholders to promote a more holistic and integrated approach to addressing the social-emotional development of students (Weist et al., 2006). Seneca has similarly engaged with school partners and county mental health agencies to develop a more broad and responsive set of expectations for mental health services on campus. Within the UE model, providing multi-tiered mental health services means that clinical experts spend time providing professional development and coaching, supporting students within the classroom itself, and providing social skills and therapeutic groups that reinforce protective factors for children who find themselves struggling.

The policy landscape described here reflects a more comprehensive and inclusive approach to educating students. The statistics presented in this chapter paint a vivid picture of an education system that is failing its most vulnerable children and families. The sheer gravity of this reality has generated a sense of urgency and commitment across multiple sectors, resulting in a comprehensive call to action from experts in the field of education, mental health, and the US Department of Justice. While many agree that an integrated approach that addresses students' academic, behavioral, and social-emotional needs is necessary, there is, as McIntosh and Goodman (2016) note, "Little research in this area to guide implementers and even fewer resources available for those interested in integrating approaches. This gap can lead to spotty implementation, in which the logic and intent are strong, but the actual implementation lacks guidance and sufficient articulation" (p. 17).

It is clear that more research is needed on schoolwide transformative approaches in order to better understand how to unify general and special education and mental health toward the cause of inclusive practices. Our hope is that this book will help to address these gaps. We have worked diligently over the past 5 years to articulate the underlying theory and the key components of a UE model and to develop a fidelity tool that guides practitioners' understanding of what structures, processes, and practices are necessary to create a truly responsive, data-driven, and transdisciplinary approach to intervention.

Building on Best Practice

To borrow from the vision statement of one of our long-time partnership schools in Oakland, "We stand on the shoulders of those who came before us." As early as 1902, John Dewey himself sought to establish schools as the center of community life. In more recent history, this idea has been built on through various frameworks, including school-based mental health models, the community schools framework, multi-tiered systems of support, and the national school social work practice model (Sosa, Cox, & Alvarez, 2017).

Various school-based mental health models promote the co-location of mental health services on public school campuses, thus increasing accessibility for students with mental health challenges by providing the staffing and services to meet their needs. The community school model builds on this concept of accessibility, aiming to transform school campuses into community hubs that can serve as "one-stop shops" for a variety of services, including various health, after-school, parent-support, and enrichment programs. This model often includes a coordinator who is responsible for assessing needs, bringing in responsive resources, and coordinating service delivery among the various provider organizations.

In addition to providing access to responsive support services, both MTSS and the national school social work practice model provide a framework to support effective delivery of those services and to build the capacity of the entire school to better meet students' needs. In general, these two models include four principles: (1) capacity building at the schoolwide level to ensure that staff are supported in implementing best practices in instruction and behavior management; (2) providing evidence-based interventions; (3) coordinating these interventions at multiple tiers, including preventative, early, and intensive levels of service; and (4) using data to inform decision-making about students' needs and progress (McIntosh & Goodman, 2016; Sosa et al., 2017).

WHAT MAKES UNCONDITIONAL EDUCATION UNIQUE?

As school principals across the country work to co-locate clinical professionals on campus and implement the tenets of MTSS, they often find themselves confronting two seemingly intractable problems: (1) inordinate amounts of time and resources being spent to meet the pressing needs of the most struggling students because robust prevention and early intervention services are not in place to support students before they fail; and (2) a collection of general education, special education, and mental health providers on campus who are working in isolation, often resulting in service gaps or overlaps. By contrast, the UE model promotes systematic shifts that ensure each school community is provided with the resources, data-informed structures, and transdisciplinary knowledge necessary to effectively and efficiently meet the diverse needs of students. The distinguishing components of this approach are described next.

Data-Informed Systems and Supports Enhanced with a Mental Health Perspective

It is well established that the melding of multi-tiered behavioral and academic supports holds great promise for addressing the needs of all students, including those with disabilities (McIntosh & Goodman, 2016; Sadler & Sugai, 2009; Sugai & Horner, 2009). Notably absent within this framework, however, is the integration of mental health supports. Traditionally, this responsibility is held solely by a clinician on campus who works with individuals or groups of students referred for therapy. In schools impacted heavily by trauma, this mental health knowledge must be transferred to the whole community. Teachers themselves are increasingly expressing this need; in a recent study, 89% reported that they felt schools should be involved in addressing mental health needs, yet only 34% reported that they had the skills to do so (Reinke, Stormont, Herman, Puri, & Goel, 2011). The UE model harnesses the mental health expertise of on-site professionals to fill out a multi-tiered academic and behavioral intervention framework with a spectrum of social-emotional and trauma-informed supports. UE infuses the mental health perspective into the student intervention planning process, using schoolwide social-emotional screening data to proactively identify and plan around student needs while monitoring goals and progress of social-emotional interventions to drive service provision and measure success.

Breakdown of Siloes and Promotion of Transdisciplinary Solutions

Standard practice across the nation is to view students with disabilities and mental health needs as a specific cohort for whom intensive interventions must be targeted and delivered in separate environments solely by trained specialists. While enriching schools by connecting them with full-service clinics is a significant enhancement of the status quo, co-locating a clinic on a school campus does not translate automatically into the infusion of a broader set of resources and expertise within the classroom (Doll, Spies, & Champion, 2012). UE changes the way in which general and special educators, school leaders, and mental health practitioners integrate their efforts to create a single, coherent system of support for students. Whereas many schools and districts pull together an impressive network of experts to work in parallel, UE relies on the integration of experts to adopt and infuse a unified approach into the fundamental structures of each school. This is achieved through intentional shifts in operational structure: (1) implementation of a transdisciplinary student problem-solving team; (2) rigorous cross-disciplinary training of staff; and (3) the introduction of new norms for adult collaboration (discussed further in Chapter 2).

Explicit Focus on Assessing and Improving Schoolwide Culture and Climate

The sheer number and severity of needs within a school can mean that even robust teams often find themselves addressing only the most pressing needs of only a handful of the most visibly struggling students at a time. Thus, one of the most crucial tenets of systems-level change is explicit resource allocation to prevention and early intervention strategies. The fact that a sound and healthy school culture and climate are an essential component of any school transformation effort cannot be overemphasized. This is particularly true for schools that serve students and families living in neighborhoods of concentrated poverty, where they may experience cumulative trauma resulting from the daily stressors of community violence, as well as from historic and structural conditions of racism and disenfranchisement (Collins et al., 2010).

In order for students to learn and grow, they and their families must feel like the school community is a safe and predictable place where they truly belong and where their needs will be met. UE provides a framework within which to explicitly assess and improve the schoolwide culture and climate, using the research-validated School Climate Assessment Instrument (SCAI) to identify areas for growth and develop measurable annual goals for schoolwide improvement (discussed in Chapter 7).

Realignment and Decentralization of Funding

The UE model requires that school leaders are willing to make systemic changes to transform the way that student support services are funded at the school-site level. Successful UE implementation requires two funding commitments. The first entails an up-front investment in tier one systems and data-based coordination capacity. This includes creating more efficient prevention and early intervention systems that, over the longer term, will reduce the need for more intensive services and therefore require less allocation of general education funding to special education and intensive clinical supports.

The creation of truly inclusive education environments requires that we rethink how and where special education and mental health dollars are allocated, namely, that we consider shifting funding that has traditionally supported students in exclusionary settings to instead support those same students at their community school sites. This reallocation provides schools with the level of funding necessary to support *all* neighborhood students within the walls of their classrooms, by bringing valuable expertise and resources (special education, behavioral, and mental health providers) to each campus. In general, decentralizing these funds gives schools leaders the ability to make data-based decisions about the constellation of supports at their school site, ensuring that resources are truly responsive to the needs of the school community (discussed in Chapter 8).

OVERVIEW OF THE BOOK

The rest of this book shares stories about students, teachers, and school leaders in their moments of both triumph and trial. It identifies critical processes that have enabled meaningful change across the schools and school systems that have adopted the UE approach. The book is divided into two parts: theory and practice.

Part I provides the theoretical underpinnings. Tracing the roots of the unconditional education from its predecessor, unconditional care, it tells the story of how direct care experiences in the mental health field have informed the development of a macro-approach to school transformation. Chapter 2 looks at the UE model through the lens of systems theory, which promotes the idea that sustainable change is enabled by the creation of strong and coherent systems that can be implemented by multiple stakeholders who lend their transdisciplinary expertise to a shared purpose. Chapter 3 examines attachment theory and the crucial role of supportive and trusting relationships in promoting environments primed for change, even when that change is terribly difficult. Chapter 4 examines behavioral learning theory, including the importance of clear, actionable goals and planning and the realization that transformative change is not always linear.

Part II introduces the framework of the UE model more concretely, providing a general roadmap for practitioners by reflecting on key features and enablers of successful implementation. Chapter 5 provides a framework for the UE approach, exploring a concrete conceptualization for a system of school supports. Chapter 6 delves into the deeper process required for rigorous service coordination. Chapter 7 outlines the formative and summative assessment process that informs high-quality program planning and implementation, and measures the extent to which the model promotes positive outcomes for students and schools. Chapter 8 examines the strategic implementation phases involved in adopting this model and provides insight into the blended funding structure that makes it possible. Finally, with a fuller picture of this model in mind, Chapter 9 discusses implementation challenges inherent within the framework and key lessons we have learned in the process of implementation.

In both parts of the book, we return to the key concepts of efficiency, intentional relationship building, cross-sector responsibility, and local decision-making. It will become evident how these concepts drive UE. For now, we simply affirm and define them as follows:

- *Efficiency:* How can we do more with what we have while maintaining or improving quality? Efficiency does not necessarily mean spending less but, instead, strategically allocating resources without wasting time or effort on tasks that have little or no impact on the lives of students. Increased efficiency may indeed create some cost savings in particular areas, allowing for reinvestment in preventative and early intervention services that will ensure a school's continued progress down the path of improved outcomes for students. Efficient systems consider how inputs can affect future needs, alongside current needs.

- *Intentional relationship building:* The foundational strength of any community can be located in its network of individual relationships. The nature and quality of these relationships is of paramount importance in the completion of any collective endeavor. The level of relational trust present within a community has a substantial impact on the everyday experiences of its members. A specific approach to building, sustaining, and repairing relationships is needed for effective change.

- *Cross-sector responsibility:* It is our collective responsibility to ensure the achievement of our communities' most vulnerable youth. Current systems of care are set up in such a way that they create a fractured experience for their participants. Students and families experience incoherent care. Opportunities for meaningful collaboration between professionals in our communities with valuable expertise in education, mental health, social welfare, and wellness are few and far between. A transdisciplinary approach is essential in addressing the complex issues facing communities that are highly impacted by poverty.

- *Local decision-making:* Those closest to a problem should be those actively involved in designing its solutions. Regardless of education, background, or training, individuals and communities are the most knowledgeable about their own needs. Program mandates by outsiders that disregard local knowledge will almost never be effective; local context matters. The role of professionals is to share expertise while providing structures in which participants can choose the approaches likely to be effective in their own lives.

We hope that the lessons we share in the following pages may offer better options for students like Joseph Starr and the dedicated professionals who surround them. We have written this book with the intention of supporting schools and districts interested in utilizing the UE approach. Currently, public systems are weighted to best support those with resources, be they financial, social, political, or otherwise. Not surprisingly, then, the systemic issues within our schools disproportionately hurt those with the least social capital. It is within these schools, neighborhoods, and districts across the nation that we intend to create a new narrative about what is possible for all students and families, particularly the most marginalized among them. We share our story in the hope that it will bring us one step closer to the promise of unconditional education.

2 Schools as Systems

WHERE WE ARE

The work of changing schools means acknowledging that we are, in fact, changing systems. Often, these are long-established systems enacted by multiple stakeholders invested in their preservation. Many efforts to promote educational equity attempt to tackle a single problematic aspect of the school in the hope that addressing an identified need in one area will improve the system as a whole. Some schools adopt a new math curriculum, hoping it will yield higher 4-year graduation rates. Other schools introduce computer-based learning, believing it will improve the ability of teachers to differentiate content. Still others practice mindfulness with students to reduce suspension rates. Efforts such as these are praiseworthy, but the piecemeal approach often fails to translate into meaningful change. At the other extreme, many schools choose to implement various reform efforts simultaneously—a new math curriculum, for instance, supplemented by computer-based learning and followed by a schoolwide mindfulness exercise. The result, generally, is mile-wide and inch-deep efforts that leave already overtaxed schools and principals with the challenge of running multiple initiatives at once, very likely without the resources to implement any one of them successfully (Cuban, 1990).

Piecemeal or duplicative approaches to school transformation are particularly troubling as they rarely produce the systemic transformation required to reduce broadscale inequities within the system. When problems are identified in isolation, solutions tend to address symptoms rather than the underlying causes of the most acute or prevalent manifestations. More often than not, addressing the root cause requires some level of attention to the system itself. When these systems-level changes are ignored, similar problems are likely to occur again in the future.

Nowhere is this more true than in the systems designed to address learning and mental health challenges in schools. Special education services rely largely on pull-out approaches to service delivery only *after* students have shown substantial deficits in their learning. The words *mental health* are often synonymous with clinicians providing closed-door therapy to specific students or supporting young people with disabilities who have been placed in specialized, segregated settings. At first glance, this may not appear to be a broken system; many children do well with specialized services or in specialized classrooms. But if the ultimate goal is for children to function fully within the general education classroom, in higher education, and in the world beyond that, the current system is broken indeed. When we choose to build the capacity of specialized staff to work in isolated settings with the most challenging youth, without preparing their natural environment or supporters to do the same, this ultimate goal is compromised (Doll, Spies, & Champion, 2012).

Troubling as this phenomenon is on an individual level, from a systems viewpoint it is far more disturbing. A seat in a specialized classroom provides intervention for exactly one child for exactly one school year at a time. It is important to note, however, that once enrolled in a specialized setting, the majority of students will remain there for several years. This is partially because funding structures invest in staff and services that are provided solely in this specialized (and isolated) setting, rather than in the bridge between children's current needs and the skills and capacity of their general education teachers and school staff to meet those needs. Simultaneously, the lack of investment in the public school environment means that the next student who struggles at a similar level will likely also be referred to a specialized classroom. This cycle leads to the continued, systematic lack of resources or expertise available to the public school as a whole. It also leads to the further marginalization of youth with mental health disabilities, who are more likely to find themselves assigned to another specialized "seat" during their adult lives—the one in prison, where individuals with mental health disorders make up the majority of the total population (Collier, 2014).

To address the root cause of these perpetuating cycles of exclusion, attention must be given to changing the system as a whole, rather than attempting to address its individual parts in isolation. Informed by the principles of systems theory, we ask the following questions:

How can a single holistic approach to the organization of student supports ensure the most efficient deployment of resources?

How can we build sustainable systems of care within schools by leveraging specialists to build the capacity of teachers and staff and promote overall health and wellness?

HOW WE GOT HERE

Piecemeal approaches to improvement are continuously incentivized by the very organization of public education in this country, notably its current funding structures. The specifics of these structures are reviewed in greater depth in Chapter 8. Here they are explored briefly to inform a discussion of systems change. Of the over 50 million young people who attend public schools in the United States, a growing number qualify for additional funds or services due to their classification as youth with disabilities, low-income learners, or English-language learners or through their involvement in the child welfare or juvenile justice systems. Funding specifically reserved for these groups has been essential in the protection of civil rights and in maximizing opportunity for our most vulnerable and traditionally underserved students. Its availability is vitally important, but it is also quite problematic in developing an inclusive approach to education.

Historically, students with disabilities were taught in segregated settings. As a result, "special education became an increasingly separate institution, with its own practices, regulations, certifications, and staff" (Conner & Ferri, 2007, p. 64). A similar set of divisions exists between schools and mental health providers, who often find it difficult to recognize their shared goals. Too often, school-based staff see their mission of education as completely separate from the community agencies' mission of child mental health, and vice versa (Stiffman et al., 2010).

Our most vulnerable students and families often have multiple needs and require support from multiple systems, necessitating cross-sector integration of resources and expertise, not rigidly siloed services governed by restricted funding guidelines. The needs of a child with a disability, for example, may be addressed through the combined efforts of general and special educators at the public school, the county's mental health or vocational rehabilitation programs, medical insurance or Medicaid, and other public benefits. Since each essential service is funded through a unique funding stream, providers within each stream are governed by separate accountability structures and are often working toward separate goals. These separate structures create a system of siloed services with few clear channels for cross-sector communication. This division among services and service providers inhibits coherence and forces an unnatural division of priorities and services, at the expense of a holistic "whole-child" approach.

More troubling still is the diffusion of responsibility, as each silo has its own accountability system, with no one person assuming ownership of the overall wellness or success the whole child. Borrowing a metaphor from McTighe and Wiggins (2007), it is as though a group of architects were commissioned individually, each to build a different room in a house. With no project manager, no blueprint for the finished project, and no centralized accountability structures, the house could end up with three kitchens and no bathrooms, to say nothing of systems that most homeowners would agree should ideally cross rooms, such as plumbing or ventilation.

An additional consequence of dividing related priorities into siloes is the competition this fuels for resources or control. This is apparent in conversations that center on whether something is "special ed.'s problem" or "admin's responsibility" and the "us versus them" talk at many district offices, where political lines are drawn and redrawn around new initiatives and additional funding requests. Significantly, it is also evident in the disproportionately low outcomes for historically underperforming subgroups of students, who are often caught in these cycles of competition among adults instead of experiencing adults as coordinated members in a "coalition of child-serving champions" (Lawson, 2004, p. 225).

While traditional public health models have, on the whole, come to recognize the importance of providing system-wide approaches to inhibit the frequency and intensity of future problems, education and mental health programs have yet to follow suit. Existing funding structures, built to safeguard resources dedicated to protected groups of students, have strict qualification criteria, requiring students to meet a certain threshold for failure before accessing the resources dedicated for support. The protections intended by these programs are essential, but they inadvertently promote a "fail-first" approach. Prevailing special education qualification criteria require students to fall up to 2 years behind before help is deployed. Similarly, to receive traditional mental health services, students must reach a medical level of necessity, signifying symptoms consistent with a psychiatric disorder. In both of these cases, our system perpetuates an inefficient approach to keeping kids healthy, by first requiring that they become very, very unwell.

In many schools a gap exists between what is offered in the general classroom and the intensive supports just described. In affluent communities, parents and families fill in this gap—with tutoring, after-school enrichment, educational consultants, or by accessing related therapies through their private insurance. However, parents who face economic uncertainty lack the resources available to their affluent counterparts to provide their children with supplementary experiences or support services beyond what is available at school. When families are unable to respond swiftly and decisively to the earliest incidences of stress, children often fall further and further behind (Conger, Conger, & Martin, 2010). The time lapse between problem identification and solution finding is critical. By the time the school system steps in, the problem will likely be more difficult to address, both because it has been allowed to linger longer and because of the student's internalized experience of failure. In the interim, many young people experience shame for needing something their family cannot readily provide and stigma for not having the resources needed to keep up with grade-level peers. They lose hope in the ability of adults to address important issues in efficient and effective ways.

The delay of services can also have a substantial impact on a school's resources. When early interventions are unavailable and special education and intensive individualized mental health services are the only supports families can access, demand for these costly services increases. Moreover, once students reach the thresholds at which to qualify for services, more substantial resources are needed to remedy the deficits that have emerged, and these resources are more likely to be provided within isolated settings that pull both students and resources away from the general education setting. Our existing system incentivizes the use of high-cost and high-intensity services, creating an escalating level of crisis that exhausts school resources and promotes failure. A systematic approach is needed to re-balance school resources toward prevention and early intervention, promoting a culture of wellness and inclusion.

A SYSTEMS APPROACH

Seneca's approach to school transformation through systems-level change comes directly from lessons learned in the mental health field. Work with clients has led to the belief that it is impossible to affect an individual's outcomes and experiences, particularly when that individual is a child, without also acting upon the family, school, and community systems within which they interact. In other words, individuals are inseparable from their complex network of relationships; a systems approach considers the entangled ecological factors at play. While systems theory now stands as one of three pillars of the unconditional care treatment model, it was not always so.

As an agency founded on the single promise of providing unconditional care to the most troubled youth in the system, Seneca's initial efforts at treatment were focused on the immediate, pressing needs of young people in crisis. Efforts focused on providing safety and building a relationship with the youth themselves. This approach was successful: many young people served in Seneca's therapeutic residential facilities had previously been projected to need long-term psychiatric institutionalization or hospitalization. However, within the walls of the residential facility, many flourished. For example, a young person who had not been allowed any contact with age-level peers for years was gradually able to join her community in sharing meals, then outings, then group therapy, and ultimately shared a bedroom with another young person, a determinant in her transition out of group care and into a family foster home.

Yet something else happened as well. Although remarkable gains occurred during their time in care, the youth struggled to transition into other, less restrictive settings. They continued to experience school discipline issues. They frequently exhibited significant assaultive and self-harming behaviors when in the community or following a transition into a foster or biological family home. And they came back in alarming numbers, seemingly more dependent than ever on high levels of supervision, support, and external intervention.

This realization was pivotal in determining strategy. A more complete continuum of services was built so that youth could receive support in different settings, from homes to schools to foster placements and crisis stabilization programs. Efforts were increased to engage parents as partners, by leveraging their extensive expertise and focusing on solutions that matched each family's unique values and goals. Parents' capacity to provide safety and responsive relationships was fostered, so that youth could experience care from their families instead of just from specially trained staff "paid to care" for them (as more than one young person has reminded us over the years). Seneca collaborated with the team of experts supporting youth in care—therapists, social workers, probation officers, psychiatrists, school personnel, and the organizations they represented. Together with these diverse professionals, the agency worked to identify and fill existing gaps in the system's ability to respond efficiently to the ever-changing needs of young people and families in crisis.

This change in practice represented a fundamental shift from the traditional conceptualization of mental illness as a condition that needs to be treated and "cured" by professionals to one in which even the most extreme challenges youth face can be mediated through thoughtful intervention that connects specialists with natural care providers to engender overall health and wellness. It was a shift that mirrored larger trends in the mental health field and has led to more positive outcomes for youth. There is no doubt as to the limited impact of 50 minutes of weekly, closed-door therapy when compared with interventions carefully infused throughout the day. Equipping a young person's natural care providers with the skills needed to reinforce behavioral change is not only effective in the moment but also leads to the increased well-being of other children, who benefit from a system now better equipped to recognize and respond to emerging needs (Doll et al., 2012).

Staff celebrated youths' increased success across multiple settings—home, school, and community. In what was perhaps the most extreme example of the impact of this fundamental shift, a residential team was working tirelessly to meet the needs of Alma, a young woman in their care. They had called on every esteemed mental health expert they could think of to consult or provide direct support. They had essentially designed an entire wing of the residential facility with Alma in mind. Still, they saw no difference in her behavior. Then, one day, her case manager found a different type of expert, making contact for the first time with Alma's biological aunt and uncle, who had lost contact with Alma when she was removed from her parents' care years earlier.

With careful planning alongside the residential team, the family began to visit the young woman. They would bring home-cooked food and exchange gifts on holidays. They began to paint a vision of what her life—their lives together—could look like outside the walls of a residential facility in a way no professional had ever been able to before. Within 2 months of their reconnection, Alma's behavior was nearly unrecognizable to the staff who had spent years with her. Within less than a year, she was living independently, attending a public school for the first time in her life, and making preparations to enroll in community college. Alma continued to receive professional support, but, more importantly, these services were now enhanced and amplified by a strong partnership with her family. The experience of Alma and those of numerous other clients have helped to demonstrate the impact of investing in a young person's natural support systems. These lessons have resulted in the formal adoption of a systems theory as one of the three pillars of unconditional care (alongside attachment theory, discussed in Chapter 3, and behavioral theory, discussed in Chapter 4).

School models that seek to serve all students must put the health and function of the system at the center of their efforts. A healthy, well-functioning system is highly efficient—that is, it produces the best outcomes for students and families with the least amount of wasted resources and effort. In the balancing act that efficiency represents, it is important not to equate increased efficiency with reduced inputs or cost savings. This mistake often leads to stagnated outcomes and even increased costs further down the line, resulting from the escalation of unmet needs. While increased efficiency may indeed result in specific cost savings when redundancies are reduced, these savings provide an opportunity for new investments to help fill the gaps in existing services.

Needless to say, the creation of a highly efficient system that meets the expansive needs of the most struggling students and families is no easy feat. However, three key tenets gleaned from similar transformation work within the field of mental health help to guide the application of systems theory in schools. They are coordination, integration, and prevention and early intervention.

Coordination

Coordination is the organization of a complex set of interrelated players in a manner that allows them to work together effectively. It maintains the importance of expertise and specialty but ensures that each expert and specialist complements the work of the other. When systems are effective in organizing different departments or providers around a single plan, youth are more likely to experience consistent messages and responses from adults, regardless of role or background, and caregivers are more likely to experience a responsive hub of services and supports.

Integration

Integration should not be assumed to follow automatically when coordination efforts are successful. Integration removes the artificial barriers between disciplines (special educators, general educators, and mental health specialists), allowing professionals and caregivers to work together in such a way that they begin to understand and learn from each person's expertise. This understanding lends itself to working together as a team to create a holistic approach capable of addressing multiple needs. When seamless, transdisciplinary supports are in place, based on real needs rather than on rigid funding mechanisms or eligibility criteria, providers are able to efficiently address interrelated challenges in behavior, social-emotional wellness, and academic skills.

The quest for highly efficient systems finds inspiration in the old adage "An ounce of prevention is worth a pound of cure." It is essential to consider both the long-term payoff of current investments and the costs that inaction will later incur. The principles of prevention and early intervention require that, when making resource allocation decisions, the future of a client and systems within which they operate are simultaneously considered alongside the current realities. In large part, efforts at prevention and early intervention focus on building the capacity of the system, strengthening existing networks of support. When funding and resource allocation mechanisms identify and respond to needs early and often, they can focus on keeping children well, not treating them only after they have experienced high levels of failure. As a colleague puts it, "We should focus our efforts on building a fence at the top of a cliff rather than parking a permanent ambulance at the bottom." These three tenets have direct applications for the work of schools.

IMPLICATIONS FOR SCHOOLS

In under-resourced schools, maximizing the effect of each and every resource dollar becomes of paramount importance. As such, the systems developed to govern the deployment of these resources must be highly efficient, preventing both a duplication of efforts and reducing gaps. School and systems leaders, who so frequently get pulled into the day-to-day work of supporting struggling students, must also have opportunities to take a 10,000-foot view. Rather than solely fighting existing fires, they must consider these existing needs alongside the future health of the system. The principles of efficient systems can guide decision-making related to this work.

Coordination

One unconditional education (UE) collaborator, an assistant superintendent in a large urban district, recently shared an experience of rushing to a large elementary school deemed "in crisis" by its principal, who made an urgent call to her supervisor for help. This particular school was located in an under-resourced neighborhood where students were regularly exposed to community violence and disrupted family relationships. The school was struggling to maintain order amidst seemingly unrelenting disturbances and fights. Arriving at the school ready to "roll up his sleeves and get to work," he found it nearly impossible to get to a single student in need. Instead, what he found was a large group of adults buzzing around, without clear direction or purpose, stepping over each other in a harried attempt to provide support.

This collaborator learned that three separate community-based organizations were working to identify emergency resources for one family in need, without realizing they were duplicating their efforts while unintentionally adding confusion to an already stressed family. And, while countless adults worked tirelessly within and across the boundaries of their individual siloes, no one at the school was positioned to hold the 10,000-foot view necessary to notice a major gap—that no effort had gone into reforming the school's chaotic recess period, widely believed to be the origin of many of the behavioral struggles at the school.

Within UE, a key approach in addressing coordination challenges like those just described is the assignment of a single point of contact—a "project manager" in the building metaphor used earlier—for all interventions at the school site. Designating a single person to hold both the bird's eye view of the school's intervention framework and the details of the individual interventions within it fosters increased system efficiency (Lawson, 2004). In the case described, the presence of such a "project manager" might have signaled the need for a coordinated response to recess challenges and drawn attention to the duplication of efforts in some areas and unmet needs in others.

In the UE model, the "project manager," or UE coach, plays a critical role in partnering with the school's principal to change systems at the school site, including the coordination, integration, and prevention and early intervention efforts detailed in this chapter. Dedicating a person to this role was one of the many lessons learned in developing the model, perhaps one of the most significant. Responsibilities for systems change and capacity building—crucial elements in the success of UE—were initially built into the existing roles of special education, behavioral, and clinical support staff at the school. However, two key points were discovered: (1) for those staff who are expected to focus most of their efforts on direct service, it is incredibly difficult to carve out time for working on proactive systems change, and (2) leading effective systems change efforts at a school site requires specific skills and comprehensive, structured, and ongoing professional development throughout the year. In other words, it is a job in and of itself.

This realization is not unique to the UE model. The National School Social Work model, which aligns with the multi-tiered systems of supports (MTSS) approach, suggests that school social workers should dedicate time to capacity building and coordination of services on-site, in addition to providing direct support to students and families. However, when surveyed, social workers report that they spend most of their time on direct care and find themselves "to be in reactive and crisis mode as opposed to a proactive or prevention planning role" (Sosa, Cox, & Alvarez, 2017, p.158). These survey results confirm the gap that often exists between theory and practice. In theory, leaders understand the value of direct-service staff dedicating time toward systems change, but in practice, they are very rarely able to carve out a sufficient amount of time to do that work well. In order to better align best practice with reality, those charged with systems change need protected time dedicated to this work, as well as highly articulated on-boarding and ongoing professional development that support their efforts. In the UE model, this work is led by the UE coach, in close partnership with the school's other leadership.

A key responsibility of the UE coach is to serve as the leader of its coordination of services team (COST), which is composed of specialists who represent a cross section of school leadership, general education practitioners, and intervention providers from within (special education teachers, school social workers, etc.) and outside (county-funded mental health specialists, on-site healthcare professionals, etc.) the formal boundaries of the school. COST (the specific processes of which are discussed in greater detail in Chapter 6) is charged with meeting weekly to address the needs of students who require extra support. When this group operates in unison, rather than as isolated players across the school, individuals become capable of doing meaningful work within their own area of expertise and no needs are left unattended because of a lack of coordination among busy school professionals. Both resource gaps and overlaps are reduced, and youth and families experience less confusion, shorter wait times, and more responsive services (Robinson, Atkinson & Downing, 2008).

To explore the silo effect and the role of coordination from the student perspective, let us return to the story of Joseph Starr. When Joseph enrolled at Ford Elementary, a UE school, his case was referred to the school's COST. This group had the authority and training to take a transdisciplinary approach in creating an intervention plan that drew in resources from the different experts who traditionally remain siloed, including special education staff, mental and behavioral health professionals, and general educators. As a result of her involvement in the coordination of services process, Joseph's primary classroom teacher, in partnership with the COST, became the "holder" of his intervention plan. This plan spelled out clearly which member of the team was responsible for which actions, as well the expectations for ongoing collaboration. When new needs were identified or successes celebrated, the team would reconvene to update the plan. As providers transitioned in and out of their roles, the plan guided their scope of work and identified other supports that had been put into place. And, every 8 weeks at the least, the team would meet to review Joseph's data, analyze the efficacy of different interventions, and formally recommend the next steps.

In traditional schools, where comprehensive coordination of services has not been established, providers' schedules are based on teacher referrals, often using a first-come, first-served approach. In these scenarios, students may or may not receive the services they need, based on the level of skill with which their teacher can advocate for their needs. In the absence of a centralized system, compassionate adults at a school would be likely to recognize needs such as Joseph's and respond. A single student may be mentored simultaneously by the school's football coach, assistant principal, and after-school provider—all well intentioned individual actors jumping in head first to provide support. Without a mechanism for close coordination, it is likely they would duplicate each other's efforts and ignore certain needs while addressing the same relatively small subset of issues. Moreover, they are likely to identify their own metrics of success, formal or otherwise, making it difficult to summarize progress objectively or to identify which interventions are moving the dial.

Without clear indicators for success or agreed-upon steps for requesting an increase in services, adults get frustrated. The feeling that "it's not getting better" can be echoed throughout the school, and indications that multiple people have become involved often send a signal that "everything that can be done has." Over time, this frustration can lead adults to point fingers at each other, fight for perceived resources, and—ultimately—lose hope that a young person can heal within the current environment. For a student like Joseph Starr, the effect is often internalized. Watching providers falling over backward to provide support, and still failing, can lead a student like Joseph to lose trust in the providers, the system in which they work, and the student's own internal worth and abilities. These experiences build on each other to create an unhelpful but deep-seated narrative about the student's inability to succeed within the public education system.

While maximizing the efficacy of individual providers, the UE coach also frees up another key staff member—the principal—to do the important work only they can do. Too often, coordinating intervention efforts fall in the lap of the school principal, who is almost always well qualified to take the lead. The challenge, however, lies not in the principal's innate ability to lead these efforts but in finding the time to do so while also balancing multiple priorities as the instructional and cultural leader of the school. As will be discussed in greater depth later in this book, the principal plays a critical role in setting and sustaining the vision for student support; the work of the school simply cannot proceed without this visioning (Bryson, Crosby, & Stone, 2006). The principal cannot successfully hold this vision if simultaneously tasked with managing every action step associated with its actualization. If the role of coordination is not properly resourced, leadership may resort to attractive quick fixes that look more like a game of "whack-a-mole" than master's-level chess.

Integration

In many ways, effective service integration is an extension of effective coordination. Service integration has begun to take hold in schools across the nation, perhaps most clearly in the community schools movement, which recognizes two important realities: (1) schools cannot independently meet the myriad needs of many of our young people, and (2) schools serve as the heart of the community; they are the place where one most expects to find and serve children and, as such, they are the natural location for integrated services to be designed and delivered (Anderson Moore, & Emig, 2014). In the full-service community school, existing services and resources are enhanced by partnerships that focus on physical and mental health, social services, parenting classes and support groups, and resource dissemination. Schools can become "one-stop shops" for community members, reducing the burden on stressed families, particularly those who are engaged with multiple systems of care and would otherwise have to shuttle across town to food banks, therapy appointments, medical clinics, and, of course, their children's school.

As in UE schools, community schools often have a schoolwide coordinator, or point person. One difference, however, is that community school efforts are almost always funded either through discretionary district funding or through grants and philanthropic contributions. They focus on bringing a collection of resources, provided by outside organizations, onto the school campus. As in most public systems, *discretionary* often signifies unpredictable, meaning that the availability of resources for community school efforts remains uncertain from one funding cycle to the next. This "come-and-go" effect takes its toll on a school community, making it more difficult for staff and students to believe that it is worth investing in new programs and building relationships with support staff who may not be around for very long (Weist, Ambrose, & Lewis, 2006). This in turn hampers the school's efforts to create a truly integrated system where providers, teachers, and school leaders have dedicated time for the in-depth collaboration that is necessary to transfer key skills and expertise across disciplines.

In stark contrast, UE does not attempt to enhance the school system through "supplemental services," a phrase generally synonymous with "discretionary funding," which itself is too often synonymous with "transitory political whims." Instead, the aim of the UE approach is to transform the education system itself, including the way in which basic education dollars, for general and special education alike, are used to meet the diverse needs of school-aged children. What this means is that in the UE model the majority of intervention providers are funded through sustainable public funding from within the school as well as through mental health dollars made available by the county, state, and federal governments. In other words, UE seeks to transform the fundamental practices of the education system, changing the way in which general educators, special educators, school leaders, and mental health practitioners integrate their efforts to create a single, coherent system of support for students.

The strategy for doing this is to create and reinforce shared decision-making processes at the school-site level. Identifying student needs and making initial decisions about how to address these begin with the teacher. This responsibility is based on a simple yet profound expectation: every kid is "your" kid, unconditionally. Setting this expectation across the school triggers the obligation to care collectively for the whole child and ensures that the values and priorities of integration permeate the entire school community and not just intervention providers and administrators. It might seem ludicrous to hang responsibility for students' holistic needs on general education teachers, many of whom lack the training and experience to work with significantly struggling students while their counterparts in special education or mental health are both equipped and eager to support them. The UE response to this reality is to expect teachers to be responsible for supporting the holistic needs of their students and, simultaneously, to work tirelessly behind the scenes to ensure teachers have what they need in order to do so. In the most successful UE schools, leaders invest an incredible amount of professional development and support for teachers in order to prepare them to identify needs and know where to seek solutions, including eliciting support from experts on campus to build their capacity.

In an integrated system, adults not only know and understand their areas of expertise but also work collaboratively to create a common language across disciplines and to lend their diversified expertise to shared goals. This integration includes the general education teaching staff as key experts at the table. Integrated efforts ensure that general education teachers can begin to expand their understanding of behavioral and social emotional interventions *and* that intervention providers can begin to better understand how their work supports teachers in their ability to create classroom community and deliver high-quality instructional experiences. Integration involves creating a truly transdisciplinary team that works to infuse sustainable resources and supports into the fabric of the school. In UE schools, the COST's orientation toward a common vision is a key differentiator that signals the evolution from a group of multidisciplinary experts to a true transdisciplinary team (see Table 2.1) (Choi & Pak, 2007).

Table 2.1 Different Team Approaches

Multidisciplinary	*Interdisciplinary*	*Transdisciplinary*
Additive	Interactive	Holistic
Draws on knowledge from different disciplines but stays within their boundaries	Analyzes, synthesizes, and harmonizes links between disciplines into a coordinated and coherent whole	Integrates multiple disciplines and transcends their traditional boundaries
Members from multiple disciplines work on solving related problems	Members use their individual expertise to develop their own answers to a given problem and then come together to formulate a coordinated solution	Members work together from the beginning and collaboratively develop solutions to problems
Members rely solely on expertise and methods from their own discipline	Members rely solely on expertise and methods from their own discipline	Members develop and combine methods from multiple disciplines to develop innovative solutions
Members engage in professional development related only to their own discipline	Members engage in professional development related only to their own discipline	Members learn from each other and engage in cross-disciplinary learning

The integrated, consultation-based approach supported by systems like COST not only promotes transdisciplinary thinking but can help to ensure that meaningful collaboration does not always begin with a crisis (Bryson et al., 2006). UE opens up opportunities for teachers, supported by a transdisciplinary team, to proactively identify the root of student challenges and develop responsive interventions. Teachers are better prepared to articulate these challenges and brainstorm solutions when the conversation happens in a preplanned COST session than when using a more traditional approach to student problem-solving, where teachers frantically reach out to the first available service provider to address the problem only after it has escalated to a level of extreme crisis.

In the fully integrated UE school, systems like COST begin to function as interventions in and of themselves, creating space at the decision-making table for vast collective expertise. They are effective enablers of integration, creating a common language across academic, behavioral, and mental health service providers and promoting a holistic approach to finding solutions.

Prevention and Early Intervention

Even schools that intentionally build their capacity for coordinated and integrated student support can find themselves overwhelmed by the sheer number and severity of needs within their school. This often means that even robust teams find themselves pouring all of their resources into addressing only the most pressing needs of the most visibly struggling students. Such circumstances perpetuate a fail-first cycle where student challenges must escalate before receiving support and then require an infusion of intensive resources to be remediated. This being the case, one of the most crucial tenets of systems-level change is an explicit focus on prevention and early intervention strategies.

The last decade has ushered in an increased focus on the importance of building systems of early intervention in schools. With the growth of response to intervention (RtI), schoolwide positive behavioral supports (SWPBS), multi-tiered systems of supports (MTSS), and the like, schools across the nation have begun to utilize data-based systems to identify students for early intervention. In addition, each of these approaches explicitly allocates time and resources to preventative, schoolwide practices meant to create an environment in which everyone feels safe, engaged, and ready to learn.

Paradoxically, UE schools that embrace the challenge of realigning resources around prevention and early intervention often begin by looking at how they organize support for the handful of students with the most intensive needs. The goal here is to conceive of exceptional intensive supports as opportunities for prevention and early intervention. In doing so, schools consider current student needs alongside the broader system needs these represent. Teams can create highly impactful plans for individual students while maximizing secondary benefits of the resources deployed. We call such solutions "the twofer," a reference to a joke that came out of a COST meeting and has gained traction ever since.

Take, for example, a student who may have been assigned a seat in an isolated, specialized program with support from a whole host of highly trained specialists. Instead, the student is matched with the same team of experts but their intensive supports are enacted within the general education environment. Under such an arrangement, the student maintains a seat in the general education classroom—itself an important accomplishment—and the school gains additional resources and expertise that reach beyond the immediate needs of the particular student to inform classroom and schoolwide practices. Rather than having the assigned clinician meet with the individual student to teach skills for emotional regulation, the clinician can join the classroom teacher to co-lead the class's weekly community meeting, where they can together lead a whole-class lesson on the topic. This approach not only creates a scaffolded skill-building opportunity for the teacher but also ensures that all 24 students are affected by the intervention, rather than just one. A behavioral specialist, instead of introducing and practicing individually the social skills needed by one student, can join the staff on yard duty to support structured games at recess that engage both the identified student and others who join in the games. These kinds of practices make an impact on a greater number of students while also providing skill building to those who need it most.

In these examples, for the same level of resources the target student benefits along with other students who have lower levels of need. In schools where these practices have been systematized over time, an unbelievably rewarding paradigm shift occurs. General education teachers begin to welcome students with the greatest needs into their classrooms. Teachers have learned that these students will be accompanied by some of the school's most talented staff, whose presence has the potential to benefit the entire classroom while also building their capacity as teachers to meet the more intensive needs of individual students.

Essential as these "twofers" are in designing an efficient system, they cannot serve as a school's sole prevention and early intervention efforts. Specific attention must also be given to the development of a strong, healthy, and inclusive school culture and climate. In this effort, it is essential that resources are assigned to a UE coach whose role, in addition to the coordination and integration efforts described earlier in this chapter, is to lead the school's Culture and Climate Committee (C3). This workgroup, which will be further discussed in Chapter 7, represents stakeholders from across the school and oversees the implementation of school-specific culture and climate initiatives. It requires an initial investment of resources that allows the UE coach to develop, implement, and refine the new systems that will ensure sustainable practices over time. This work includes developing the COST and C3 teams, structure, and processes, supporting the adoption of new data-informed systems to identify student needs and progress, and providing a foundation of training and coaching to staff that will support them in adopting new mindsets and practices aligned with the principles of unconditional education. Over time, as effective schoolwide systems are put into place, fewer students require Tier 2 and Tier 3 supports, freeing up those resources to be reinvested into ongoing culture and climate efforts.

CONCLUSION

Schools that operate as effective systems understand their local ecology and forge meaningful partnerships aligned with the community's values, goals, strengths, and needs. They do not yield their independence to external motivations or passing fads. Members of the community understand how all the pieces fit; they know how to ask for and receive help; they continually experience the school's values in action as demonstrated by the way the school operates, accesses resources, and integrates expertise and support. In such a system, students are seen as more than the sum of their parts and there is a cross-sector commitment to the wellness of the whole child and the whole community.

This commitment can transform more than students' individual math or reading scores. Implementing a systems approach specifically geared toward coordination, integration, and prevention and early intervention provides social and fiscal benefits beyond the educational realm. A system focused on wellness provides improved long-term outcomes for youth, which include higher income levels, increased health, and reduced reliance on costly interventions, including specialized educational settings, institutions, hospitals, and prisons (Collier, 2014). Furthermore, when overtaxed public schools or districts overcome dysfunction and organize for collective impact, they begin to change the very narrative about what is possible within public systems (Karnia & Kramer, 2011).

3 Schools as Relational Networks

WHERE WE ARE

Changing the economic and structural systems of schooling, as explored in the previous chapter, is essential. But systems change, in and of itself, is insufficient for true transformation (Elmore, 2007). Our schools are more than structural systems. They are communities—networks of human relationships that inform the trajectory of students' future lives while defining their current experiences. As discussed in Chapter 2, under-resourced, siloed systems create a fractured framework troubled with economic inefficiencies. These same conditions simultaneously promote a splintered relational network.

In other words, schools with the greatest opportunity gaps face multiple layers of resource-related stressors that shape not only their physical and systematic design but also the psyches of entire school communities. Parents come to expect that schools lack either the willingness or the ability to help their children and engage with schools in a manner consistent with this underlying belief. Students make sense of the system by figuring out what others expect from "students like them" and acting out their assigned role accordingly. Staff squabble over the few resources that do exist and blame each other for the gaps in support and services available. To mitigate the effects of resource-related stressors we must cultivate school communities of safety, acceptance, and belonging. In this chapter, we ask:

How can specific intentional approaches to relationship remediate past experiences of exclusion?

HOW WE GOT HERE

Childhood poverty is widespread in the United States and income inequality has become increasingly pronounced in recent years. According to a report published by the National Center for Children in Poverty, nearly half of our nation's children (30.6 million) live in families classified as "low income," many without consistent means to meet their most basic needs (Jiang, Ekono, & Skinner, 2016). Nowhere is America's class divide more evident than in our nation's schools.

Low socioeconomic status has time and again been linked to reduced educational outcomes. Ultimately, students from low-income families nationwide are less likely to graduate on time than their peers (National Center for Education Statistics, 2015). However, it is not low-income status alone that correlates with poorer school outcomes—researchers have found that the single most powerful predictor of disparities in educational achievement is the extent to which students are surrounded by other low-income students (Poverty & Race Research Action Council, 2015). This is where our nation's long history of residential segregation by race comes into play: "Because American neighborhoods are highly segregated by race and income, children of color are far more likely than their White counterparts to attend schools where the vast majority of students live in families who are struggling economically" (National Equity Network, 2016). All of this paints a troubling picture of an educational system fraught with inequities that fall along the lines of race and class.

Substantial national and local policy shifts are most certainly needed to ameliorate larger patterns of social stratification in residential and school segregation. In the meantime, school leaders are faced with the real and present charge of creating educational opportunity for all students. The work of building equitable and inclusive schools cannot be accomplished without giving explicit attention to the important connection between relationships and learning. Given the additional stressors high-poverty communities face, intentional relationship building is particularly important both to rework past experiences of trauma and to build resilience in facing current challenges.

There are predictable life stressors correlated with poverty. Of low-income children, 52% have immigrant parents, 70% reside with parents who lack full-time, year-round employment, 40% live with a single parent, and 7% are uninsured (Jiang, Ekono, & Skinner, 2016). These circumstances, when compounded by economic insecurity, produce a substantial level of pressure. An understanding of challenges poor families face, known as the family stress model, has grown out of the work of Glen Elder and Rand Conger's research group (Conger, Conger, & Martin, 2010). Masarik and Conger (2017) describe a trajectory where (a) economic hardship leads to economic pressure, (b) economic pressure leads to parent emotional distress, (c) parent emotional distress leads to conflicts between family members and disruptions in parenting behaviors, and (e) disruptions in parenting behaviors lead to child maladjustment. Or, as summarized by Melissa Barnett (2008), "economic disadvantage triggers feelings of economic pressure, which in turn lead to psychological distress in parents that ultimately negatively impacts child development" (p. 2).

For children and families living in high-poverty neighborhoods, this experience of chronic stress is often intensified by specific traumatic incidents. To better understand the impact of trauma, we look to the adverse childhood experiences (ACEs) study for guidance. The original ACEs study, conducted by the Centers for Disease Control and Prevention (CDC) and Kaiser Permanente, surveyed over 17,000 participants regarding their childhood experiences of abuse, neglect, and disrupted relationships, as well as their current health status and behaviors (Feletti et al., 1998).

ACEs tend to appear together, and frequently alongside the experience of economic hardship, with "poor children [being] more than twice as likely than their more affluent peers to have three or more ACEs" (Child Trends, 2013, p. 5). What's more, these adverse experiences in childhood, especially when experienced in clusters, are linked to poor health and social and economic hazards throughout the lifespan (Blodgett & Harrington, 2012; Sacks, Murphey, & Moore, 2014). It is important to acknowledge that economic hardship does not, of course, always result in poor life outcomes. Research demonstrates, and many students and families have proven, that powerful protective factors exist that can mitigate these adversities, resulting in healthy development. However, economic hardship does increase the conditions of stress and has the potential to alter parent–child bonding and shape the ways in which parents are able to participate in their children's education.

While the importance of parent engagement is commonly understood, a deeper look at the impact of poverty on parent engagement in schools reveals why it is that parents with higher levels of education are more likely to be involved than parents who live below the poverty line (Sacks el al., 2014). Here too, income alone doesn't represent the whole story, but financial security does have a substantial impact on parental availability and the ways in which parents can and do participate in their children's education. It is the type, more than the frequency, of engagement that matters. Still, schools fail to address the barriers to the types of engagement that are most impactful. While schools commonly promote parent activities related to school involvement (contacts between parents and school personnel, attendance at school events, volunteering, etc.), these activities have been shown to have an insignificant impact on student attainment. Activities that require a high degree of home involvement (discussing school activities at home, monitoring out-of-school activities, direct support with school work, parents' modeling of expectations and aspirations) contribute substantially to a students' educational attainment (Desforges & Abouchaar, 2003). The latter, of course, require a substantial investment of time and consistent parent availability. It is no wonder, then, that when parents face economic difficulties compounded by other challenges, such as job and housing instability, they are less available to participate in meaningful school engagement (Britt, 1998).

School-based interventions aimed at engaging parents often fail to address the challenges of daily living that prevent meaningful engagement. Supporting families to address these challenges requires a foundation of relational trust that comes from taking the time to develop a genuine connection with parents. Unfortunately, low-income parents do not always experience school staff as making efforts toward genuine connection and often perceive blame for student failure leveled in their direction despite the heroic efforts they may be making to tackle profound life challenges. As a result, low-income parents report few reasons to engage with school staff, finding "home–school contacts empty, contrived, insubstantial and awkward" (Harry, 1992, from Desforges & Abouchaar, 2003, pp. 45–46).

Beyond the challenges related to family income, students in high-poverty neighborhoods face a "double-jeopardy" phenomenon. While individually affected by chronic stress and trauma they are simultaneously funneled into the schools least prepared to meet their needs. These "high-poverty" schools lack sufficient resources, including staffing, facilities, and social capital (Editorial Projects in Education, 2004). Just as poverty affects family networks, resource scarcity has a substantial impact on the relational networks of high-poverty schools. Schools with the greatest opportunity gaps face multiple layers of resource-related stressors. Mirroring Masarik and Conger's (2017) pathway from poverty to maladjustment, under-resourced schools face a seemingly parallel trajectory: (1) resource scarcity leads to resource pressure, (2) resource pressure leads to educator distress, (3) educator distress leads to conflicts between school staff and disruptions in effective student engagement and instruction, and (4) these disruptions lead to reduction in student educational attainment.

Those who are charged with supporting students are often themselves suffering from the emotional toll of chronic stress and experiences of trauma. Forty-six percent of teachers report high daily stress, which compares only with nurses for the highest rate among all occupational groups (Gallup Education, 2014). A review of teacher stressors found that the majority stem from poor school organization, low trust of colleagues and leadership, inferior school climate, high job demands, a limited voice in decision-making, and difficulties managing student behavior (Greenberg, Brown, & Abenavoli, 2016).

In high-poverty neighborhoods, stress in the teaching profession comes not only from within the school walls but from the streets beyond. Teachers are participating members of the communities in which they work. Some may live nearby, while others may commute to work from wealthier neighborhoods, but all spend a significant portion of their waking hours in neighborhoods where it is not uncommon to witness acts of community violence, including the exchange of gunfire. Police-initiated lockdowns can be a routine occurrence. In addition to this direct exposure to violence, teachers often play the role of confidant for their students and in doing so repeatedly hear stories of trauma and loss. Over time it is not uncommon for school personnel to experience symptoms of traumatic stress, often referred to as secondary or vicarious trauma (Treatment and Services Adaptation Center, n.d.). Long understood as an occupational hazard in the field of mental health, secondary trauma is rarely acknowledged in the field of education, and little is done to educate teachers on how to prevent or alleviate symptoms of stress that may occur.

The stressors just described contribute to the long-standing challenge of teacher attrition. Forty-two percent of teachers leave the profession within their first 5 years. Teacher turnover has a negative impact on the academic scores of students in all schools, but it has a disproportionate impact on high-poverty, urban schools. Annual teacher turnover in high-poverty schools is over 22%, compared with just 13% in schools serving more middle- and upper-class students (Gray & Taie, 2015).

These high rates of teacher attrition destabilize low-income neighborhood schools by consistently disrupting relationships within the school community (Greenberg et al., 2016).

The occupational hardships described here result in a large number of teachers leaving the profession each year. They also have considerable impact on teachers who choose to stay and the students they teach. Notably, research on teacher stress demonstrates a link between teacher-reported feelings of burnout and the academic and social adjustment of students. Not surprisingly, teachers who demonstrate increased indicators of burnout have classrooms where students more frequently misbehave and show decreased academic and social performance (Hogland, Klingle, & Hosan, 2015). Furthermore, teachers who report higher levels of burnout have students who, when tested, demonstrate increased levels of the stress hormone cortisol, indicating an important connection between teachers' occupational stress and students' physiological stress regulation (Oberle & Schonert-Reichl, 2016). This "stress contagion" is no doubt cyclical in nature. Teachers of students who are highly stressed become stressed themselves and struggle to provide the types of consistent and nurturing relationships needed to regulate highly stressed students.

Despite growing agreement that addressing the extensive social and emotional needs in high-poverty schools requires a comprehensive approach, prevailing strategies rely on a medical model of care in which a small number of students are assigned to individual treatment with specialists. That problematic logic relies on seeing schools as peripheral to the social-emotional development of young people. Yet, after their parents, school staff are often among the most significant people in children's lives. More than any specialized treatment, healing and resilience develop from children's day-to-day relationships. An approach rooted in relationship is needed if schools are to become places in which all members experience unconditional acceptance and belonging.

A RELATIONAL APPROACH

For over 30 years, Seneca's work with youth and families facing profound emotional challenges has been guided by attachment theory and relational intervention. That is, Seneca's treatment philosophy is grounded in the belief that the emotional bonds between children and their caregivers have a substantial influence on their development. The origins of this approach may be traced to the demographics of the agency's earliest clients: adolescent foster youth with a history of disrupted placements and fractured relationships with their caregivers. Having worked with some of these youth in their previous group home, Seneca's founders recognized a disturbing pattern. A young person would enter the program and almost immediately challenge the staff and structures of the new placement. Adolescent clients would become physically aggressive, sexually provocative, or otherwise engage in actions likely to cause significant harm within the home. They would do whatever was necessary to send a clear message to the new adults in their lives: "Don't bother rejecting me; I've already rejected you." In prior placements, these behaviors had predictably resulted in a notice of discharge and removal to another placement in which a similar pattern would occur. Seneca's founders had made a commitment to change the familiar patterns of rejection and exclusion youth had internalized as the norm. When a young person asked, "What do I have to do to get kicked out of here?" the only possible answer was, "You must get better."

When a young person hit, punched, spit, kicked, brandished a weapon, displayed sexualized behavior, or spewed hate language, the staff stayed engaged. Staff did not yell or threaten loss of placement; instead, they intervened before, during, and after the crisis. They reaffirmed that nothing the young person could do would cause them to detach or disengage. Stability in relationships was crucial and the most powerful form of treatment. Young people who had been rejected or let down by adults so many times before eventually stopped trying to get the new adults in their life to reconfirm this experience.

This approach is directly informed by attachment theory and illustrates the ways in which relational treatment is at the heart of unconditional care. Attachment is a deep and enduring emotional bond that connects one person to another across time and space (Bowlby, 1969). Early theories of attachment stem not from the work of psychology but from the world of ethology, in the now famous experiments of Konrad Lorenz and his fledgling geese. Seeking to understand animal behavior, Lorenz demonstrated the phenomenon of imprinting. By placing himself in the role of the caretaking mother goose and observing the goslings' response to him as they grew increasingly attached, Lorenz established the existence of the innate patterns of proximity seeking, which in some species compels the development of a bond between mother and child (Sprinthall, Sprinthall, & Oja, 1994). Lorenz's work gave way to the prevailing notion that patterns of proximity seeking serve an evolutionary function. Notably, he demonstrated that the sense of safety we associate with close proximity between parents and their young is hardwired within us. From an evolutionary perspective, healthy attachment signals increased physical protection from predators and improved access to nutrition, thus influencing the chance of survival.

By the 1940s the documentation of a series of puzzling phenomena began to raise questions about whether attachment was purely a physical need. Observations of children in institutionalized settings revealed that infants who were well fed and physically cared for but deprived of human contact had weakened immune systems, failed to thrive, and sometimes simply died (Robertson, 1953; Spitz & Wolf, 1946; discussions in Karen, 1994). These observations indicated that there was more to be understood about the early experiences of care.

British psychoanalyst John Bowlby (1969) sought to explain the evolutionary connection between infants and mothers. Bowlby proposed, and many others in the field have helped to confirm (Cassidy & Shaver, 2016; Greenberg, Cicchetti, & Cummings, 1993; Oppenheim & Goldsmith, 2007), that a maternal bond develops not solely to meet an infant's physical requirements but also to fulfill a hardwired need for nurturing. In fact, human beings come into this world with a biological need for relationship. Proximity and connection to a responsive caregiver provide a sense of safety and equilibrium, whereas separation or disconnection results in an increased state of anxiety or distress. Further, infants utilize certain behaviors such as crying or smiling to elicit engagement with a caretaker, reflect emotions, and communicate needs. The success with which these cues are interpreted and responded to by a caregiver begins to shape the child's view of relationship, which then serves as a pattern for future relationships into adulthood. Finally, it is important to note that these early connections with a responsive caregiver establish an internal sense of safety, known as a "secure base" (Bowlby, 1988). Once this is established, children feel more comfortable in exploring the world and taking risks, which creates the foundation for learning.

Internal Working Model

Central to understanding and applying the principles of attachment theory is the concept of the internal working model (IWM). First proposed by Bowlby in 1973, this concept is useful in describing how, through early interactions with caregivers, individuals internalize messages about their own sense of safety, self-worth, and capacity to engage in relationships with others. IWMs arise from patterns of what has "worked" in previous relationships to secure the emotional engagement and proximity of others. Children who have been raised in relatively responsive settings likely had to do very little to initiate engagement with their adult caregivers. Thus, these children may have a certain understanding about the world—that it is a safe place, that they are worthy of love and care, and that adults have their best interests at heart and will respond to their needs. Children who have experienced disrupted, unresponsive, or threatening early relationships will likely hold a different set of assumptions— that the world is unsafe, that they are not worthy of love and care, or that they might need to go to great lengths to get what they need from their relationships with adults.

Children who have experienced traumatic or inconsistent engagement with adults have, out of necessity, shown ingenuity in employing strategies to engage in relationships, even if these strategies prove to be maladaptive in other settings. Take, for example, a baby whose mother struggles with significant clinical depression and as a result demonstrates a withdrawn demeanor or is wholly unresponsive in the daily act of caring for her child. The child who is rarely picked up from her crib or changed, and usually attended to only as a result of loud and sustained crying, will likely learn early on that "I have to work hard to get adults to see me." Fast forward 2 years down the road. This now toddler, inevitably encountering obstacles, may rely on violent temper tantrums to secure the proximity of adults. As a school-aged child, she may begin to demonstrate additional acting-out behaviors designed to get her noticed.

Because sense-making is a natural human tendency, children who have encountered more severe traumas may enact behaviors designed "to elicit reactions from others that confirm the implicit beliefs of [their internal working model]" (Sprinson & Berrick, 2010, p. 37). In other words, IWMs tend to work as self-fulfilling prophecies. For example, the behaviors of a child whose IWM is "I do not belong" or "I am not worthy of care" may elicit feelings of frustration, anger, or repulsion from adults, who then confirm these beliefs by pushing the child away.

Disconfirming Stance

From an attachment theory perspective, treatment thus becomes the process of disentangling children's unhelpful IWMs and gradually providing new experiences that "disconfirm, contradict, or in some way throw into question their beliefs and expectations" (Sprinson & Berrick, 2010, p. 59). The provision of a disconfirming stance "creates the possibility of altering those beliefs and, in turn, altering the behavior that flows from them" (ibid, p. 59). Children with disrupted attachments are keen observers of the world around them and are particularly good at reading the adults with whom they interact. It is the most struggling students who are most able to test the limits of new relationships by highlighting insecurities, provoking difficult emotions, and knowing just what to do or say to make adults want to push them away. Challenging behaviors that children display must be seen as "invitations" by the child to confirm their implicit, often unfavorable, beliefs about themselves.

In the work of unconditional care, adults must intentionally decode the underlying beliefs of a child's IWM, identify behaviors the child uses as "invitations" to confirm existing models, and articulate and practice interventions that will "disconfirm" unhelpful beliefs about the child's own self and place in the world. Take, for example, the child just described who knows that protesting loudly might just convince an adult to take notice. Conventional discipline strategies may label the child's behaviors as "attention seeking" and coach adults to ignore these behaviors until the child utilizes polite communication to make her request. However, for the child whose experience tells her "my needs will not be noticed," this approach will likely elicit an escalation rather than a decrease in the behavior. Instead, one might focus on providing consistent, proactive opportunities for teacher–student interactions throughout the day that send the message "you do not need to act out to noticed." We have seen talented teachers successfully institute systems of verbal and non-verbal cues designed to subtly remind students that they are seen and their needs considered, from the use of thumbs-up and other hand signals to the practice of leaving sticky notes on students' desks during work periods to show them that even when they are focused on the task at hand their teachers are still focused on them. Simple to implement, these interventions can be highly effective when incorporated in conjunction with explicit coaching for the child on new, more appropriate communication strategies for requesting a caregiver's time and attention. Engaging with the child throughout maintains a relational connection, sending the message that "your needs are important" and "you will be taken care of here."

Self-Regulation

Essential to the discussion of trauma-informed care is the concept of emotional regulation. If we conceive of misbehavior as an attempt to communicate an underlying need, then our first response must be decoding the message and attending to the need at hand. Too often, adults rush to correct the disruptive behavior of a young person in the midst of an emotional crisis, further exacerbating the child's escalation. A trauma-informed approach seeks first to restore the young person's sense of safety and equilibrium by attending to internal or environmental triggers fueling the behavior. In-the-moment intervention efforts must prioritize de-escalation, offer comfort, lend control, and incorporate physiological interventions that regulate breathing and heart rate, all of which allow thoughts and emotions to stabilize. Then, and only then, will attempts to modify behavior through the teaching of new and desired responses prove to be effective.

With practice, youth may be able to learn a variety of self-regulation strategies, including mindfulness techniques and incorporating healthy replacement behaviors and coping skills into their routines. Yet, many students require the assistance of a skilled and caring adult to restore emotional equilibrium. Sprinson and Berrick (2010) explain how this process of co-regulation helps the undeveloped, unregulated brain of the child make use of the developed, regulated brain to seek comfort and relief. The attuned adult can "reflect back to a child her own emotional states and thereby assist her in learning to recognize and modulate them" (Sprinson & Berrick, 2010, p. 43). During typical development, children shift away from reliance on an adult attachment figure for equilibrium and, increasingly, develop internal self-soothing strategies. When a connection with a regulating adult is disrupted or absent, children's "capacity for self-regulation is inadequately developed and they have a great deal of difficulty responding to the usual (and unusual) stresses, transitions and disappointments of daily life. In the face of these challenges, their behavior may become disorganized, impulsive, or aggressive (or 'dysregulated') and usually gets them into a great deal of trouble with those around them" (Sprinson & Berrick, 2010, p. 43). Young people who have experienced disrupted attachments and the adults who work with them both require special assistance in developing capacities related to self-regulation.

Returning to the example of the child who was raised by a caregiver with clinical depression, as an infant, her cues of distress and dysregulation (crying, fussing) too often went unanswered. Under similar circumstances, a more attuned caregiver might instead have opted to pick up a distressed child, rock her, talk in a soothing voice, or provide verbal assurance that everything would be okay. These attuned responses are capable of helping young children to regulate their emotions in the moment and eventually help them to understand how to self-soothe when distressed. If this transition is absent during that formative period, they may continue to become easily dysregulated as they grow older. Mild distress manifests in tantrums and other more severe behaviors that appear to be out of proportion to the visible trigger. These behaviors in children naturally evoke strong emotional reactions in their caregivers. As such, adults who work with dysregulated youth require explicit training and opportunities to practice promoting their own self-regulation. It is the role of the adult to resist these emotional triggers and instead demonstrate a well-regulated, consistent, emotionally contained response that communicates safety and aides young people in learning to regulate their own emotions.

While the principles of attachment theory have primarily been applied to individuals, they also inform our approach to educational systems transformation in highly resource-stressed communities. Substantial efforts are needed to more equitably resource high-poverty schools (to better understand how the unconditional education [UE] model leverages publicly available cross-sector funding, see Chapter 8; for strategies for increasing the efficiency of existing resources, turn to Chapter 2). Here, however, we consider how, in addition to procuring and aligning resources, the UE approach works to mitigate the relational effects of resource scarcity in high-poverty environments by applying an intentional approach to building and sustaining relationships, guided by the principles of attachment theory. In doing so, UE promotes school systems in which adults are available, attuned and responsive, and where children develop the secure relationships they need to take risks, explore the world, and engage in the important work of learning.

IMPLICATIONS FOR STUDENTS

The limits of UE are frequently tested when a school leader and community grow overwhelmed by the needs and resulting behaviors of one or more students, such as our very own Joseph Starr. The principal at Ford Elementary wanted to do everything possible to serve her students in their community school. However, she knew she was on the cusp of losing the trust of her faculty and parent community if change did not quickly occur. As is quite often the case, the principal was one of few remaining adults to maintain regular contact with Joseph and, therefore, to sustain a meaningful relationship with him. And by this point she started questioning her own ability to maintain unconditional positive regard. She was no less committed to Joseph than she had ever been, yet she began to express feelings of guilt at how a single student pulled her away from other duties and at the impact this was having on the school community as a whole. The more Joseph struggled, the more she herself felt emotionally depleted and the harder time she had thinking through creative interventions or implementing them with the necessary fidelity. It was time for a different approach. Joseph's team began working to unpack his IWM so that they could devise the most appropriate disconfirming stance and help Joseph heal and thrive.

When a student demonstrates a significant level of struggle, it can be tempting for teams to simply jump into action, employing interventions that may have worked for other students or in other settings. Pausing instead for a brief and powerful stage of empathy building can reconnect stressed and frustrated educators with the foundation of love and compassion that, as mission-driven individuals, brought them to their work. Building empathy begins by cultivating a state of curiosity that helps educators see the individuality of the student and to better understand and articulate the context in which the student is struggling. When Joseph Starr's team arrived at this stage, a trained facilitator led them to formulate a map of how he understood himself, his relationships, and the world around him—in other words, his IWM.

It is from this lens that relational connection, repair, and, ultimately, treatment are possible. In a session dedicated to the formulation of a student's IWM (see Appendices 3.1 and 3.2), the team is first asked to share what they know about the student's life and relationships outside of school. In this session, the team hypothesizes about how students' individual experiences may have shaped their core beliefs about themselves and the world. Considering past life experiences and relationships allows school-based teams to reflect on what unhelpful IWMs a student may hold. Finally, the team reflects on what reactions students' specific behaviors evoke in them and how these behaviors may be invitations to confirm the student's existing core beliefs, even when these beliefs are unhelpful or destructive. As mentioned previously, children who grow up in relatively secure and responsive settings develop helpful IWMs and assumptions, unlike students who have experienced traumas or unhealthy relationships. Table 3.1 lists common examples of both helpful and unhelpful IWMs.

Joseph Starr's team (including his service providers, teacher, and parents) sat down to reflect on his past experiences and his current behaviors and narratives. They discussed Joseph and his history at school. The team started with his strengths, noting that Joseph was bright, articulate, and persuasive. Joseph's parents described him as "attentive," "advanced for his age," and "someone who takes care of other people." School staff reported that he was a fast learner, with an infectious smile, who had built strong bonds with trusted adults. The team then reflected on his personal experiences and trauma history, recalling that from the time of Joseph's birth, his parents had engaged in significant conflict in their relationship with one another, which had included verbal and physical altercations, both before and since their separation. Within the past year, Joseph had witnessed fights between his mother and step-mother, as well as shouting matches between his parents, and had been denied access to one or the other parent at different times. Joseph's behavioral problems started when Joseph was in kindergarten. His mother attributed the onset of his emotional dysregulation to an early traumatic experience in which Joseph shot a

Table 3.1 Helpful and Unhelpful Internal Working Models (IWMs)

Assumption	Helpful IWM	Unhelpful IWM
My own safety	The world is a relatively safe place and adults are here help keep me safe.	The world is unsafe and I have to protect myself.
My ability to control my own outcomes	The world is somewhat predictable and I have the ability to control what happens to me.	The world is completely unpredictable and I have no control over what happens to me.
The motivation and intention of others	People have my best interests at heart and are here to help me and care for me.	I cannot trust others to help me or care for me and my best interests.
My own essential goodness as a person	I am a good person.	I am a (bad, unworthy, uncontrollable, unwanted) person.
My ownership of my own body	I can control what happens to my body.	Other people control what happens to my body. I cannot keep my body safe.
The capacity to control my own thoughts and emotions	I can control my own thoughts and emotions.	I cannot control my own thoughts—bad memories or thoughts and emotions intrude unexpectedly.

gun and accidentally hit his grandmother in the foot. The behaviors escalated significantly in second grade when his grandmother passed away.

The team hypothesized that, given these experiences, Joseph held a number of unhelpful core beliefs, including "I cannot be controlled" (I shot a gun that hit my grandmother in the foot but could have killed her), "I cannot do anything right" (I keep getting kicked out of school), and "no one cares about me" (my parents' fighting is the focus of their attention). The collaborative reflection and formulation of Joseph's IWM was a crucial first step in his team's ability to develop an effective relational approach to their work with him.

Joseph Starr's internalized perceptions about himself and the world in turn influenced behaviors that were making his school placement untenable. He appeared unresponsive to consequences, often minimizing the impact of his behavior on others or dismissing the impact they had on his own developing sense of self. The presence and frequency of these behaviors instilled fear, anger, frustration, and even disgust in the adults at Ford Elementary. When these difficult emotions surfaced, they provoked an innate desire in the adults around him to push those emotions, and with them Joseph, out of the school. They had been unknowingly accepting Joseph's invitations to reconfirm his beliefs that he could not be controlled, that he could not do anything right, and that the community would struggle to continue to care for him. Reflecting on Joseph's unwanted behaviors through the IWM lens provided a new perspective. A new approach to intervening would be required, making it clear that success would depend on developing a clear and consistent counter-message to Joseph's entrenched, unhelpful beliefs about himself.

Perhaps among the most interesting invitations identified by Joseph's team were his attempts to keep the adults with whom he worked from communicating with each other. When two adults would talk to each other, Joseph would yell, hum, and even try to physically separate them, inevitably provoking frustration in the adults involved, who would turn their attention to addressing his behavior instead of each other. In essence, this reaction from adults confirmed two of his IWMs—that he could not be controlled and that the adults in his life would not persevere in the face of adversity to pursue his care. The team hypothesized that Joseph was noticing that (for the first time in his educational experience) his teacher, his therapist, his behavioral interventionist, his mom, and his dad were making genuine efforts to create a cohesive, collaborative support plan. While this collaboration in and of itself provided an initial disconfirmation of his core belief that he could not be cared for, it also proved to be anxiety-provoking to have this belief challenged. Joseph did everything in his power to keep this collaboration from happening.

It is important to note that this collaboration between Joseph's parents and school also required a great deal of empathy. Just as the team focused its attention on uncovering Joseph's IWM, an understanding of his parents' IWMs about the intention of educators and the school system in regard to their son was paramount. His team recognized that, for families, messages about acceptance and belonging begin long before students walk through the school doors. Joseph had previously been rejected from a number of school placements, and an exploration of his parents' school history revealed similar experiences of exclusion. Parents' own IWMs and core beliefs about education are shaped by their own experiences of school, as well as prior personal and communal experience with schools and public systems at large. The team hypothesized that Joseph's parents held beliefs that included "the school system has consistently failed and excluded the students of our community" and "this school will not make efforts to understand and support my son." Thus, an equally important step in disconfirming Joseph's unhelpful worldviews was to concurrently rework the IWMs that prevented his parents from engaging at school.

The beliefs held by Joseph's parents are not uncommon and require acknowledgment of what has been problematic about prevailing approaches to education and mental health services in high-poverty neighborhoods. Education systems derive from a tradition of assimilation, with the purpose of indoctrinating children and families into the culture of power in the name of democracy. Similarly, traditional mental health approaches have long focused on "saving" clients from the "damage" done by their parents, relying on approaches to treatment that involve the removal of students from their natural support networks, such as residential treatment or other forms of out-of-home care. These traditional approaches end up creating further confusion and trauma and disrupt attachments within a child's primary network. It is no wonder that many families question the motives of professional "do-gooders" whose racial and cultural background is often very different from their own. Families are not blind to the inequitable outcomes produced by their neighborhood schools, nor to the experience of blame that accompany them. Given this history, schools hold a responsibility to engage in intentional relationship building as a means to disconfirm experiences of rejection or, worse yet, institutionalization.

Disconfirming Stance

Work with parents builds on what we know about the ways in which parent engagement affects educational attainment, identified earlier in this chapter. It is twofold. First, schools must establish a culture of shared responsibility, with a foundation of relational trust. Second, schools must actively rework prior rejection and alienation experienced by families. A growing body of research highlights the powerful role that relational trust between site leaders, teachers, and parents plays in supporting students. This research specifically acknowledges that the element of trust most essential to learning is the collective belief school staff put in the parents and students with whom they work (Bryk & Schneider, 2002; Forsyth, Adams, & Hoy, 2011; Tschannen-Moran, 2014).

As Bryk and Schneider (2003) explain, "Regardless of how much formal power any given role has in a school community, all participants remain dependent on others to achieve desired outcomes and feel empowered by their efforts" (p. 41). This is true when for interactions between school leadership and staff, and equally so when the discussion broadens to include an understanding of the shared investment by parents and school staff in the success of their children. To fully realize the potential of a trauma-informed approach, schools must create pathways by which families can authentically participate alongside practitioners in developing and implementing plans for their children. This inclusion of parents as partners requires a shift in mindset for many educators, who have come to see themselves as the "experts." They must embrace the belief that parents have something of high value to offer and are equally a part of the team, thus building relationships that are genuine rather than perfunctory. Reflecting on the experience of Joseph Starr's parents, and particularly the relationship between service providers and Joseph's mother, it was precisely these attempts to go "beyond the perfunctory" that eventually convinced his mother that this relationship would be different and might be worth engaging in. Instead of writing her off as "uninterested" or "unwilling to support" after an obligatory phone call or two, Joseph's team did their best to physically show up, time and time again, to express their genuine interest in her insights into her son, sending her the message that the plan's success depended on her genuine participation, knowledge, and support.

In addition to these baseline processes for teams, focused efforts must be made to disconfirm prior experiences of harm enacted by school systems. Schools in which parents have been historically marginalized and discounted must make intentional efforts to disconfirm these expectations by demonstrating something different is possible. The message parents need to hear and feel is that they matter, that they are valued and appreciated, and that they have something to offer. As a part of relational treatment, UE has come to call these practices, quite simply, practices of *mattering*. Drawn from the sociological construct developed by Rosenberg and McCullough (1981), the idea is to convey in small but meaningful ways that each member of the community is important and is valued. This framework helps staff to consider the key areas in which individuals frequently hold unhelpful beliefs about belonging and the ways in which small actions can help to send a message of inclusion (see Table 3.2).

In the case of Joseph Starr, taking time to establish relational trust between his parents and the school was a crucial component of providing a disconfirming stance. What also became apparent early on was that efforts to address Joseph's unhelpful belief that he would not be cared for necessitated further development of trust within the family itself. The deep-seated tension and disagreement between Joseph's mother and father affected their ability to fully participate in and support their son's educational experience. For this reason, Joseph's therapist dedicated considerable time and effort to working with his parents to develop a shared understanding and collaborative approach to his care, and to help them acquire new skills and strategies for successful co-parenting across time, location, and philosophical beliefs. Witnessing his parents' efforts to work as a team to support his needs helped lay the groundwork needed for Joseph to experience them as active, hopeful participants in his education.

While collaboration was at times rocky, it became clear that Joseph Starr's team of caregivers would persist, repeatedly sending him the message, through their collective words and actions, that "we are going to work together to help you take control of your situation, to support you in doing the right thing, and to show you that you have a team that cares very much about you and your well-being." This consistent disconfirming stance eventually prevailed and, over time, the child who would once use his own body as a block to prevent adults from talking about him now stopped trying to sabotage their efforts to work as a team, even going so far as to trust his parents to meet and talk with service providers in his absence. In addition, the support of this team sent a message to Joseph that he was not alone in his struggle. He now had a team that would not only support him but would also work to support his family, relieving him of the burden of holding their collective pain and anxiety and freeing him to focus on the work of being a student.

It is important to stress that empathy building and the formulation of an IWM and interventions to provide a disconfirming stance are only one piece in the very

Table 3.2 Practices of Mattering for Families

Realm of Mattering	Examples
Attention *I notice when you are here.*	Schools can be busy places, and the front office is usually the hub of activity from which parents and families come and go. The front office staff play an important role in welcoming families but are often forgotten when training in family engagement is provided. Some unconditional education schools have done specialized "customer service" training for their front office staff, shaping their role as welcoming committee for the entire school. Members of one front office team, in an effort to remind themselves that this duty extended to their phone interactions, placed a small mirror next to their computer. That way they could turn to it and smile when they answered the phone, ensuring that the smile would come through in the tone of their voices and provide a friendly connection to whoever was on the other end.
Appreciation *I value your efforts.*	When a student is struggling, school personnel may express frustration, and parents frequently feel they are being blamed for the student's behavior. Parenting is difficult work at the best of times. Noticing and naming all the things parents are doing to support their children is an important first step.
Importance *Your fate is important to me.*	Families struggling with the chronic stressors of poverty engage with schools when schools are able to provide support in meeting the problems they face in daily life. Practitioners who work with families must recognize the issues that are pressing and try to engage with these first. A parent who is facing eviction, for example, is unlikely to be able to give full attention to a parent–teacher meeting convened to discuss incomplete homework.
Dependence *I need you.*	Parents are important partners in their children's education and know their children far better than school staff ever could. Providing the time, space, and attention to elicit their observations about their children's strengths and weaknesses demonstrate that parents' participation matters. When staff and parents speak different languages, quality interpretation underscores the message of dependence.
Ego extension *I will celebrate your successes and be saddened by your misfortunes.*	Families and practitioners often set goals together to guide their work and find successes and setbacks along the way. Celebrating achievements and ultimate success is an important step. Celebrations such as a trip together to the corner store to buy special ice cream bars may be small but the process of celebrating together is monumental.

difficult work of changing patterns of engagement. It is essential that these actions be paired with an exploration of the systems within which students operate (see Chapter 2), a deeper analysis of the behavioral function and skills and knowledge needed (see Chapter 4), and thoughtful leveraging of the necessary resources for intervention (see Chapter 8). The totality of this exploration provides powerful insights and allows a team to individualize actions so that those interventions that are enacted are more likely to be effective.

IMPLICATIONS FOR STAFF

Relational approaches to supporting highly traumatized youth have been at the heart of Seneca's work since its inception. It became apparent early on that this approach could be sustained only if the same principles of relational engagement were applied to the adult caregivers within the system, while informing the overall policies and decisions of the agency. At the heart of the UE model sits the belief that schools' foundational work must be to create a sense of belonging among community members through the cultivation of genuine relationships. While the work is in the service of students, it cannot be done without equal attention to adults.

Like some students, educators may come to school with unhelpful internal beliefs, and over time in highly stressed systems it is not uncommon that they develop two specific unhelpful IWMs as a result of their experience: (1) "What I do is not valued" and (2) "I am not able to be effective." Administrators must work to disconfirm these unhelpful beliefs with concrete actions that demonstrate the value of teacher insight, particularly when it comes to developing plans to support the most challenged students.

Internal Working Model: What I Do Is Not Valued

Not unlike families, many teachers have had prior experiences of alienation within the school system. The recent era of high-stakes testing, valuing singular assessments, and ignoring teachers' insights illustrates what scholar Deborah Meier (2002) refers to as our collective radical distrust of public education, including teachers. Teachers' contributions are devalued. They have significantly less input than other professionals in important aspects of their work, and most efforts at school improvement are designed by administrators and policymakers for teachers rather than with them (Bryk, Gomez, Grunow, & LeMahieu, 2015). It is not surprising that, according to a 2014 Gallup poll, 70% of teachers report feeling unengaged with their work, meaning that they are emotionally disconnected from their workplaces. This reality is disturbing not only because of its potential impact on students' growth and learning but also as a reflection of the value we place on the life experience of those committed to the important work of teaching.

Disconfirming Stance: Building Relational Trust and Practicing "Mattering"

Building from its roots in the therapeutic realm, UE specifically supports leaders in cultivating the relational network within schools. This work builds on the idea that whatever we are asking our teachers to do with students should be modeled by administrators in their relationship with teachers. Roland Barth, founding director of the Principals' Center at Harvard University, sums it up in this way in *Educational Leadership* (2006):

> If the relationships between administrators and teachers are trusting, generous, helpful, and cooperative, then the relationships between teachers and students, between students and students, and between teachers and parents are likely to be trusting, generous, helpful, and cooperative. If, on the other hand, relationships between administrators and teachers are fearful, competitive, suspicious, and corrosive, then these qualities will disseminate throughout the school community. In short, the relationships among the educators in a school define all relationships within that school's culture. Teachers and administrators demonstrate all too well a capacity to either enrich or diminish one another's lives and thereby enrich or diminish their schools. (p. 8)

Just as effective teachers nurture relationships, rather than relying solely on content knowledge or pedagogical wizardry, so must school leaders immerse themselves in improving working conditions and teacher motivations beyond the world of instructional and curricular coaching (Leithwood, Day, Sammons, Harris, & Hopkins, 2006). In the midst of day-to-day challenges, a foundation of relational trust can help to protect against the relational divides in under-resourced schools.

A significant factor in the development of relational trust between administrators and teachers is teachers' participation in shared decision-making (Tschannen-Moran, 2014). Teacher voice is especially important in the often emotional work of supporting struggling students. However, the prevailing notion among teachers surveyed by Gallup is that their opinions rarely seem to count. Teacher voice (or lack thereof) is consistently identified as a key factor by teachers leaving the profession. The pattern of teacher attrition and its disproportionate effect on high-poverty schools highlights yet another reason why shared decision-making is a central tenet in the implementation of UE. Shared decision-making values the power of relationships, manifesting in the belief that those who have the closest relationships with students, most often teachers, can provide the greatest insight into students' needs and identify the most applicable solutions. Further, teacher participation in decisions about students' care strengthens the immediate relationship between teacher and student and increases the potential for stable relationships across the community by contributing to teacher retention.

However, this foundation of relational trust and promoting a team-based approach in a school is not sufficient in and of itself. Larger shifts aimed at decentralizing decision-making across districts and schools are necessary, but so are smaller, daily practices of mattering (see Table 3.3). These can help to rework unhelpful core beliefs that teachers may have concerning how they are valued and cared for, particularly with regard to the responsibility of supporting our most struggling students.

Table 3.3 Practices of Mattering for Staff

Realm of Mattering	Examples
Attention *I notice when you are here.*	As staff go through their busy days, it can become the norm to scurry past each other in the hallways or by the copy machine without acknowledging each other's presence. Simple practices of making eye contact and offering a greeting to colleagues go a long way toward being seen. One UE leader made a particular effort to take a "lap" of her school each afternoon after the closing bell, with no other purpose than to notice and acknowledge her staff. Some days this meant a quick "Hello" in a dozen classrooms and on other days it meant focusing on one or two deeper connections.
Appreciation *I value your efforts.*	Many community rituals have been designed to provide staff opportunities to appreciate the efforts of their colleagues. Some teams end each meeting with 5 minutes to "shout out" the good work of another, while others may post handwritten appreciations on a bulletin board somewhere in the school. Some UE schools have adopted the practice of asking staff to complete a short "likes and loves" survey at the start of the school year, soliciting information about how each staff member likes to be appreciated (public acknowledgment, private notes, etc.) and a list of favorites that staff can reference to further appreciate each other. One leader we worked with went so far as to keep a spreadsheet, recording to whom she'd sent an email appreciation after observing people doing something great during the course of a day. More than telling her who was standing out, this routine gave her valuable information about which of her staff were not on the spreadsheet. Since she spent most of her days in the classrooms of struggling teachers, she found she was cheerleading their efforts and improvements but often failed to appreciate the teachers who were excelling.

Table 3.3 Continued

Realm of Mattering	Examples
Importance *Your fate is important to me.*	Teachers and school staff are professionals with a desire to learn and grow. Specific and individualized efforts to aid in their continued personal and professional development demonstrate the valuing of their future selves, alongside their current work. Some UE schools provide each supervisor with a set of structured interview questions to engage the staff with whom they work directly in short- and long-term personal and professional goals. A process such as this provides valuable time within an otherwise busy schedule to "matter" the future of staff who commit tremendous effort in the present.
Dependence *I need you.*	Genuine efforts by school leaders to solicit feedback on important decisions and opportunities for shared decision-making demonstrate to staff that their input matters.
Ego extension *I will celebrate your successes and be saddened by your misfortunes.*	Staff spend most of their waking hours at school but have lives outside as well. A community can practice mattering by taking the time to recognize and celebrate important milestones and personal accomplishments, including weddings, the birth of children, and completion of advanced degrees, and similarly to acknowledge personal losses, such as the death or significant illness of family members. A simple card, a small gift, or brief celebration activity at a staff meeting can all serve to show team members that they are valued.

Internal Working Model: I Am Not Effective

Related to teachers' beliefs regarding the importance of what they say and who they are is their perception of whether they can make a difference. Feeling effective as a teacher is challenging, particularly when tasked with creating a cohesive, functioning community within a classroom while also attending to and addressing individual needs. Teachers increasingly struggle to feel effective when students present the more intensive social, emotional, and behavioral challenges discussed in this book. A growing body of research links teachers' positive perceptions of their own efficacy to increased levels of engagement (including retention) and emphasizes the importance of finding ways to increase teachers' sense of effectiveness throughout their careers (Forsyth et al., 2011; Tschannen-Moran, Hoy, & Hoy, 1998).

Disconfirming Stance: Investing in Teacher Capacity Building

In UE the development of teacher efficacy is specifically considered, building in sufficient support for teachers to feel confident in addressing the needs of all students in the classroom. For high-needs students, who frequently require the assistance of trained specialists (mental health therapists, school psychologists, speech pathologists, behaviorists, and counselors), UE proposes enlisting the support of these specialists in working toward the explicit goal of fostering secure attachments. The UE framework recognizes the real and powerful role that trained specialists can and must play in a coordinated, integrated system. Rather than acting as a replacement, this expertise is most effective when it shores up existing relationships in a child's school life, notably with their primary teacher.

For younger children or those who have struggled previously with engagement, having a trusting relationship with a single adult with whom they spend the most time at school can be essential to reshaping their connection to school as well as to repairing any trauma they may have experienced with previous caregivers (Sprinson & Berrick, 2010). Yet, all too often, as soon as students show signs of struggle they are ushered away from their teacher, a primary support provider, to the office, to specialized programs, or, in extreme cases, to hospitals, mental health institutions, and prisons. A system set up to send students away is harmful to teachers as well. It disempowers teachers and implicitly reinforces the notion that they are lacking both the skills and the trust of the school to connect with or help students who are experiencing significant challenges. Rather than sending students to higher levels of care, UE proposes that this same level of care and resources be embedded within the school environment, with specialists entering classrooms where teachers can observe and learn from the specialists' expertise. This approach provides relational stability for students while simultaneously making an investment in the skill and efficacy of teachers and the capacity of the entire school community.

As discussed in Chapter 2, serving high-needs students requires a team-based approach, with teachers occupying a central role in the functioning of this team. Intentionally including teacher voice in team collaboration efforts can provide a powerful forum from which to build innovative intervention strategies. It is the quality of relationships within these teams that informs the quality of the interventions they are able to provide. Teams with a high degree of relational trust provide the foundation for continuous improvement and the support needed for adults to persist in finding solutions, even when doing so proves difficult.

A team-based approach to treatment relies heavily on giving and receiving feedback, which must be explicitly taught and practiced through professional development activities. A culture of feedback means that team members commit to seeking out honest reflections from others and take risks to offer the same. A culture of feedback protects practitioners from designing interventions blinded by the biases inherent in their own IWMs. In addition, regular practices of giving and receiving feedback provide practitioners with the skills and opportunity to resolve inevitable difficulties in their relationships with each other, freeing them up to more readily focus on interventions with students.

Finally, a team-based approach provides a safe and supportive place to engage in the iterative work of relational intervention. While the earlier discussion of IWMs may have implied that formulation was a one-time phase of empathy building, the fact of the matter is that the path is far more circuitous. The work of relational intervention requires consistent revision and a great deal of vulnerability. As such, time and space must be carved out through ongoing professional development for practitioners to self-reflect on the impact they have had on the interventions employed, explore the difficult emotions that arise in their interactions with students, share successes and failures, give and receive feedback about their relational approaches, and devise new responses. By consistently returning to their foundation of empathy, they also return to hope and, with it, the commitment and courage to build inclusive schooling.

IMPLICATIONS FOR SCHOOLS

Beyond individual treatment and teacher capacity building, there has been growing interest in applying the principles of attachment theory across organizational settings, referred to as creating *trauma-informed environments*. This desire to look beyond one-to-one interactions with individual students and to apply trauma-informed principles across entire school environments is promising, for two reasons. For individual students like Joseph Starr, it is critical that the adults who support him throughout his day understand and apply trauma-informed principles in their interactions with him. What is equally important, however, is that these individual interactions occur within a school environment where attention to relationship, engagement, and repair is infused into *all* interactions with *all* students across *all* locations and times of day. In this way, Joseph and his classmates do not rely on specific adults for the predictability, consistency, and sense of safety and responsiveness they need. Instead, adults respond with a unified approach as youth move through their day, regardless of what they are working on or with whom they are engaged. Further, when schools develop a coherent set of trauma-informed practices, their reliance on expensive, external specialists diminishes as all adults become more capable of responding to students' individual needs.

The importance of this schoolwide approach became apparent during the first year of work at Ford Elementary. A new clinician there, who knew about the high rate of traumatic events students at the school had experienced, offered a targeted group for fourth-graders, using the Cognitive Behavioral Intervention for Trauma in Schools (CBITS) curriculum called Bounce Back.[1] The curriculum contains a

---

[1] See www.bouncebackprogram.org.

screener to determine which students have been exposed to a traumatic event (or events) and currently demonstrate post-traumatic, anxious, or depressive symptoms. From screening data the clinician planned to identify a handful of students to participate in the group. While the clinician expected to identify more students than she could serve, when the screeners were returned the results were astounding—over 60% of the hundred plus students screened met criteria for participation, signaling the need for a broader and more expansive approach.

For schools like Ford Elementary, where the majority of students experience some symptoms of post-traumatic stress, this whole-school approach is a critical component in ensuring that trauma-informed principles address the level of need in a school community. These guiding principles cannot be implemented by one clinical expert on campus. They must be infused into the mindsets, policies, and practices of day-to-day operations. Consistent with Seneca's approach to systems transformation, trauma-informed practices foster relational engagement across the school network. Whole-school approaches informed by principles of attachment theory help to ensure that students who have experienced toxic stress or trauma receive consistent interventions while at school and that the entire school experience serves as a therapeutic setting. The National Center for Trauma-Informed Care (NCTIC) identifies a trauma-informed approach as one that:

- realizes the widespread impact of trauma and understands potential paths for recovery;
- recognizes the signs and symptoms of trauma in clients, families, staff, and others involved in the system;
- responds by fully integrating knowledge about trauma into policies, procedures, and practices; and
- seeks to actively resist re-traumatization.

Building on content developed by the American Institute for Research, Seneca has developed a trauma index (see Appendix 3.3) that helps schools assess the extent to which they are promoting a trauma-informed environment. Three critical areas of examination are professional development, physical environment, and schoolwide policies.

As is the case with most initiatives addressed at the systems level, professional development plays a large role in developing schoolwide consciousness around trauma-informed practices. Training in trauma-informed education includes the knowledge and skills outlined by the NCTIC and is essential in the following areas: classroom practice, promotion of self-regulation, examining implicit bias, and the connections between self-care and self-control.

- *Classroom practice*—Professional development and coaching resources must be dedicated to helping staff adopt consistent discipline practices and integrate social-emotional learning into their day-to-day practice in the classroom. These supports provide staff and students with a common language for talking about behavioral and social expectations, further enforcing a sense of predictability and consistency campus-wide.

- *Promoting self-regulation*—The ability to respond in predictable and consistent ways brings us back to an important concept central in discussions of attachment: self-regulation. Intentional self-regulation can aid practitioners in their provision of a disconfirming stance. At the same time, through the use of additional strategies educators can offer emotional availability to aid a dysregulated student in developing self-control. Stress, anxiety, and feelings of powerlessness are among the many factors that increase emotional reactivity and decrease regulation. Teachers, especially those in high-poverty schools, are routinely subjected to all three. The cumulative effect of stress from working in an underresourced environment, coupled with the emotional toll of caring for students who have experienced significant trauma can have a powerful effect on teachers' ability to employ the foundational relational approaches described thus far. Training must support educators in gaining a better understanding of their own IWMs and emotional states and in developing self-control and self-care strategies to modulate their own responses, even while under stress.

- *Implicit bias*—Educators' knowledge of their own IWMs is essential for the provision of relational treatment. Teachers, like students, carry around their own beliefs and expectations for social relationships, including those between adults and children and between teachers and students. When children enact their own IWMs, it can be disconcerting to adults whose culture, background, and personal experiences have led them to see the world through a different lens. Many teachers enter the profession with IWMs like "I'm a natural with kids," for example. It makes sense, then, that such teachers might struggle with a student who is not naturally won over, just as it makes sense that a teacher who believes "the world is designed for adults to lead and children to follow" might feel constantly frustrated by a young person whose worldview maintains that "adults' rules can't keep me safe and thus don't need to be followed." Often, this mismatch can provoke difficult feelings, such as annoyance, frustration, or even disgust, which can pose a significant barrier to empathy for the adults involved. By exploring their own IWMs in a structured setting, educators have a chance to uncover their implicit biases and confront their own unhelpful beliefs. In addition, professional development activities, such as the one shown in Appendix 3.2, guide school staff in identifying when these feelings arise and to control their own behaviors in response to these, and other, difficult emotions.

- *Self-care*—School practitioners, particularly those working in under-resourced communities, must also be supported in practicing self-care, which promotes the habits required to engage in self-regulation and maintain wellness, motivation, and longevity. Self-care helps teachers to respond with emotional consistency and combat the long-term effects of stress, preventing burnout. Bessel van der Kolk, psychologist and leading researcher on traumatic stress, has identified several shared traits among "stress-resistant persons," in his book *Psychological Trauma* (2003). These include (1) a sense of personal control; (2) pursuit of personally meaningful tasks; (3) healthy lifestyle choices, including exercise, sleep, and healthy eating; and (4) socially supportive relationships with others who can serve as a protective buffer in difficult situations. In training dedicated to this topic, school staff reconnect with the motivations and meaning that brought them to the profession, learn to identify early symptoms of vicarious trauma and burnout, and develop self-care plans to revisit throughout the year. Teachers are one of the most important assets in creating healthy, thriving school communities. An investment in their well-being is an investment in the well-being of every community member.

CONCLUSION

When the principles of attachment theory are applied to school systems, all members of the school community develop strong, healthy, and supportive relationships. There is a common understanding that these relationships are essential for both future growth and learning and to rework past experiences of harm. When attention to relationships permeates a school, members believe that they each have the other's best interests at heart and that their efforts and participation are a vital part of building a strong community. Strong relationships can help buffer the effects of the many stressors facing under-resourced schools, allowing all participants to focus more freely on the important work of growth and learning. At the same time, relational quality matters in and of itself, ensuring that the experiences children have in school are pleasurable and contribute to an overall sense of self-worth and community engagement.

With a shift to focusing on intentionality of relationship, school staff better understand the impact of prior personal experiences on students, families, and each other and apply this knowledge in daily interactions, even while under stress. Skillful participation in relational approaches relies on adult self-regulation, facilitated by the policies and practices that promote self-control and self-care. In addition, new systems must be developed to promote individual efficacy, engaging all stakeholders in decisions that affect their daily lives.

APPENDIX 3.1
SAMPLE INTERNAL WORKING MODEL WORKSHEET

Trauma History		Student Strengths
		• e.g., Likes showing new students around the school

Behaviors	Our Stuff	Invitations
Describe the student's observable behaviors.	What thoughts, feelings, and assumptions do these behaviors bring up for YOU?	How is the child inviting you to respond? What does it seem like he or she wants you to do?
• e.g., Physically aggressive with peers and adults (hits, pushes, kicks)	• e.g., This student takes up too much time and energy.	• e.g., Student is inviting me to avoid and ignore him.

Internal Working Model Hypothesis	Disconfirming Stance	Intervention Strategies:
Use first person to describe students' core beliefs about themselves, their relationships, and their world.	What approach can we take to correct unhelpful beliefs about themselves, their relationships, or their world?	What specific strategies can you use in your classroom to disconfirm unhelpful beliefs?
• e.g., I have to be in control in order to feel safe. • e.g., No one likes me.	• e.g., Adults are here to keep you safe. • e.g., We like you.	• e.g., Create a calm corner in the classroom (student is still welcome in the classroom even when feeling upset)

INTERNAL WORKING MODEL WORKSHEET

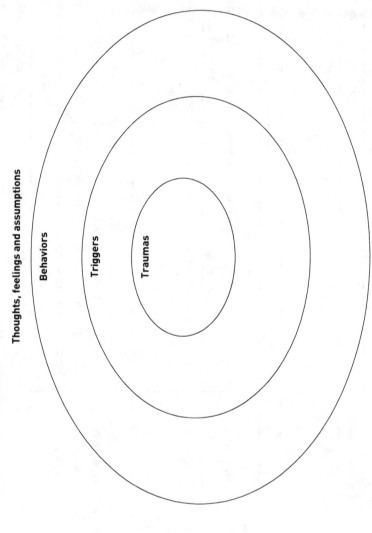

Thoughts, feelings and assumptions

Behaviors

Triggers

Traumas

Student Strengths		
Behaviors: Describe the student's observable behaviors	**Our stuff:** What thoughts, feelings and assumptions do these behaviors bring up for YOU?	**Invitations:** How is the child inviting you to respond? What does it seem like he/she wants you to do?
Internal Working Model Hypothesis: Use first person to describe the student's core beliefs about themselves, relationships and their world	**Disconfirming Stance:** What approach can we take to correct unhelpful beliefs about themselves, relationships or their world?	**Intervention Strategies:** What specific strategies can you use in your classroom to disconfirm unhelpful beliefs?

More information on Seneca's trauma-informed approach to care and the Internal Working Model can be found in the book *Unconditional Care: Relationship-Based, Behavioral Intervention with Vulnerable Children* by John S. Sprinson and Ken Berrick

APPENDIX 3.3
BUILDING TRAUMA-INFORMED SCHOOLS: KEY DOMAINS

For each category listed below, please mark one of the following options:	Not in Place	Somewhat in Place	In Place
SUPPORTING STAFF DEVELOPMENT			
Training for staff in understanding and responding to symptoms of trauma			
Training in vicarious trauma/burnout and supporting self-care			
Ongoing trauma-related consultation and support			
CREATING A SAFE AND SUPPORTIVE SCHOOL ENVIRONMENT			
Clean, well-maintained, accessible classrooms and common areas			
Adequate monitoring of classrooms and common spaces			
Clear policies for violence and bullying that are understood by staff and students			
Clear expectations and routines and clear plans for transitions			
Staff responses are consistent, predictable, and respectful			
Staff use praise and reinforce positive behaviors			
Staff work to identify and reduce potential triggers for children and parents			
Designated safe spaces for children to go to when feeling overwhelmed/triggered			
Clear crisis prevention/management plans that include de-escalation techniques			
Cultural background of students is reflected in artwork, language, and materials			

For each category listed below, please mark one of the following options:	Not in Place	Somewhat in Place	In Place
ADAPTING POLICIES			
School regularly examines and adjusts policies and procedure in light of trauma principals (e.g., understanding safety, choice, control, and empowerment)			
School identifies procedures and policies that are potentially triggering or re-traumatizing to students (leave them feeling, anxious, vulnerable, out of control)			
INVOLVING CHILDREN AND FAMILIES			
Children and families have input into school rules, policies, practices, and programs			
Families are partners in decision-making around child needs and plans			
Families are educated on making referrals to school and community-based supports			
ACCESSING AND PLANNING SERVICES AND BUILDING SKILLS			
All school-based assessments (educational, functional behavioral, psychosocial) consider history of trauma and its potential impact on learning, behavior, testing results, and diagnosis			
All individualized plans (Individualized Education Programs [IEPs], behavior plans) include trauma-specific components when applicable (e.g., triggers, trauma-related responses, trauma-sensitive supports)			
School maintains a holistic view of students and facilitates communication within and among service provider systems			
School offers trauma-specific individualized services			
Staff consider the relationship between culture, trauma, and recovery and use interventions that are considerate of cultural background			
School builds and maintains connections with community-based agencies with expertise in trauma and can provide in-service trainings and consultation as needed			

4 Schools as Centers for Behavioral Learning

WHERE WE ARE

Organizing for effective change requires an understanding both of formal systems and of intimate human relationships. It requires that efforts be intentionally embedded within local context while remaining attuned to the human dynamics that breathe life into these very communities. Chapter 2 proposed that true educational reform requires deep and sustained systems-level change. Chapter 3 explored the impact that relationships have on the sense of connection, trust, and vulnerability necessary for the transformative process. Building on a systems-level lens and an investment in human relationships, this chapter will explore the tenets of behavioral learning theory to better understand how behavior change contributes to transformation within students and school communities.

Changing behavior is difficult; it is a slow, often circuitous, journey. It requires real people, with their own personal preferences and habits, to change behaviors that they may have grown strongly accustomed to overtime. What's more, school professionals responsible for shaping the behavior of others within the education setting often lack the foundational knowledge and skills to do so. In the process of reshaping student behavior and inspiring adult learning, educators frequently start with ambitious goals that lack a clearly articulated plan for promoting the changes necessary to achieve them. Without a roadmap, it is commonplace for educators to become convinced that efforts at change are going nowhere, to lose hope or give up along the way, and tell themselves that "we just can't help this difficult student" or "this schoolwide initiative won't work here." This chapter proposes that the principles of behavioral learning theory can be applied to (1) teach students the social-emotional skills they need to become successful scholars and citizens and (2) build the capacity of adults to improve the overall culture and climate of a school campus. Guided by the tenets of behavioral learning theory we ask the following questions:

How do we approach challenging behavior as an opportunity to engage with students and build new behavioral skills?

How do we create proactive discipline systems with the explicit purpose of creating a sense of predictability, consistency, and equity?

The essential elements of behavioral learning theory—assessment and planning, implementation, and progress monitoring—are well established in education in regard to acquiring academic knowledge and skills. When a student is struggling with reading, educators are quick to assess the problem and develop a plan for additional support and targeted skill-building. All too often, however, when a student's behavior is the subject of concern, there is a missed opportunity to take a skill-building approach. When a young person's behavior disrupts the learning environment or damages relationships within the classroom, the first instinct is to punish or remove the "offending student" from the classroom setting. This go-to response compromises time devoted to learning and leads to further removal through the assignment of exclusionary consequences, including suspension and expulsion.

These effects are magnified for youth of color, students with disabilities, and those living in poverty, who over the course of their school careers average a greater number of instructional days missed due to exclusionary discipline practices than their classmates without these traits (Sosa, Cox, & Alvarez, 2017). Among middle-school students, Black youth are suspended nearly four times more often than White youth, and Latino students are roughly twice as likely to be suspended or expelled as their White counterparts (Losen & Martinez, 2013). High school students with disabilities of any sort are nearly three times more likely to receive an out-of-school suspension than their non-disabled peers (Kang-Brown, Trone, Fratello, & Daftary-Kapur, 2013).

This pattern of disproportionate exclusionary discipline practices contributes to the persistent achievement gap that exists along the lines of race and disability status. While struggling socially and behaviorally clearly has an impact on time spent learning, research indicates an even more specific and perhaps unexpected relationship between behavioral challenges and success at school. One longitudinal study showed that lower academic achievement is not directly associated with misconduct itself but rather with the disconnection from school that occurs as a result of this misconduct (Hoffmann, Erickson, & Spence, 2013). This finding suggests the importance of keeping young people engaged in school, even when, and *especially when*, they are having behavioral problems.

Before covering the principles of behavioral learning theory in depth, it's important to reflect on the origins of the problem, namely our nation's overreliance on exclusionary discipline practices in schools and the disproportional inequities these practices perpetuate. Taking time to understand the context of a problem is, after all, one of the main tenets of behavioral learning theory. Two factors, in particular, contribute to this problem: the legacy of zero-tolerance behavioral policies and the impact of implicit bias.

The proliferation of exclusionary discipline practices can be traced, in part, to the 1994 passage of the Gun-Free Schools Act and the introduction of zero-tolerance policies. This Act created a contingency for states to receive federal education funding, requiring them to mandate all school districts to expel, for at least 1 year, any student who brought a weapon to school. The "hard on crime" tidal wave of that era spurred the proliferation of a zero-tolerance mindset that was adopted much more broadly, resulting in implementation of policies promoting suspensions for a variety of offenses, from the more objective act of "possession of a controlled substance" to the most subjective acts of "insubordination" or "disorderly conduct." Further mirroring the punitive criminal justice system, school campuses began to host more formal law enforcement personnel. Between the 1996–97 and 2007–08 school years, the number of public high schools with full-time law enforcement and security guards tripled (Kang-Brown et al., 2013). The increased involvement of law enforcement in school discipline has only helped perpetuate the notion that students who exhibit challenging behavior are perpetrators who should be punished and isolated from their peers rather than children who need to learn more acceptable behaviors. Students of color have been particularly impacted by this way of thinking. Notably, the schoolyard behavior of Black boys is adultified and their youthful "transgressions are made to take on a sinister, intentional, fully conscious tone that is stripped of any element of childhood naiveté" (Ferguson, 2000, p. 83). This adultification of normal childhood behavior systematically perpetuates exclusionary discipline practices and limits opportunities for necessary social development.

Our educational system is slowly awakening to the troubling repercussions of the zero tolerance policies. An emblematic turning point occurred in 2014 with the release of the *School Discipline Guidance Package*, a joint effort by the US Department of Justice and Department of Education. However, these are still mere recommendations being embraced by individual schools and districts with varying levels of urgency and dedication. In practice, even schools with the best intentions are slow to shed the legacy that over 25 years of zero tolerance has imposed.

As previously noted, students of color and students with disabilities are far more likely to experience a punitive, exclusionary response when exhibiting challenging behavior, and these persistent and well-documented patterns of disproportionality in discipline practices are evident from the time students enter school. In fact, researchers at Yale University found that preschool students are expelled at three times the rate of all kindergarten through 12th-grade students and that among this age group African American children are expelled at twice the rate of their White peers (Gilliam, 2005). Even more recently, the US Department of Education (2016) showed that while Black children comprise only 19% of the preschool population, they account for nearly half of all suspensions. As part of an effort to understand the reasons behind these eye-opening statistics, researchers at Yale conducted an experiment with early childhood educators. The results of this experiment strongly suggest that implicit bias—that is, attitudes or stereotypes that are activated unconsciously or involuntarily—plays a role in disproportionate disciplinary practices. Social scientists believe that implicit biases are learned as young as age 3 and may be fueled by stereotypes perpetuated in the media or beliefs passed along by parents, peers, or other community members (Gilliam, Maupin, Reyes, Accavitti, & Shic, 2016).

In the Yale study, early childhood educators were asked to watch videos of preschool children in the classroom setting and to be prepared to signal when the first signs of behavioral challenges occurred. In reality, none of the children in the videos displayed behavioral challenges. Instead, the researchers were tracking the eye movements of the educators to see which students drew their attention. What they found was that teacher participants spent more time looking at the Black children than the White children, and they spent the most time watching the student who was an African American boy (Gilliam, Maupin, Reyes, Accavitti, & Shic, 2016). Not surprisingly, when teachers spend more time studying the behavior of a particular student they expect to misbehave, they more readily identify incidents of misbehavior. This study demonstrates just one way in which implicit bias deeply affects students of color. Decades of punitive approaches to discipline have perpetuated oppressive structures that harm our most vulnerable children. An approach that shapes behavior, rather than punishes it, is needed to build equitable organizations of learning.

A BEHAVIORAL LEARNING APPROACH

As its name implies, behavioral learning theory has long existed at the forefront of both behavioral health and educational theory. Rising to prominence during the first half of the twentieth century, psychologists and theorists such as John B. Watson, B. F. Skinner, and Ivan Pavlov strove to understand how humans learn through interaction with the environment. Together, they created a canon of research that demonstrated how human behavior is influenced by its antecedents, as well as by the positive reinforcement or negative consequences that result. Combined with more recent findings in the fields of cognitive learning theory and social learning, educators and researchers have begun to understand how to help shape and reshape behavior through a strategic, planned approach, referred to here as *behavioral learning theory*.

Alongside systems theory and attachment theory explored in previous chapters, behavioral learning theory has long stood at the foundation of Seneca's work with youth. From the agency's earliest days as a residential services provider, great emphasis was placed on creating predictable environments where young people were met with consistent behavioral responses from adults. Similarly, unconditional education (UE) equips schools to shape the behavior of students and systems using the guiding tenets of behavioral learning theory: (1) strengths-based assessment and planning, (2) thoughtful and explicit skill building and coaching, and (3) regular progress monitoring. Creating discipline systems that integrate these tenets helps to reinforce a restorative and positive approach to discipline, engaging rather than excluding students. Seneca's experience working with youth and families within the realm of mental health treatment has produced valuable insights in this regard. These three tenets are described in greater detail in the next sections.

Strengths-Based Assessment and Plan Development

As outlined in Sprinson and Berrick's (2010) *Unconditional Care*, there are core components of behavioral learning theory that influence Seneca's treatment approach to behavioral intervention with children and youth. The first step to engaging with a child in a high level of behavioral crisis relies on a strengths-based assessment that leverages input from the client and family and engages them as experts in identifying their own strengths and challenges as well as meaningful goals for treatment. When skillfully completed, this initial engagement with the child and family is an integral part of the intervention itself and an opportunity to initiate a relational intervention. In the process of assessment, some or all of the following questions arise: What strengths and capacities can be further developed in the child? What are the ingredients that have been associated with the child's success? What resources does the child have that have not been fully recognized and that can be developed? What do I as a service provider need to know of the child's cultural background to understand how my efforts are perceived? What values, dreams, and hopes for the future do this child and family have? What interventions have been successful? Who are the people who have important relationships with this child and how can they be included? (Sprinson & Berrick, 2010, pp. 6–8).

As goals are co-created by the service provider and the client, specific, observable behaviors and the context in which they occur must be identified. Thereafter, staff can pinpoint specific strategies as they formulate a treatment plan. A client in one of Seneca's early residential programs, Isabella, serves as an example. Isabella was a 6-year-old girl who had been cared for in more than a dozen placement settings since being separated from her biological father at the age of 2. The final decision to move Isabella into dependent care was driven by substantiated findings of frequent and pervasive physical and sexual abuse. When she arrived in the program, staff read accounts from her prior placement, from which she had been expelled. These reported on her behavior in vague terms—for example, "She never listens to anything staff say"—which had no doubt led to watered-down solutions and a continued escalation of her crisis behaviors. Working to develop a more specific problem statement, Isabella's new team articulated a more specific definition of her behavior: "She ignores me when prompted to start getting ready for bed and will respond with verbal refusals and tantrum-like behavior when I ask her to brush her teeth or get in the shower." This descriptive problem statement helped the team to develop more targeted and specific action steps.

In efforts to shape maladaptive behaviors in children, it is essential to focus on understanding the function of such behavior. As Sprinson and Berrick (2010) remind us, "All relationships with clients must begin with the default assumption that their problematic behaviors worked for them in some way in other settings and relationships" (p. 128) and "all behavior is, at least in part, established and maintained by rewarding events or escape from negative events that may follow it" (p. 6). If Isabella had a history of being abused at night while in her bed, her current behaviors serve the (understandable) function of avoiding bedtime. Part of grasping the full context of behavior requires staff to ask where, when, and why the behavior occurs. In other words, not "Why does this behavior happen?" but "Why does this behavior happen in this context?" Table 4.1 provides an overview of common behavioral functions, enabling practitioners to ask the question, "Does this behavior primarily serve as access or avoidance of particular stimuli?"

Gathering observable data regarding unwanted behaviors can tell us a great deal about "what," "when," and "where," but not "why"—the hardest question to answer and the one with the least obvious collectable data. Studying our collected data, and making connections to what we know about a client's personal history and internal working model (IWM), forces us to develop a hypothesis of the "why." What makes this so difficult is that the reward sought or negative event avoided may be external and observable (e.g., "I don't want to go into my dark room alone"), but it may very well be related to a client's IWM (e.g., "I cannot trust adults to keep me safe at nighttime"). A child may be seeking a reward or avoiding a threat that is a very real possibility for the child, given their prior experiences, but one that we would never think to consider. Identifying the "why" is crucial if we are to develop an intervention that addresses the root of the problem. In our attempts to understand the function of behavior, we must be prepared to make use of observational skills while also asking questions that might help us understand any internal motivations that may exist.

Implementation and Coaching

Once we've identified the context of the problematic behavior, we work to explicitly teach discrete skills, replacement behaviors, or both. The end goal is to promote

Table 4.1 Functions of Behavior

	Access	Avoid
Item, outcome, or preferred activity	Occurs when a preferred item or activity is removed or is unavailable	Occurs when presented with a non-preferred direction, task event, outcome, or activity
Attention	Occurs when attention from another individual or group of individuals is unavailable	Occurs when high rates of attention are available
Sensory	Occurs because the behavior satisfies the performer	Occurs to distract from a non-pleasurable sensation

mastery of skills across environments that clients can use in their day-to-day experiences at home, in the classroom, and in the community. In adapting this approach to Isabella, the team might work to teach her concrete skills to address her anxiety (e.g., relaxed breathing), rather than trying to change her behavior through punitive strategies like timeout that may only increase her anxiety by leaving her alone and unsupported while in a vulnerable emotional state.

The process of teaching and learning requires a big investment on the part of the service provider and a great deal of willingness on the part of the client to try something new and challenging. Because we are asking our clients to take risks, try new things, and aim for ambitious goals, it is crucial that this work take place within an environment that is inherently rewarding and where clients are offered positive feedback about their progress. The provision of positive feedback, rooted in learning theory, can be guided by the following principles:

1. Use quantitative measures of performance.
2. Give feedback as immediately as possible.
3. Give feedback frequently.
4. Make feedback positive.
5. When applicable, provide group feedback (based on a group goal that will have the effect of improving individual performance).
6. When appropriate, post positive feedback publicly.

Finally, we must ensure that the support provided through this process and the relationship between service provider and client is not contingent on the client's success. We are asking clients to take big risks and try new things, and we must be honest with ourselves and with them: there will be setbacks, mistakes, and temporarily insurmountable barriers along the way. We should not give the impression that support relies on success but, rather, the opposite. A child's inclusion in the program and the availability of relationship with its staff are explicitly *unconditional*. This reframes challenges as opportunities to grow, and enables clients to reflect on their mistakes, revise their approach, and try again, knowing we will be there to support them.

Monitoring for Effectiveness

The circuitous path of change often means moving "one step forward, two steps back," as a result of unforeseen and unpredictable obstacles that arise along the way. Human beings and organizational systems are complex, ever-evolving organisms. We resolve one issue, we conquer one goal, and we learn a new skill only to find that fresh challenges have arisen that require our attention. Indeed, by digging into one area of improvement we often unearth several more. It is in the context of this phenomenon that a structured, incremental approach to assessing needs, identifying goals, and measuring progress is critical.

Making change measurable and anchoring it in observable differences helps combat the perception that "nothing is improving" or "it just isn't working." Staff work to create a treatment plan that specifically states the baseline behavior and sets realistic goals for improvement within a set time period. For Isabella, a measurable goal was "Isabella will increase the pace of her bedtime routine, completing it in 15 (rather than 45) minutes." The team could monitor and track Isabella's progress on this goal, as well as reflect on the progress at agreed-upon intervals (e.g., every 2 weeks). While nighttime staff continued to feel overwhelmed when Isabella engaged in tantrums or other crisis behavior, the objective progress monitoring data served as a welcome reminder that overall progress was being made in the right direction and that Isabella was learning new replacement skills over time. These lessons gleaned from work with students in intensive treatment environments can be similarly applied to students and schools.

IMPLICATIONS FOR STUDENTS

Providing differentiated and personalized approaches to instruction to support the various academic motivations and learning styles represented in a classroom is becoming more commonly understood as best practice. UE takes this one step further by applying the concepts of personalization and differentiation to the behavioral and social-emotional development of students. As with academic readiness, students come to school with different levels of mastery of a wide range of social and behavioral skills. Some have the foundation to be successful in the traditional classroom environment, while others struggle. Consequently, some students will require explicit instruction and ongoing opportunities to practice new behavioral and social skills in order to access the academic curriculum.

Teaching behavior requires a certain mindset, a level of dedication, and a specific skill set that will be highlighted in the text that follows. If efforts are to be successful, the relational and ecological concepts presented in the previous two chapters must also be considered. To more readily illustrate this complementary interplay between the ecological, relational, and behavioral streams of intervention, we return to the story of Joseph Starr and, in particular, the ways in which Joseph's one-on-one behavioral coach was able to seamlessly weave together the relational and ecological work of establishing trusting relationships while building the capacity of natural supports through behavioral interventions.

Integrating Relational Theory: Relationship as the Foundation for Effective Behavioral Intervention

While there are specific assumptions and strategies that guide both behavioral and relational interventions, arbitrary divisions between these two realms, in practice, become problematic. In schools and other youth-serving programs, providers may address the behavioral and emotional realms as separate and distinct. Instead, attention to the inherent duality within a student's internal experience and external response requires professionals to interweave these approaches in a complementary manner. Joseph Starr's notable progress over time was undoubtedly a team effort, but it was jump-started by one particularly skilled veteran staff, Coach Santos, who had mastered the art of integrating behavioral and relational interventions.

When Santos arrived at Ford Elementary, it was clear that he was working with a student who had grown to distrust the school system and that those feelings of distrust were reflected back by the school community. Joseph's relationships with staff and students were strained, to say the least. As Santos began meeting with staff to introduce himself and explain his role, he was met with responses like "Good luck working with him, because everyone else has failed." Adults on campus were tired, having spent the last drops of their empathy reserves, and they had clearly developed a picture of Joseph as an "impossible" student with whom they could not connect. Santos understood that any attempts to teach behavioral intervention in earnest would be futile without first helping Joseph to reestablish trust and connection with his community. For the first few weeks, he focused almost exclusively on helping Joseph to hold himself accountable for healing damaged relationships. Santos would track these behavioral incidents and coach Joseph in reconnecting with staff and students to take ownership of his actions and their impact. This work was difficult for Joseph, but he quickly learned that no matter how hard he pushed back, Santos would consistently record incidents that occurred and reinforce the process of relational repair.

After a time, a number of things started to shift. First, Joseph became more able to recognize the impact of his behavior and to take responsibility for repair. Second, staff and students who witnessed Joseph's development in this area and experienced these restorative conversations began to shift their perception of Joseph, easing some of the tension and creating space for connection, curiosity, and trust. Finally, Joseph learned something valuable about Santos. It became clear that Santos wasn't going anywhere. No matter how hard Joseph pushed or how much he struggled, Santos showed up every day. He brought consistency and predictability to the relationship repair process that in turn created space for Joseph to experience himself as someone capable of healing and deepening relationships.

While some behavioral interventionists might be eager to dive into the more traditional behavioral-shaping strategies, such as setting up structures for rewards and consequences, Santos's vast experience led him to understand that behaviorally based strategies can only be carried out by adults who have built a level of trust and proven their dedication to a client. Establishing such a relationship takes time, but providers like Santos demonstrate that effective outcomes depend on this initial and ongoing investment. Furthermore, not only are behavioral interventions more effective when carried out within the context of a strong relationship, but the quality of relationships is fueled and deepened by the predictability inherent in an effective behavioral intervention. When a caretaker is able to use positive and pro-active means to guide a child to more acceptable behaviors, it leads to an enhanced sense of competence and control for the caretaker, which, in turn, reinforces the experience of regulation and safety on the part of the child. This cyclical connection between behavioral regulation and relational engagement is a critical aspect of the intervention process.

As we will see in the next section, a large part of Santos's work with Joseph's teacher involved helping her to regulate her own responses to Joseph's unwanted behaviors. Self-regulation (covered in Chapter 3) is a key concept in our relational work with students and families. Implementing a structured behavior plan, with consistent and predictable responses to challenging behavior, is one of the most effective ways to support staff in the important and challenging task of self-regulation.

Integrating Systems Theory: Building the Capacity of Natural Supports

One of the most common mistakes schools make when securing professional behavioral supports for students with significant social-emotional challenges has to do with sustainability. Staff often feel such a sense of urgency for services, and relief when they are secured, that they view this support as the ultimate solution. A behavior interventionist is often assigned sole responsibility for the student's progress, and this person's ongoing presence is a presumed prerequisite for the student's success. While a skilled interventionist can provide much needed relief, the eventual work must also include an ecological approach. As discussed in Chapter 2, sustainability in intervention planning requires explicit attention to strengthening a child's natural networks of support.

After the initial phase of relationship building, Santos's main goal was to build the capacity of Joseph's caregivers to successfully address Joseph's behavioral needs. From the beginning he began in earnest to "work himself out of a job," planning how each intervention step would help build Joseph's independence and garner the support of his existing network of caregivers. This focus on building the capacity of others, once again, brought Santos back to relationship.

Joseph's main classroom teacher, Ms. Castillo, had the heart and dedication of most people who choose teaching as their profession. It was clear that she wanted to do her best for Joseph however, her ongoing struggles with him in the classroom had resulted in a predictably contentious relationship. Santos knew that any attempts to build Ms. Castillo's repertoire of successful behavioral intervention strategies would be fruitless without successfully building relational trust. First, he coached Ms. Castillo in developing her own self-control, helping her find emotional distance from Joseph's words and behavior while modulating her emotional reaction in the moment. He also coached her to take a stance of curiosity and in creating proactive moments of connection.

Aside from the more obvious points of engagement, like stepping out at recess to play with Joseph, Santos worked with Ms. Castillo to create a wellness check routine each morning. This consisted of taking a few moments before class started to hand Joseph his hygiene kit and ask him a quick set of questions, such as "How are you doing? How are you feeling? Did you get enough sleep last night?" and "Are you hungry?" This checking in would provide the team with a chance to intervene if Joseph arrived tired or hungry and create the space for a quick, proactive moment of connection between Ms. Castillo and Joseph each morning. This simple strategy not only helped Ms. Castillo to start shifting the nature of her relationship with Joseph but also added a strategy to her toolbox of social-emotional supports to be used with future students in need of personal connection. As she became more successful at engaging Joseph in relationship, she became more able to adopt a new repertoire of behavioral techniques.

In addition to building the capacity of school staff, family engagement and connection is an important component of any ecologically focused treatment plan. As described in Chapter 1, Santos and the school team worked persistently over time to create a connection with Joseph's parents, gain their trust, and join with them in developing a plan for Joseph's treatment. Capitalizing on this strong foundation of trust, Santos spent a considerable amount of time collaborating with Joseph's parents around the creation of clear and consistent rules, consequences, and rewards to guide Joseph's behavior at home. This partnership was a crucial component in developing the consistency that Joseph craved, ensuring that he experienced an aligned response to his behavior, regardless of his location.

Much of Santos's work with Joseph's parents was to help them see the value of this close collaboration and alignment and to facilitate their working together as a parenting team, despite their separation and their own interpersonal challenges. While Santos took a lead role in early meetings with Joseph's parents, guiding conversations about how to address certain challenges at home, over time he was able to step back and let them lead the conversation. By taking a step back, Santos was able to ensure sustainability in his interventions, handing the reins over to Joseph's natural system of support.

Strengths-Based Assessment and Plan Development

While Santos took time to ground his approach in the context of relationships and systems, his end goal was to help Joseph learn new, more socially acceptable behaviors. Given that there are many formal and informal avenues to employ behavioral supports for individual students, the strategies used with Joseph provide a useful frame for demonstrating how the behavioral intervention concepts outlined earlier can play out in the school setting.

As a general practice, behavioral intervention begins with the development of a functional behavioral analysis and individualized treatment plan through collaboration among the youth, the family, treatment team, and school staff. Santos spent time reflecting with Ms. Castillo and Joseph on meaningful behavioral goals for the classroom. One identified goal was to increase Joseph's ability to communicate effectively when he was overwhelmed with emotion. In order to help track progress, the team focused on identifying specific, observable behaviors and establishing an understanding of the baseline occurrence of these behaviors. The team summarized this information as follows:

The *mild* form of the behavior occurs 10 times per day and consists of ignoring directions by saying "no," contradicting directions, arguing with caregivers, attempting to redirect or distract caregivers, singing, humming, and making distracting noises. The *moderate* form of the behavior occurs 5 times per day and consists of Joseph banging objects on his desk in class, swearing, and threatening caregivers and peers. The *severe* form of the behavior occurs 2 times per week and consists of Joseph hitting peers and leaving the classroom without permission.

The team then worked to identify the function of the behavior—what needs Joseph was fulfilling through his engagement in the targeted behaviors. Taking into account what they knew of his IWM ("I cannot be controlled," "I can't do anything right," and "No one cares about me"), the team hypothesized that Joseph's behaviors were a result of wanting to regain control of his environment, especially in moments when he felt disempowered. The team also recognized that when Joseph started to feel emotionally escalated, he struggled to express himself verbally, which increased his sense of helplessness and, in turn, fueled emotional escalation. With this understanding of the function of the behavior, the team was prepared to introduce new, more socially acceptable strategies for Joseph to gain control of his environment and to implement natural consequences and positive rewards with consistency, transparency, and predictability.

While the team was clear on Joseph's challenges, it was important to understand his strengths in order to formulate meaningful, positive rewards. Fortunately, his strengths were also easy to identify. The team was able create an extensive list via input from his therapist, therapeutic behavioral services worker, school staff, parents, and peers. Some of these included: "Joseph connects with others through performance, jokes, and play," "Joseph is attentive to others," "Joseph is sensitive," "Joseph enjoys being helpful and having a job," "Joseph is a performer and loves to rap and write music," "Joseph has proven to be a great leader," and "Joseph is very supportive when it comes to helping others." These identified strengths were noted and used as the basis for designing intervention in Joseph's treatment plan, described in greater detail next.

Implementation and Coaching

Once Joseph's behavioral team had identified his strengths, target behaviors, and antecedents, it was time to get creative and find effective ways to teach explicit skills and replacement behaviors. To this end, Santos worked once again to build on existing practices in the classroom. Ms. Castillo was teaching a geometry unit in which her students created three-dimensional, six-sided cubes. Santos was inspired to help Joseph transform his cube into a communication tool, using the six faces of the cube to identify Joseph's commonly experienced, challenging emotions (mad, tired, hungry, etc.) as well as effective strategies to address them.

For example, the strategy to address "angry" would be a 5-minute break. Each side of the cube had a corresponding color (e.g., angry = red). The idea was that Joseph could use this tool any time during class to communicate his emotions and needs to his teacher in a way that would allow him to maintain a sense of control while not disturbing the learning environment. When Joseph felt angry, he would quietly hold up his cube toward the teacher. She had a matching cube on her desk and when she saw the color of the emotion and need he was holding up, she would hold up hers with the same color facing him, acknowledging that she understood his emotion and giving him permission to use the agreed-upon strategy to address it. Joseph would then get up, grab a timer, set it for 5 minutes, and walk out with Santos for a 5-minute break.

In the beginning, Santos accompanied Joseph on these breaks to help create structure and guarantee that they would last just 5 minutes. When time was up, he would prompt Joseph to quietly return to the classroom. Over time, Ms. Castillo and Joseph built a level of trust and Santos faded out his support, allowing Joseph to complete his 5-minute breaks independently. In this way, Santos intentionally worked to build Joseph's mastery of skill and his sense of responsibility and ownership of his newly developed replacement behaviors.

While Joseph worked to adopt these new behavioral strategies, he experienced the predictable successes and setbacks that come with learning a new skill. Santos and the team worked tirelessly to acknowledge his success with positive feedback and earned rewards and to consistently respond to unwanted behavior with logical consequences. These rewards and consequences were collaboratively developed with the understanding that they would change only with input from the team and Joseph, proactively reinforcing that sense of transparency, control, and predictability that were an important part of the team's disconfirming stance.

To leverage Joseph's passion and talent for spoken word, writing, and poetry, the team put out a call to staff across their network to identify an adult skilled in the same areas. A staff member from the IT department volunteered to teach Joseph how to use his turntable and Joseph was able to earn time toward making music. Eventually, other students found out and took an interest in the opportunity, and Joseph was able to pick a friend to join him for each session. This positive reward provided the opportunity for Joseph to practice his pro-social skills with friends and to express himself and his emotions in a safe and positive way through poetry and writing. The team also established a set of consequences for unwanted behaviors, choosing responses that were logical, consistent, and included opportunities for reflection and skill building. When Joseph was suspended, the team created a formal reintegration protocol where the administrator met with Joseph, his family, and his teacher to welcome Joseph back to school, rebuild relationships, and reflect on what further skills and support he would need to be successful.

Monitoring for Effectiveness

In order to ensure that behavioral interventions like the ones provided by Santos are time-limited and lead to sustainability, it is crucial for the team to establish a realistic definition of success. Perhaps one of the most important strategies that staff can employ to this end is to identify meaningful, realistic goals and a way of measuring progress toward them. One of the aims of goal setting is to establish shared expectations about what the student can accomplish over a given period of time. This approach, ideally, clarifies that assigned interventions are intended to result in progress in specific areas rather than overall absolute improvement. The important question teams must consider is: Which goal(s) must be met in order for the student to step down from the current level of service? If this is not clear from the beginning, it is easy for staff to feel as though services must continue indefinitely.

The first step toward service termination should occur during the assessment and plan development phase, when staff assess needs and establish a clear baseline of behaviors. With this clearly established baseline, teams are able to articulate behavioral support goals. For example, given the baseline just described, Santos and the team developed the following goal:

Joseph will decrease his engagement in defiant behaviors from 10 times per day at a mild intensity to 5 times per day, from 5 times per day at a moderate intensity to 2 times per day, and from 2 times per week at the severe intensity to 1 time per week. Joseph will follow directions of adults at the initial request in 4 out of 6 opportunities.

Once a measurable goal is established, service providers can build the capacity of the team, including teachers, to help monitor progress toward these goals on a regular basis.

Such concrete, observable, regularly collected data help teams to monitor student progress objectively and celebrate successes. Staff might otherwise rely on anecdotal evidence of progress, asking teachers and staff about "how so and so is doing." In this scenario, it is natural to be influenced by the most recent, emotionally charged incident and to respond that little progress is being made, even if things are getting progressively better. It is not uncommon for a team to be caught off guard and pleasantly surprised (and proud and happy) to see an objective graph that marks a student's progress over time in specific behavioral goals.

This collaborative marking of progress allows for moments of celebration and for developing a shared understanding of when a student has reached the targeted goal and is ready to reduce the intensity of support or move on to the next goal. With the dedication and support of his entire team, Joseph was able to reach his behavioral goals. At this point, Santos started a 30-day phase-out plan. He intentionally stepped down his services while continuing to monitor Joseph's use of replacement behaviors. By the end of this period, Joseph was spending his entire time at school independently in the classroom. Santos was available to support Joseph if necessary but was fully removed from the classroom setting. At the end of the 30-day period, Joseph had demonstrated his ability to maintain use of his replacement behaviors, and a graduation ceremony was held to celebrate this huge milestone in Joseph's (and the school team's) journey.

IMPLICATIONS FOR SCHOOLS

Built on the principles of individual behavior change, organizational learning occurs in much the same way and can be used to guide cycles of learning across the school. Chapter 7 describes how this learning process is adapted to improve school culture and climate more broadly; here we focus on how learning theory can be applied to systems-level change, including the factors that lead to exclusionary discipline practices. The alarming rates of disproportionality in discipline practices referred to at the beginning of the chapter have a significant impact on students' experience at school. In order to create a strong foundation of safety, predictability, and inclusion, schools must willingly acknowledge patterns of racial exclusion that exist on campus, reflect critically on their root causes, and take concrete steps toward more equitable outcomes.

The groundwork for such practices can be laid using evidence-based interventions like positive behavioral interventions and supports (PBIS), in which schools clearly define and teach behavioral expectations, create clear and consistent responses to unwanted behavior, and track office discipline referral incidents in such a way that the data can be analyzed to better understand who is being referred, from what location on campus, and for what behaviors.

Since Joseph Starr graduated from Ford Elementary the school has undergone several shifts in leadership. Efforts to implement UE have continued to evolve, including addressing the issue of disproportionality head on. The example described next illustrates how, using the tenets of behavioral learning theory to help frame and structure this initiative, Ford's most recent school leaders were able to break down this daunting work into thoughtful and achievable steps.

Strengths-Based Assessment and Plan Development

Ford Elementary has continued to serve a community with substantial needs. In recent years, Ford Elementary has focused on refining schoolwide discipline procedures. Implementing the principles of PBIS, the school has developed a consistent and predictable school environment and set of expected responses to challenging behaviors. Students have a strong understanding of what is expected of them across various locations within the school. Building on this foundation, the equity-focused leadership team was ready to engage in courageous conversations about the troubling pattern of disproportionate discipline they saw emerging across their school

Utilizing the existing coordination of services team (COST) and adding a few other key members who oversaw discipline at the school ensured participation and input from all stakeholders. When the team reviewed office disciplinary referral data, a disturbing trend emerged: over one-third of referrals were for Black students, who represented only 14% of the overall school population. As the team grappled with this information, they had to reckon with a difficult question: "How could a team so dedicated to equity and the inclusion of all students be unintentionally replicating national patterns of exclusion?"

Just as they did when confronting a student challenge, they began with curiosity. First, they engaged in a strengths-based assessment of the situation, which later informed their plan development. By analyzing the data they were able to determine that referrals of Black male students came from across the school, not a single classroom, and were not solely of one or two high-needs students, as they had at first suspected. Referrals largely occurred during instructional time, as opposed to the lunch room or playground. To better identify observable behavior and the context in which it occurred, the team used the PBIS team-implemented problem-solving (TIPS) protocol to drill down into the data until they developed a precise problem statement: "Since the beginning of the year, there have been 64 referrals for 21 African American students for minor disruption in the classroom (0.58 referrals per day). African American students are more than 3 times more likely to receive this type of referral than their peers." The team used faculty meeting time to share the data with the larger school team and gather additional input about the problem's root causes. What was also acknowledged was that of the school's 28 teaching staff, only a handful were themselves Black, which meant that most Black children spent the majority of their day with educators who looked different from them. While teachers espoused a theory of instruction and discipline consistent with equitable practices, it became clear that teachers, and perhaps the established schoolwide behavioral practices themselves, embodied a level of implicit bias leading to a problematic pattern of exclusionary discipline for Black students.

Implemention and Coaching

The team thus set to work. They designed a training session in which teachers explored their own IWMs, including the mindsets and beliefs that triggered their responses to the students in their classrooms. The team taught specific new skills and strategies for intervening with students who demonstrated challenging behavior. Further, they identified three goal areas derived from root causes: (1) supporting new teachers, (2) addressing implicit bias, and (3) acknowledging and identifying different cultural norms.

For each of these goal areas, a variety of action steps resulted from the inquiry process. For example, as a means of supporting new teachers while positively acknowledging and recognizing those teachers with standout skills in classroom management, the team created a schedule in which these two groups were paired and could spend time co-teaching, so that new teachers learned from their skilled colleagues. To address implicit bias, the team established a voluntary book club for staff to meet and discuss books like *Pushout: The Criminalization of Black Girls in Schools*, by Monique W. Morris (2016), and *Culturally Responsive Teaching and the Brain*, by Zaretta Hammond (2014). They also conducted a schoolwide professional development series on implicit bias, providing brave space for staff to reflect on their own experiences and to learn strategies to mitigate the implicit bias playing out in their classrooms. And, in an effort to acknowledge different cultural norms that may exist between staff and students and their families, the school developed a family survey that provided a structured way for teachers to take a positive, curious stance in getting to understand the values and goals that individual families held.

Monitoring for Effectiveness

In their efforts to address disproportionality, the team made sure to take an in-cremental approach to assessing needs, identifying goals, and measuring progress through regular monthly meetings. In their first meeting, the team identified a real-istic, measurable short-term goal: to reduce referrals for Black students in the class-room for minor disruption from an average of 0.58 referrals per day to 0.25 referrals per day. In consecutive monthly meetings, the team first reflected on progress made on the short-term goal, celebrating any success or improvement. If progress wasn't made, they assessed the extent to which they had carried out their action steps, asking themselves, "Did we do what we said we were going to do?" The answer to that question helped shape the action steps for the coming month. The team would decide whether to recommit to previously agreed action steps that were not carried out or to develop an alternative approach. After a year, discipline data revealed that Ford was able to reduce the rate for this type of referral to 0.20 times per day, not only meeting but exceeding their goal.

CONCLUSION

Schools that utilize the concepts of behavioral learning theory understand that just as we structure the learning process for reading, writing, and arithmetic, so too must we structure the learning process for social and behavioral development. These schools are able to transition from practices of exclusion to practices of inclusion, confirming for students that they are capable of learning new social and behavioral skills. These learning communities become skilled in the art of critical reflection; they use schoolwide data to inform structured shifts in practice that address disproportionality and promote equity. What's more, they understand how to break down these difficult tasks into measurable milestones, tracking progress toward goals in a way that encourages joyful celebration and inspires hope for the future. They build the stamina and persistence required to finally move toward long-term goals for students and their school.

Making this shift requires schools to adopt new mindsets and learn new skills applied to shaping behavior. It requires communities to take shared responsibility, interweaving the tenets of the ecological, relational, and behavioral streams. It requires that the individuals most closely affected by a problem are an integral part of the change process, providing insight into assessment, planning, and goal development, and understanding and sharing in progress and success along the way.

5 Unconditional Education Framework

The first half of this book has helped lay the theoretical foundation on which the unconditional education (UE) model stands. Building off of the three pillars of unconditional care (systems theory, relational theory, and behavioral learning theory), the second half of this book transitions to providing an overview of what it concretely takes to implement this model in schools. The following chapters will provide insight into the architectural framework, the data-informed processes for ongoing assessment and evaluation, the stages of implementation, the funding mechanisms that support such work, and the challenges that inevitably arise when promoting complex change of this nature. We begin in this chapter with an overview of the model itself.

UE functions as a unifying framework in which to consider an array of interventions designed for students and schools. This framework incorporates a set of systems and processes that leverage needed expertise and resources, align funding sources, and articulate a strategy for serving all students. By implementing this framework, schools are better prepared to promote equitable access to quality education for all students, with the greatest impact experienced by the most marginalized youth—those whose achievement is hindered by complex stressors including disability, trauma, poverty, and institutionalized racism. UE concerns itself less with the particulars of intervention type, instead assuming that many sorts of intervention programs have the potential to be effective so long as they are based on research, are well implemented, and are chosen to meet the particular needs of a student, family, school, or community context. In other words, UE is centered on the belief that the effectiveness of specific interventions is enhanced when implemented within a cohesive framework that promotes four central enablers for school transformation: increased efficiency, intentional relationship building, cross-sector responsibility, and local decision-making.

The essential structure behind UE draws heavily from other multi-tiered frameworks. UE articulates three levels of service, described in greater detail in the next sections: universal (Tier 1), targeted (Tier 2), and intensive (Tier 3) (Figure 5.1). Where UE differs from other approaches is in its application of this tiered framework across disciplines: academic, behavioral, and social-emotional. In so doing, UE is organized to identify and address multiple barriers to students' success in schools, rather than merely responding to academic skill deficits with

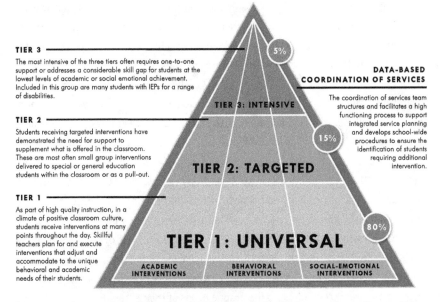

TIER 3
The most intensive of the three tiers often requires one-to-one support or addresses a considerable skill gap for students at the lowest levels of academic or social emotional achievement. Included in this group are many students with IEPs for a range of disabilities.

TIER 2
Students receiving targeted interventions have demonstrated the need for support to supplement what is offered in the classroom. These are most often small group interventions delivered to special or general education students within the classroom or as a pull-out.

TIER 1
As part of high quality instruction, in a climate of positive classroom culture, students receive interventions at many points throughout the day. Skillful teachers plan for and execute interventions that adjust and accommodate to the unique behavioral and academic needs of their students.

DATA-BASED COORDINATION OF SERVICES
The coordination of services team structures and facilitates a high functioning process to support integrated service planning and develops school-wide procedures to ensure the identification of students requiring additional intervention.

TIER 3: INTENSIVE — 5%
TIER 2: TARGETED — 15%
TIER 1: UNIVERSAL — 80%
ACADEMIC INTERVENTIONS   BEHAVIORAL INTERVENTIONS   SOCIAL-EMOTIONAL INTERVENTIONS

FIGURE 5.1 The unconditional education (UE) framework. The UE framework provides a unifying approach to the provision of school supports and services.

academic-based interventions. This holistic approach increases efficiency and helps ensure that even the most vulnerable students, who often struggle in more than one domain, achieve success.

THE UNCONDITIONAL EDUCATION TIERS
Tier 1—Universal Supports

It may seem obvious, but students' experiences in school matter a great deal. They matter as predictors of their academic and social success. They matter because children's experiences at school help shape their future participation as citizens in a vibrant democracy. They matter because education has the potential to shift the balance of power and create a more just society. Most simply, they matter because all children deserve to spend their days in safe and nurturing environments in which they and their families are respected and cared for. Few of us, when given the choice, opt to go to places where we feel unwelcome or unsuccessful, let alone return to these places 180 days in a row, for a minimum of 13 years. Yet for far too many students, particularly those whose families have limited choice in which schools they will attend, a sense of alienation is all too real.

UE schools invest significant energy in creating and sustaining schoolwide practices that deliver an unequivocal message to students: you belong here un-conditionally. Tier 1 interventions are the programs and practices of a school that affect all students. Core instructional practices, schoolwide discipline policies, social-emotional curriculum, and a school's culture and climate are all aspects of Tier 1. In a highly functioning, efficient school, it is expected that 70–80% of students would have their needs met through the school's universal program. This essential school culture and climate work is everyone's responsibility. The front office team greets all visitors warmly—by name and in their preferred language, when possible. The custodial team takes meticulous care to ensure shared spaces at the school are clean, well maintained, and inviting. The fact that UE is a community effort does not, however, diminish the reality that the single most important adult a student will encounter in school is their classroom teacher (Committee on Education and Labor, 2007). While other staff may have touch points with students throughout the day, it is the classroom teacher who spends the greatest amount of time, and therefore has the greatest potential to build meaningful and impactful relationships, with the students in their care. Thus, UE staff spend the bulk of their efforts carefully tailoring Tier 1 interventions that will enable teachers to shape the experiences students have in school. This work aims to develop teachers who plan for and execute interventions that adjust to the unique needs of their students.

Professional Development

Building the capacity of school staff to create a safe and nurturing environment for students is the foundation of UE's Tier 1 interventions. As an entry into sharing professional development across disciplines, schools new to the UE approach often launch with a 2- to 3-day "Foundations Series" training prior to the start of the school year. This training introduces all school staff to some of the important markers of an effective school culture and climate and includes an introduction to trauma-informed education, an overview of instructional and behavioral strategies and interventions, and an inquiry into how the school will organize itself and its participants for the transdisciplinary work that lies ahead.

Yet, formal professional development offerings only account for a small part of teachers' growth into skillful UE practitioners. While certainly important, formal professional development is limited in its ability to influence sustainable changes in teacher practice. For this reason, the UE approach conceives of its capacity-building role both within formalized professional development opportunities and outside of them. Much of the professional development that teachers receive comes from ongoing support provided by professionals at the school site, either through their participation on structured teams or in their side-by-side planning and data analysis with transdisciplinary specialists. The UE model encourages expert service providers to take advantage of such opportunities to collaborate with teachers. Through either planned collaboration time or drop-in office hours, providers are able to support teachers in implementing the concepts and tools introduced in formal professional development sessions to address actual challenges that have arisen regarding classroom management or individual students' behavior.

While strong Tier 1 practices result in fewer students requiring additional services, it is expected that some students will still need supplementary supports to thrive. That is not to say that high-quality schoolwide practices are not crucial for the success of those students who require more. A strong Tier 1 foundation is, in fact, the greatest predictor of such students' success, even with the careful infusion of the sorts of targeted and intensive interventions we will describe here (Browning Wright & Gurman, 2001).

Targeted supports can be defined as those interventions and programs within a school that aim to provide direct assistance to students who are beginning to show signs of struggle. These Tier 2 services can be thought of as mid-course corrections aimed at remediating specific challenges by building protective factors that will prevent the escalation of more serious problems. Students receiving targeted interventions have demonstrated the need for support in specific areas to supplement what is offered more globally in the classroom or school as a whole. Interventions are most often delivered in small groups, either by a general education teacher or by an intervention specialist, within the classroom or outside of it. It is expected that about 15–20% of students will require some type of targeted supports at any given time. The intention of these early intervention services is to provide the opportunity for students to move fluidly in and out of Tier 2 as their immediate issues are addressed, making room for additional students to receive targeted supports in their own unique areas of need.

Students with more intensive needs often require one-to-one support to address considerable skill gaps in academic, behavioral, or social-emotional achievement. Included in this group are students with disabilities and those with intensive mental health needs. It is expected that 5–10% of students will require Tier 3 levels of intensive supports in order to ensure their academic success and overall well-being. The UE approach to designing effective interventions at the Tier 2 and Tier 3 levels is rooted in research from across the field, which shows that the key to quality intervention consists of (1) evidence-based curriculum, (2) implemented with fidelity, (3) by a high-quality instructor (Rice, 2003).

Student-Centered, Evidence-Based Approaches Implemented with Fidelity

Numerous intervention choices exist for the provision of tiered academic, behavioral, and social-emotional supports. When developing a school's menu of potential interventions, it is important to strike the right balance between having a range of offerings from which to choose and limiting the number of options, to ensure that intervention providers, teachers, and school leaders can develop a level of expertise in their delivery. When choosing a promising or evidence-based practice, it is important to understand the context in which these interventions have proven successful. There are no "one-size-fits-all" options. Practitioners must be aware of whether the chosen intervention has been proven effective within a similar context and whether the school has the capacity to implement it with fidelity. For example, has the intervention worked for students with similar demographics and at similar stages of development as your students? Are the time and resources available to provide the recommended amount of service? Are providers able to complete any formal training needed to carry out the intervention?

One common mistake schools make in their initial attempts to provide tiered supports is assuming that there is a single curriculum or intervention that will meet the needs of all students within the school community. This was a lesson learned at one implementation site. Keen to embrace a tiered intervention approach, the school's newly appointed UE coach was made responsible for regularly collecting and analyzing aggregate data regarding students' responses to different interventions. It was a task that had never been assigned to a member of the school community before. What the coach noted was striking. For years, the school had invested a significant amount of resources in a community-based organization that pairs students with trained reading tutors. Ample anecdotal evidence left no doubt that the intervention was a remarkable model for success. Many students who participated demonstrated reading growth. Understandably, then, the waiting list for students to be assigned tutors was long and demand rarely matched the supply. Yet, upon further investigation, the coach uncovered an important trend. While the reading tutor intervention worked brilliantly for students in grade 3 or above who were between 1 and 2 years behind in reading, it was virtually ineffectual with younger students or with those who had more significant skill deficits. In light of the new information, the school was able to make a shift in the way it assigned students to tutors. Students who fit the newly identified profile gained access to tutors more quickly, while those who were less likely to make progress were assigned to other interventions that were better tailored to their specific needs. Over time, this realization and others like it helped the school raise its overall achievement rate in dramatic ways, significantly increasing the number of students who scored proficient in state standardized tests for English language arts.

Intervention providers must give careful consideration to not only the type of intervention chosen but also the duration of services provided. One surprising shift schools make upon implementation of UE is to shorten the amount of time spent on direct intervention to 8- to 12-week cycles, which are punctuated by 2-week cycles of data analysis. This time dedicated to analyzing data between cycles to inform the next configuration of intervention has been known to cause anxiety in educators who worry that this "pause" results in lost intervention time for students. Yet, in resisting the temptation to move more quickly, schools commit to working smarter. In calculating caseloads and designing intervention cycles, schools can allow time for specialists to conduct a careful analysis of data so that they can identify gaps in students' skills and knowledge and compare these to what is known about the effectiveness of potential interventions. Schools that take on this disciplined work with fervor have demonstrated a pattern of early, identifiable acceleration in student outcomes and a sophistication in specialists' conceptualization of need-matched interventions.

Instructor Quality

Much has been written on the impact that instructor quality can have on student learning outcomes (Committee on Education and Labor, 2007). More than just pedagogical skills and knowledge of the curriculum are at play here. At the foundation of this finding is instructor mindset (Shindler, 2009). As more fully explored in Chapter 3, for students who are already struggling, adult mindset is all the more essential. Many students arrive at school having experienced their caregivers and teachers reacting to their attempts at engagement with anger, harsh judgment, or disappointment—or, perhaps even worse, failing to respond to their needs at all. These previous experiences can lead students to develop unhelpful internal beliefs, or internal working models, about themselves which they come to school expecting, and even asking, to have confirmed. In the case of Joseph Starr, for example, he came into the classroom with the belief that "I cannot do anything right" and "nobody cares about me." The ability of an instructor to provide a disconfirming stance to these sorts of unhealthy self-conceptualizations is at the core of their ability to support a student in making academic progress. For this reason, mindset is foundational and non-negotiable in the hiring process and should be assessed in interviews. This can be accomplished by providing case study examples and questions that gauge a potential staff member's approach to addressing students' unhelpful internal beliefs. Providing opportunities for interactive interviews in which potential hires spend time in the classroom with students is another helpful way to assess this essential skill. Furthermore, specialists' pre-service preparation, ongoing professional development and training, and high-quality supervision by an experienced mentor are needed to move from mindset to daily practice.

THE UNCONDITIONAL EDUCATION STRANDS

Other established multi-tiered frameworks have been developed from distinct disciplines, focusing on interventions for a particular type of student support, most often either academic (response to intervention [RtI]) or behavioral (positive behavioral interventions and supports [PBIS]). UE, by contrast, integrates multiple treatment perspectives to achieve a holistic approach to student support, rather than solely considering one aspect of a student's experience at a time. While in practice this approach is transdisciplinary, to aid in conceptualization UE can be considered as three strands of multi-tiered support: an academic strand, a behavioral strand, and a social-emotional strand. Each strand draws from research in its unique discipline to illuminate field-specific best practices. The interplay among the three strands blends to improve the health of every child and of the system as a whole.

Academic Strand

The academic strand is the most familiar to schools. Academic achievement measures have traditionally been the primary indicators of school success, and the development of multi-tiered interventions aimed specifically at bolstering academic skills significantly predates UE. What is known now, of course, is that threats to academic achievement do not always originate as challenges within academic content and thus are not always remedied through academic supports. It is not uncommon for schools to begin implementing an academic RtI framework, only to find its singular focus on academic interventions too limited to meet the multiple needs of students. UE builds on the foundations of the RtI framework, strengthening schoolwide instructional practices by utilizing the principles of universal design for learning (UDL) and implementing best practices in the field of special education. An overview of the components within the academic strand are discussed in greater depth in Table 5.1.

Behavioral Strand

Informed largely by the work of schoolwide positive behavioral supports (SWPBS), multi-tiered behavioral interventions are built on a foundation of schoolwide discipline practices that promote a safe, predictable, and positive school environment for all students (Cole et al., 2005; Walker & Cheney, 2004). Behavioral expectations are made clear, and all students are explicitly taught how to meet them. When students manifest behavior that does interfere with their ability to learn, schools implement interventions that build students' skills and promote greater self-regulation over time. Practitioners rely heavily on data, such as office discipline referrals, to identify areas of need and then choose what schoolwide, classroom, and individual student-level interventions will best meet the needs of the community. The ultimate goal of these interventions is to create a more restorative (versus punitive) response to challenging behavior. The main components of this stream in each tier are highlighted in Table 5.2.

Social-Emotional Strand

Until recently, social-emotional services have operated largely outside the core function of schools. An increasing number of schools embrace the concept of social-emotional learning as a schoolwide intervention (Tier 1), coupled with the

Tier 1
- **Universal design for learning.** Classrooms are designed with the *why, what*, and *how* of learning in mind, and an understanding that successful students must be engaged in their own learning (understand and embrace the *why*), be resourceful and knowledgeable (through different representations of *what* they are learning), and be strategic and goal-driven (by making decisions regarding *how* they will pursue and express new learning).*

- **Differentiated instructional support and training.** Classroom teachers offer differentiated supports. Particular attention is given to the language needs of students, including English-language learners and students with disabilities. Effective teachers utilize strategies that ensure high cognitive rigor while allowing multiple pathways for students to engage with material within their instructional range so that they are neither working repetitively on material that they already know with automaticity nor spending time with material that is outside their current developmental or academic bandwidth. Either will only lead to frustration (Vygotsky, 1962).

- **Professional development in pedagogical approaches and core curriculum.** A common phenomenon that follows a focused look at Tier 1 academic interventions is the adoption of new curriculum or the insertion of additional pedagogical approaches. It is important to recognize that these investments are meaningless unless accompanied by the necessary professional development, including embedded coaching, for classroom teachers to gain familiarity with new approaches and receive meaningful feedback that pushes their practices forward (Hawley & Valli, 1999).

- **A culture of learning.** In UE schools, a culture of curiosity and learning is present. Meaningful processes for teachers to meet together for planning and problem-solving purposes are predictors of successful instruction. Creating structures that allow teachers to participate in careful data analysis with their colleagues enhances teachers' ability to reflect on their own practice. In addition, doing so helps ensure a more unified experience for students as classroom teachers develop common language and expectations around academic work production (Hawley & Valli, 1999; Kruse, Seashore Louis, & Bryk, 1994; Warren-Little, 2006).

(continued)

Table 5.1 Continued

Tier 2	• **Targeted intervention groups.** Students receive targeted, supplementary instruction from highly trained intervention providers, focused mostly in the areas of language arts and mathematics.
	• **Co-teaching and push-in support.** Intervention providers collaborate with classroom teachers to maximize classroom instructional time through meaningful co-teaching opportunities, including small workshops, parallel teaching, or a centers model.
Tier 3	• **504s and Individualized Education Program (IEP) planning.** Many, though not all, students in need of Tier 3 Interventions are students with identified disabilities. For this subgroup of students, careful attention to planning for their 504s or IEPs can be an influential intervention. Students can advance when these specialized plans align with the overarching experiences they have in school, are well communicated to all adults who interact with them throughout the day, and are based on research regarding the appropriate type and dosage of intervention.
	• **Research-based, multisensory instructional approaches.** For students with intensive academic deficits, the use of multisensory instructional approaches, such as reading interventions based on the Orton Gillingham method, can be influential in closing existing gaps and allowing access to learning through channels that may have not previously been accessed.
	• **Related services that promote academic attainment.** Students receiving intensive interventions often benefit from related services in areas such as speech and language pathology and/ or occupational therapy that develop strategies that enable them to more readily access educational content in the regular school program.

* www.CAST.org.

increased availability of intensive mental health therapy as a specialized intervention for the handful of students with the most extreme needs (Tier 3). However, it remains rare to find fully built-out, multi-tiered models that include early intervention services (Tier 2) and allow for mental health providers to become integrated, embedded members of the wider school community. UE aims to address this gap (see Table 5.3). While UE's integration of trained mental health staff into the very fabric of the school itself is important for all students, astute attention to this aspect of service is essential in communities disproportionately affected by chronic stress

Tier 1 • **Consistent schoolwide system of discipline.** The core principle behind schoolwide positive behavioral supports (SWPBS) at the Tier 1 level is to develop common expectations for all students across the school, ensuring that these expectations directly reflect the school's core values. To this end, UE schools focus on creating structures for recognizing students for following agreed-upon expectations, maintaining a ratio of five positive engagements with a student to each single correction offered. Still, it is inevitable that there will be times when students do not follow agreed-upon rules. In these instances, the school's ability to utilize a consistent response to challenging behavior helps to create safety and predictability, as well as to decrease the likelihood that consequences will be assigned disproportionately among the school's diverse subgroups.

• **Restorative discipline practices.** Rather than focusing on establishing blame and determining punishment, systems of restorative practices provide students with opportunities to repair harm and rebuild relationships. Interventions are considered effective when students can express a new understanding about how their actions may have affected others in the community and practice new skills for coping with challenging situations in the future. Key questions for guiding students in a restorative approach include identifying:

  • What happened?
  • What thoughts or feelings were you having at the time?
  • What skills could you use to express these thoughts or feelings differently in the future?
  • Who was affected by your actions?
  • How can those relationships be repaired?

• **Logical consequences.** Students' actions demonstrate the amount of responsibility they are capable of holding in certain situations. In other words, when students demonstrate that they are not yet ready to hold a certain level of responsibility (e.g., walking independently from one class to the next while maintaining positive interactions with peers in the hallway), then restrictions on the expanse of that responsibility must be put into place (for instance, having to walk with an adult in the hallway while the student practices and the adult observes until that support can be thoughtfully faded away). It is important that the restriction offered be directly related to the area in which a student needs additional guidance so that intervention continues to build the student's internal locus of control in the specific areas of need. In the same way, it is also important that students clearly understand what levels of responsibility they must demonstrate in order to regain privileges at school.

(continued)

Tier 2 • **Environmental interventions.** When students are repeatedly struggling to demonstrate desired behaviors, most frequently it is because they are not set up for success. Often, there is an inherent mismatch in the behavioral skills we are asking students to perform and their level of readiness or skill acquisition. As educators, we commonly understand that there is a progression to learning essential concepts for academic development and understand that it would be unreasonable to ask a student to perform calculus if he had yet to master multiplication. However, classrooms are often set up in a manner where students are asked to perform the behavioral equivalent of calculus when they are, in fact, missing many basic skills. Environmental interventions are used to review the classroom behavioral supports offered to a struggling student, group, or class and support the teacher in employing new instructional strategies to provide additional structure in which students can build and practice self-regulation. Take the student who was seldom able to move from one class to the next without ending up in some sort of altercation with a classmate. The average middle- or high-school transition period is highly chaotic, with hallways full of jostling students, erratic noise, and abrupt social interactions. A student who struggles with sensory or emotional regulation may easily become triggered in this level of stimulus and thus may benefit from an environmental intervention. For example, this student may benefit from a plan where he waits until the end of passing period to move from one class to the next, when the halls are quiet. While it means he'll arrive at his next class a few minutes later than other students, it increases the chances that he'll do so ready to learn.

• **Social skills group interventions.** There are many promising intervention options that can be used to support students who are struggling with academics, relationships, or both because they lack behavioral regulation. For elementary students struggling with self-regulation, UE schools often turn to methods related to Michelle Garcia Winner's Social Thinking approach,[*] including the zones of regulation, or the Alert Program's "How Does Your Engine Run?"[†], both of which break down abstract executive functioning tasks, such as identifying and regulating one's response to difficult stimuli into concrete, easily digestible steps. Other students benefit from the SWPBS structure of check-in, check-out (CICO), where students begin and end their day in one-on-one reflective conversations around their individualized goals with a designated adult on campus. CICO cycles of intervention are often accompanied by a behavioral tracker that students carry throughout the day to aid them in measuring and reflecting on their progress made toward goals. A strong family component accelerates the efficacy of this intervention, ensuring home and school are communicating regularly to encourage consistency among settings.

Table 5.2 Continued

93

Unconditional Education Framework

Tier 3 • **Behavior support plans.** Well-crafted, individualized plans can effectively address undesirable behaviors by systematically identifying what needs are being met by students' engagement in undesirable behaviors and providing direct instruction in functionally equivalent replacement behaviors (Browning Wright & Gurman, 2001). The implementation of behavior support plans generally requires the initial support of a specialist who conducts a thorough assessment of students' baseline behaviors, antecedents that lead to engagement in undesirable behaviors, and preferred reinforcers that may aid in introducing new routines capable of supporting behavioral change.

• **Individualized intensive interventions.** Individualized interventions draw on decades of behavioral intervention practices, including in applied behavioral analysis (ABA) and its related methodologies (Baer, Wolf, & Risley, 1968; Sulzer-Azaroff & Mayer, 1991). The predecessor to this book, *Unconditional Care*, by Sprinson and Berrick (2010), further outlines the behavioral interventions that guide UE schools in meeting the intensive behavioral needs of their most vulnerable students.

* https://www.socialthinking.com

† https://www.alertprogram.com

Table 5.3 Components of the Social-Emotional Strand at Their Corresponding Tiers

Tier 1 • **Schoolwide social emotional learning curriculum.** Because we believe in the importance of local decision-making to ensure cultural relevance, the UE model remains intentionally agnostic as to what specific curriculum is implemented. School teams are encouraged to consult the CASEL* website and the What Works Clearinghouse,† two publically available, federally funded warehouses that compare and contrast different curricula and provide available empirical research to aid in decision-making. By using these resources, school teams can ensure they are choosing an evidence-based, culturally appropriate approach, while considering what will best match the needs of the school and its students. In schools where trauma is common, investment should be made in approaches that are aligned with trauma-informed practices. Professional development will help reinforce these concepts and enable teachers to integrate them into their daily work in the classroom.

(continued)

- **Consistent set of practices to support relationship and engagement.** School culture exists regardless of whether or not we make intentional efforts to create it. So, as a sign in one of the UE school's staff lounge reads, "As adults, we have a responsibility to be right in our relationships with one another in service of our students and families." Indeed, the importance of creating and sustaining a staff culture that blends high expectations with explicit space to make, and safely learn from, mistakes is a critical marker of a functioning school culture. Just as we build clear behavioral expectations for students, so must we do for adults. Simple practices that are clearly articulated in staff trainings, such as greeting students at the door of the classroom or responding to emails from caretakers within 24 hours, help schools to come to common expectations around staff-to-student and staff-to-family relationships and define a clear pathway for the school's engagement efforts.

- **Psychoeducation for teachers and school staff.** One of the pathways to building schools capable of meeting the broad range of social-emotional needs of its students is to partner educational practitioners with skilled mental health specialists. These specialists are able to provide psychoeducation on youths' presenting challenges and suggest strategies for addressing these challenges. In many UE schools, the ready access to mental health professionals for consultation is paramount to teachers' feelings of efficacy in meeting the social-emotional needs of students. This is not surprising, given that research has reliably shown that while 89% of teachers believe that schools must infuse mental health interventions into the classroom in order to be effective, only 34% of them felt they had the capacity to do so, expressing a strong desire for training in recognizing and addressing mental health challenges, designing effective classroom management strategies that incorporate these considerations, and fostering effective partnerships with families (Stormont, Reinke, & Herman, 2010).

Tier 2
- **Therapy groups.** A broad range of targeted interventions and modalities exist to support the development of emotional regulation skills through group interventions at the school level. Mental health therapists design and lead therapy groups that provide intervention to students sharing common challenges, such as building coping skills to deal with loss and grief, developing friendship skills, or using alternatives to aggression in times of frustration and turmoil.

Table 5.3 Continued

95

Unconditional Education Framework

- **Parent classes and/or support groups.** In addressing mental health challenges in youth, UE practitioners recognize the need to tailor interventions to support students' families. As such, many schools design parent classes or support groups into their plan for Tier 2 intervention at the school. These workshops or support groups may include topics such as dealing with stress and promoting self-care, establishing positive discipline at home, and understanding the social-emotional developmental stages of their children.

Tier 3
- **Individual and family therapy and case management.** Counseling services and supports are an important element of a comprehensive, school-based mental health program. Services that emphasize the transfer of skill and collaboration with the students' primary caregivers—classroom teachers and families—are promoted in the UE model.
- **Wraparound and wraparound-informed interventions.** For some students, the primary factors that limit their ability to successfully access educational content lie outside the school building. This is particularly true in communities highly affected by multigenerational trauma. When families are caught in cycles of crisis, dysfunction, and/or abuse, specific intervention must be employed to address the mental health symptoms that interfere with student learning. In such cases, teams of professionals and natural support providers come together to identify relevant goals for a particular student and family and work together to make progress on those goals. Interventions are comprehensive, and skill building in the home environment may be a necessary component of a successful intervention plan.
- **Personalized learning spaces/collaborative programs.** Students with the most intensive needs often require significant support within the general education classroom to provide high levels of consistency and a sense of safety throughout the school day. For students with social-emotional needs, this may involve additional support to help practice new coping strategies and self-regulation skills in the natural environment. In such cases, personalized therapeutic programs can be created that include individualized supports and high levels of team coordination, mirroring the levels of support traditionally offered in segregated settings, while allowing a student to remain in his or her school of origin.

* https://www.casel.org

† https://ies.ed.gov/ncee/wwc/

and frequent incidents of violence. These "trauma-informed" practices, including things like creating predictable routines, promoting student and family voice, and creating an orderly and welcoming physical environment, are good for all youth *and* are particularly beneficial for those students who have experienced trauma. In other words, a strong focus on the social-emotional strand is absolutely necessary to ensure high academic achievement of all students.

Data-Based Coordination of Services

The three strands of UE, layered in its three tiers, account for a total of nine modules of services. Yet, the tenth and most essential element of UE lies at the core of the framework: data-based coordination of services. While schools may elect to implement UE with one or more module(s) at a time from the list of the previous nine, it is imperative that an early and sustained emphasis on coordination of services accompany all planned efforts. Discussed more fully in Chapter 6, a structured coordination of services process includes the collection and analysis of student and schoolwide data, which in turn drives decision-making about intervention selection and delivery methods. Even when schools are well resourced with a host of interventions available, significant inefficiencies develop if they lack strategic coordination, often resulting in students being haphazardly assigned to interventions that are just as likely to interfere with their core instruction as they are to support it (Robinson, Atkinson, & Downing, 2008).

A MODULAR APPROACH

Thinking of the UE framework in terms of its various modules enables schools to employ strategic and measured practices of implementation, phasing in new modules of service as readiness is developed. For instance, for a school that has recognized that their greatest current barrier to affording an excellent education to all students is the lack of social-emotional interventions, an early adoption of UE's social-emotional strand may make great sense. By focusing all of its attention on this one area, a school team should experience significant progress and improvement. This early sense of success can, in turn, propel forward the adoption of additional modules, using the lessons learned from early implementation efforts in the social-emotional strand to build out the rest of the framework (DuFour, 2002; Schmoker, 2004).

The modular nature of the framework also allows schools to consider how to best utilize the expertise of partners, including other public service departments and community-based organizations, to provide needed support within different strands and/or tiers of service. While this modular framework is intended to help schools define and articulate their practices within each strand and tier, in reality, the modules of service have permeable boundaries and are inextricably related to and dependent on each other. Students rarely fit neatly into these nine boxes, and the best interventions and services cut across strands, as students who struggle the most often require a transdisciplinary approach in order to locate and address the root causes contributing to their current areas of difficulty.

Think back to Joseph Starr. While the manifestation of his struggles was behavioral in nature, the root of his challenges stemmed from previous trauma. Simply providing Joseph with a behavior intervention staff, while a critical piece of the intervention puzzle, would not have promoted the kind of transformation we witnessed. As you may recall, the approach was far more comprehensive, involving a therapist who worked with Joseph to address the symptoms of his traumatic experience, a special educator to support his academic development, and a principal and general education teacher who joined with these experts to convey to Joseph that they were not going to give up and that he truly belonged in this community (a powerful intervention in and of itself). These providers did not work in isolation but as a team, collaborating with each other and supporting the other adults on campus to understand the function of his behavior and how best to meet his needs. This transfer of skills to the general education teacher was a benefit not only to Joseph during that school year but also to the students who would walk through that teacher's door in the years to come.

CONCLUSION

With its modular organization, the UE model supports schools and districts in installing sustainable structures that align resources and expertise both horizontally (across strands) and vertically (across tiers). This alignment helps address students' needs holistically at the most opportune points of intervention. The point of convergence between different disciplines and providers is the coordination of services team (COST), to which we turn our attention in the next chapter.

6 Coordination of Services

Issues of coordination, integration, and early intervention are addressed throughout this book. Within the unconditional education (UE) framework, they come together in practice most visibly through the coordination of services team (COST). While the idea of a COST is not unique to UE, the framework's explicit articulation of certain processes and protocols have helped to ensure that the myriad decision-making and data analysis processes that drive UE coexist in a coherent manner. Such carefully structured coordination is essential, given that barriers to academic success are most often multifaceted. A highly functioning COST ensures that individual student and schoolwide supports are coordinated and build on each other in a meaningful way, rather than competing with each other for a student's valuable time. In addition, COST integrates services so that they create a seamless and comprehensive experience for students and families, rather than promoting supports that feel fractured or redundant. Of equal importance, COST allows schools to respond with early interventions, ensuring that services are quickly deployed and responsive to the evolving needs of schools and staff throughout the year.

TEAM PARTICIPANTS

One of the key factors in ensuring that effective solutions are developed within a COST is, quite simply, making sure that the right people are sitting around the table. As we have established, barriers to school success are often difficult to identify. What manifests as a struggle with math could instead be a response to intense anxiety, and what manifests as defiant behavior could also stem from being asked to read a text that is too difficult. When it comes to identifying the root cause of student challenges, the possibilities are endless, as are the unique solutions that may be developed to address them. For this reason, it is important that a diverse, transdisciplinary team of specialists collaborate with teachers and administrators to identify the true origins of a problem and responsive action steps to address them. To enable this transdisciplinary transfer of knowledge, teams in UE schools usually consist of the following team members:

- COST facilitator (often the UE coach)
- School administrator
- Special education teacher

- Behavioral and mental health support specialists
- Other intervention/support service providers (from the school and community)
- Experienced classroom teachers

Table 6.1 provides an overview of roles and responsibilities of team members.

ROLES OF THE COORDINATION OF SERVICES TEAM

The COST holds three main roles: (1) schoolwide intervention assignment and monitoring, (2) reviewing and developing plans for individual student referrals, and (3) thematic analysis of rising schoolwide trends. Within these three areas what is important, above all else, is the team's visibility as a body of accountability for prompt and responsive action. The most frequent complaints we hear from schools new to UE is that prior requests for intervention took too long, did not match the request of the teacher making the referral, and/or were insufficient to meet the needs of the student or students. A COST is highly functioning when others at the school see this body as a genuine support they can turn to for help and are confident that they will receive a response that provides partnership and builds their skills to address the real-life challenges that unfold within the classroom.

Intervention Assignment and Monitoring

A key function of COST is the collection, review, and analysis of schoolwide and student-level data to identify students in need of additional support and assign them to targeted Tier 2 and/or intensive Tier 3 interventions. To facilitate the coordination of progress-monitoring efforts, UE schools define 8- to 12-week cycles of intervention (usually a total of three to four cycles per school year) that are punctuated by time to review student outcomes and make decisions about what levels of services need to be considered in designing the next cycle of intervention. For example, students who experience success in a Tier 2 social skills group may be moved to Tier 1, while students who continue to struggle may be considered for more intensive intervention in the next cycle.

While the entire team is involved in the collection and analysis of data and the development of responsive intervention plans, it is important to note that it is the school principal's ultimate responsibility to guide these decisions by defining the school's theory of action for assigning students to resource-limited intervention options. For example, the principal may decide that the school will focus academic intervention efforts on ensuring that all students are proficient in reading by third grade, or social-emotional intervention efforts on those students experiencing internalizing symptoms of anxiety and depression. Once the intervention strategy for the cycle is developed and students are assigned to responsive levels of support,

Table 6.1 Coordination of Services Team (COST) Roles and Responsibilities

	Role of the Principal	Role of the COST Coordinator	Role of Team Members
Training of school staff	Ensure all staff understand the role and responsibility of the COST and the school's theory of action around how students will be targeted for specific interventions	Ensure all staff know when and how to use the student referral form and are aware of the menu of existing Tier 2 and Tier 3 interventions	Engage in all interactions with teachers and staff with a capacity-building mindset
Data collection and analysis	Provide the centralized and coordinated messaging to staff about data-collection expectations and deadlines	Facilitate the preparation process by developing a plan for the timing, messaging, and collection process for schoolwide screeners	Provide support to teachers as needed, based on expertise (i.e., teachers may reach out to the clinician with questions about completing the social emotional screener)
Intervention assignment	Define theory of action on how to target and assign resource-limited interventions	Collaborate with principal to identify intervention approaches that will maximize existing resources	Within realm of expertise, analyze data from screeners and progress monitoring and make recommendations for student assignment
Evaluation and review of student growth	Participate in all review sessions and provide theory of action for the upcoming cycle of intervention	Coordinate end-of-cycle review sessions with the appropriate team members for students in academic, behavioral, and social-emotional interventions	Present on the end-of-cycle progress for students on their caseload and provide suggestions for next steps for each student

it is the responsibility of service providers to set goals and track progress for all of the students with whom they work. At the end of every cycle, these data points are reviewed to assess student success and make decisions about next steps.

Data Collection and Analysis

A key goal of the UE approach is to create increased efficiency in selecting and implementing interventions so that limited school resources are well matched to needs. The careful collection and analysis of data is the essential strategy for achieving this goal. As is the case with other multi-tiered frameworks, UE looks at various data points to assess these needs.

Universal Screening Universal screeners are an important tool used to identify student struggles early and often so that responsive interventions may be provided at the earliest opportunity. Universal screeners are used to assess the performance of all students within a particular area. Screening involves collecting data for all students at regular intervals throughout the year, aligned with each cycle of intervention. Using the social-emotional strand as an example, schools may have teachers complete the Student Risk Screening Scale (SRSS) for all students in their class. The SRSS is a publicly available and validated screening tool that helps teachers quickly report on both externalizing and internalizing social and behavioral challenges of students. Data can then be analyzed to identify which students fall below established thresholds of performance and are in need of intervention. Universal screeners ensure that the needs of all students across the school are balanced equitably. When universal screener data are not used to guide the assignment of interventions, schools tend to rely on teacher referrals alone. While this source is an important one for identifying student struggles, it can create a system where "the squeakiest wheel gets the grease." That is, students whose teachers are most skilled at advocating for their needs are the ones to receive additional services while other students with the least able teachers lack access to additional support.

Dig-Deep Screening After universal screenings have been completed and it has been made clear which groups of students could use additional support, further assessment is often needed. While universal screenings give a global picture of a student's performance in a particular area, "dig-deep" screening offers additional insight about the particular areas of deficit that need to be targeted through intervention. This more nuanced information informs the COST's decision about specific intervention content. Building on the previous example from the social-emotional strand, all students identified on the SRSS as needing social-emotional support may be additionally screened using the more nuanced and detailed Strengths and Difficulties Questionnaire (SDQ). This tool provides information on exactly what areas of social-emotional development should be supported, and aggregated information from all of the completed SDQs should help identify common themes among groups of students.

Initial Intervention Assignment

The rich information provided from the screening process assists the COST to develop the most responsive, tiered intervention approach for that particular cycle of intervention and to best determine the particular curricula and/or skills to work on within each group. For example, within the social-emotional strand, a school might decide to develop Tier 2 interventions that include a kindergarten "friendship group" focused on self-regulation and cooperation skills and a fifth-grade "cognitive-behavioral interventions for trauma in schools (CBITS)" group for students demonstrating symptoms of exposure to trauma. Based on information from the screeners, the COST may also identify 10 students with more unique and intensive needs who would benefit from Tier 3 individual therapy services.

The UE coach at each school works with service providers to build a "menu" of evidence-based and promising intervention practices that are available to choose from as the schoolwide intervention plan is developed for each cycle. As the COST is working to identify responsive interventions that address the identified themes of need, they may ask themselves these guiding questions:

1. Will we be able to implement this intervention with fidelity?
2. Are there particular populations for which this intervention has previously been most effective?
3. Is this intervention culturally responsive to our population?
4. Is this intervention developmentally appropriate for our population?
5. How does this intervention match specific skill gaps identified by the dig-deep screeners?

Progress Monitoring

Once students are assigned to targeted interventions, the service provider is responsible for defining measurable goals for the intervention and ensuring that the highest leverage skills are taught. Student progress is monitored frequently to ensure there is sufficient growth toward goals and to inform any midcourse corrections or adaptations. Intervention providers are responsible for identifying objective, reliable, valid, and sensitive measures to assess progress toward intervention goals. Assessments are administered at regular intervals (e.g., weekly or bi-weekly) and student progress is charted for each student receiving intervention.

The rate at which providers collect progress-monitoring data should be based on the frequency of the intervention. For intensive one-to-one intervention, progress monitoring data may be collected on a daily basis. For those interventions that occur less frequently (for example, weekly 1-hour social skills groups), providers might collect data monthly. In general, progress-monitoring data should be collected for every 4 hours of service provided.

Review

Appropriate subgroups of the COST are responsible for meeting at the end of each cycle of intervention to review student progress and determine next steps. Usually this subgroup consists of an administrator, the COST coordinator, and the service providers from a particular strand of service. Evaluation of student growth and intervention effectiveness is based on three measures:

- *Attainment of intervention goals*—Did students meet the goals set for their intervention?
- *Acceleration of growth*—Did the intervention change the trajectory of students' learning? This measure analyzes the rate of growth on a global screening measure (usually the assessment used for universal screening) and compares it to the rate of growth the students previously demonstrated throughout their school career.
- *Closing of the gap*—Are students closer to expected targets for their grade or age? This measure compares students' performance on a global screening measure (usually the assessment used for universal screening) and compares the gap between students' scores and grade-level expectations at the start of intervention with the gap between students' scores and grade-level expectations at the end of intervention.

When students are either making great growth or failing to make growth as expected, it is important to reconsider the type of intervention and its dosage. The following questions can be helpful in this process:

- *Implementation fidelity*—Did the student receive at least 85% of the intervention assigned? Did the student demonstrate a high level of engagement during intervention lessons?
- *Appropriateness of goals*—Did the student meet intervention goals, but not make expected progress on the global screening measures? In other words, were the goals developed for specific interventions helpful in moving the dial forward in students' overall performance in the classroom?
- *Dosage*—Did the student make some progress, but may need increased frequency or intensity of the existing intervention to make greater gains?

- *Approach*—Does the presentation of intervention match the learning style and needs of the student?

Transdisciplinary Approach with a Focus on Collaboration and Transfer of Skills

One key feature of transdisciplinary teams is the careful and consistent communication of progress to key stakeholders (teachers, parents, and the treatment team) in such a way that everyone is informed about what is being worked on, what progress is being made, and how they can further support the student within their respective roles (for example, considering what one can do at home as a parent or in the classroom as a teacher to build on the work being done in therapy sessions). Consistent consideration of how current interventions will not only build specific skills but, more importantly, transfer into broader contexts is essential to the UE approach. Promoting skills transfer from specialists to classroom teachers and parents begins with the development of intervention strategy. It is often the case that prior to UE implementation interventions were executed in isolation. Reading groups happened separately from classroom instruction. Outpatient therapists provided mental health interventions in a separate room and shared little with school staff about the goals of their work. The UE approach, in contrast, holds that while the work done outside of the classroom can be an important part of the big picture, true progress depends on students' ability to take what is learned back into the general education classroom, where they spend the vast majority of their day. In other words, if it is believed that a 50-minute closed-door therapy session weekly is capable of improving student outcomes, how much more of a boost can result when these interventions are infused throughout the remaining 30 plus hours of their school week?

In traditional systems, even ones flush with resources and services, staff who may be dismissed as not true "specialists," including teachers' aides, recess support staff, and even classroom teachers, are often underutilized. The fact is, students spend a substantial portion of their day with these staff, who are thus best positioned to act as agents of change in their lives. Similarly, when schools are not mindful to engage parents as true and equal partners in intervention planning and implementation, the opportunity for carryover skills to be practiced at home or to learn from the parents' expert insights into what works for their child is lost. With UE's integrated approach, predictable structures that foster this collaboration ensure that intervention becomes a mindset and mission, rather than a time and location, and all team members share a responsibility for all goals rather than only those specific to their area of expertise.

While teachers are almost always on board with their students' receiving tiered supports, they understandably view interventions as precious time away from the general education learning environment and want that time to contribute to the

Box 6.1 Sample Introductory Note to Classroom Teachers

Dear Ms. Conlon:

Based on data from the social-emotional screener and our follow-up consultation, Crystal has been invited to join a social skills group from September 13th through December 5th. The group will meet every Monday from 1 to 2 pm at lunch recess. The social skills curriculum will focus on the following skills:

- *Coping skills that promote emotion regulation, including deep breathing, requesting to take short breaks, meditation, etc.*

***Intervention goal**: By the end of this intervention cycle, participating students will be able to name and demonstrate five emotion-regulation coping skills.*

Each week, I will email and place in your box an update informing you of the skill being targeted, progress made toward our goal, and ways that you can reinforce the work we are doing in group. Please talk with me about any questions or concerns you may have.

In partnership,

Ms. Banks

overall success of their students. To support this aim, UE promotes a few simple steps to help build a common understanding of what skills a student is learning and what progress they are making toward goals. All service providers are expected to send this information to teachers and parents at the beginning of the intervention. See Box 6.1 for an example.

Intervention providers are then expected to send regular progress-monitoring updates that give specific information on how students are progressing (or not) toward goals and what next steps are recommended, based on the data (see Box 6.2).

Simple protocols such as these help teachers and parents in their efforts to reinforce new skills throughout a students' day and to understand the impact and effectiveness of tiered interventions provided.

Individual Student Review and Plan Development

Despite the careful, proactive planning that goes into identifying student needs and planning for tiered intervention cycles, unforeseen student challenges inevitably arise at various points throughout the year. The second major responsibility of the COST is to support teachers in addressing these student needs as they develop, particularly for those students whose complex challenges require a transdisciplinary approach. As a strategy for this, the COST mandate is profound yet remarkably

Box 6.2 Sample Weekly Update

Hello, Ms. Conlon,

We had another meeting of our social skills group and I'd like to update you on what we learned this week.

Today we worked on: *deep breathing techniques*

The students have the following homework: *practice pausing and taking three deep breaths when they get frustrated in class*

Update on progress: *Crystal is now able to identify and demonstrate three (of five) emotion-regulation coping skills.*

Remember to give her a high-five if you see her practicing any of these new skills. Thank you for doing what you do!

Please let me know if you have any questions or would like more information about our social skills group!

In partnership,

Ms. Banks

simple: to create a centralized "one-stop shop" for teachers to access a range of experts ready and willing to help address the complex needs of their students.

The student review and plan development process can be broken down into six steps (see Figure 6.1):

(1) A universal COST referral form (Appendix 6.1) is available to teachers who are instructed to fill one out any time a student would benefit from supports

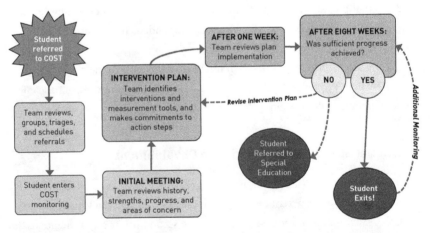

FIGURE 6.1 The process of individual student review within the coordination of services team (COST). A student is initially reviewed by COST to identify goals and interventions and later to monitor progress and assess needed adjustments to the student's individualized plan. SPED stands for special education.

that teachers cannot provide within the classroom—everything from eyeglasses and learning supports to social skill development and housing resources.

(2) New referrals are reviewed weekly by the UE coach, who is responsible for triaging requests to identify immediate interventions that can be put in place without delay, such as an outside referral to replace lost reading glasses, and to determine the urgency of requests that warrant student presentation with the COST. The UE coach then creates a schedule of these student presentations and communicates which students will be reviewed on what dates.

(3) COST meetings begin with a focus on student presentations, with approximately two 30-minute student presentations per week. After teachers present students' strengths, intervention history, and needs, the COST members ask clarifying questions, identify measurable goals for student growth, and commit to specific action steps that will support the student in making progress toward those goals.

(4) Following the student presentations, the meeting concludes with two follow-up accountability checks: one in which team members review the action steps that were agreed on for students discussed the previous week, to ensure that all required action has been taken or is underway, and another in which the team reviews students who entered COST monitoring 8 weeks prior and discusses student progress and identifies next steps.

(5) Outside of meeting times, expert service providers within COST hold regular office hours—our favorite branding by far is one school's famed "COSTumer Service Hours"—or join designated grade-level or department meetings to collect updates on student progress and unresolved concerns.

To fully understand the impact of this structure, let's explore the experience of one of our colleagues who attempted to assemble support for her student before the implementation of COST. Ms. Reyes had a student in her classroom named Simon who frequently got out of his seat, pushed others in line, and from time to time erupted into tantrums during work periods. After a particularly challenging afternoon in which Simon had torn up his reading journal and thrown the pieces off the edge of his desk, Ms. Reyes was at a loss and decided to seek guidance from others on the school staff. The next morning, while she was making copies, she ran across the school's mental health clinician, who suggested that Simon needed individual therapy to explore his underlying emotional issues. While Ms. Reyes was waiting for her class to line up after morning recess, the school's behaviorist suggested she introduce a strict reinforcement schedule to incentivize desired behaviors. During reading period, the reading specialist, who pulled this student and others from her class in a small group, offered that since Simon was struggling with core reading concepts she should provide him with extra practice to boost his confidence and skills. Later, over lunch in the staff lounge, she mentioned Simon's struggles to the occupational therapist, who suggested that he might be having difficulty integrating sensory and emotional stimuli into his physical being and suggested some grounding body exercise. By the end of her investigation, Ms. Reyes had spent a large chunk of her day tracking down these various experts. She had four suggestions but no idea how to make any of them a reality, especially since she was already working late until the evening just to prepare her regular lessons for the next day. Ms. Reyes felt more hopeless than when she started.

In schools without a formal process through which teachers can access support from specialists, teachers spend a great deal of time and energy attempting to identify and employ useful strategies, often with minimal success. Master teachers who, after many years of experience, have a strong grasp on instruction of the core curriculum and day-to-day classroom management, may have the bandwidth to seek out new techniques on their own. However, teachers who are just starting out in the field, which is a significant proportion of those assigned to the highest needs students and schools, are rarely able to juggle the expansive needs of their many students entirely on their own. As a result, students' needs are seldom addressed promptly and new teachers are left feeling overwhelmed and ineffective, often leaving the field in fewer than 5 years (Greenberg, Brown, & Abenavoli, 2016).

Some schools have adopted teaming in the form of student intervention teams (SITs) or student study teams (SSTs), but these are often time-consuming, rarely lead to immediate action steps, and too often are conceived of only as gatekeeping processes for special education referral (Weist et al., 2012). There are four key elements, largely missing from existing teaming structures, that when implemented ensure increased efficiency in individualized student intervention:

(1) Teams must consist of a coordinated, transdisciplinary group of specialists focused on identifying and addressing the needs of a particular student.

(2) Teams must focus on capacity building for the teacher by employing interventions that are first carried out in an integrated partnership between the teacher and specialists and gradually released to the teacher as intervention techniques are mastered.

(3) Meetings must lead to immediate actionable interventions in order to intervene early and prevent an escalation of need.

(4) The process must involve consistent attention to tracking and monitoring, including scheduled follow-up on specific, measurable goals and the completion of identified action steps.

Coordinated, Transdisciplinary Team

There are numerous benefits associated with locating transdisciplinary experts around one table. First and foremost, the time and energy this saves for classroom teachers ensures that they have more time and energy to focus on the actual implementation of interventions. Additionally, it is common for professionals within individual disciplines to approach similar problems in particular ways, using the tools of their own discipline. In the example of Ms. Reyes, each of the perspectives she collected were likely true, yet each only a small piece of the puzzle. This common downfall brings to mind the more popular adage "If all you have is a hammer, everything looks like a nail" (Maslow, 1966). In typical systems, such as the one experienced by Ms. Reyes, where specialists work in isolation, there is no chance to combine these various forms of expertise. Collaboration provides an important opportunity for specialists to expand their own horizons and gain new perspectives in their own work with students. It is common after the implementation of the COST structure for specialists to begin to use interventions from other disciplines in their own work. This creativity can be further fostered by providing ready opportunities for specialists to engage in professional development activities within other disciplines. Practitioners who participate in such cross-discipline training have more tools at their personal disposal and therefore develop a more flexible approach when choosing interventions. In addition, they can work successfully on transdisciplinary teams to create student-centered, out-of-the-box solutions not bound by the limitations of any specific discipline.

Capacity Building for Teachers through an Integrated Partnership

An important element of training for new COST members is that this role requires an element of customer service. That is, their job is to make teachers feel comfortable participating in a collaborative conversation about the root cause of the problem and the solutions that will begin to shift the student's experience toward success, asking. How can teachers feel welcomed into this space? How can they become an integral part of the conversation? How do we help them identify classroom supports that are feasible and efficient? What can be done to help scaffold their experience and provide teachers with the coaching and support necessary to make sure that the implementation of the intervention is successful? How can specialists act as partners rather than simply provide a checklist of additional tasks for the teacher to do?

In other teaming structures, it is not uncommon for a teacher to hear a standard barrage of suggestions from the team, such as "move the student closer to the front of the room," "provide modified assignments," and "make a positive phone call home!" When cookie-cutter interventions are employed without a transdisciplinary analysis, they are not likely to identify root causes or influence much positive change in experience for the student or teacher. Additionally, in other teaming structures, teachers frequently leave meetings with a lengthy list of to-dos, but without any additional time or support to put these interventions into action. Either outcome leaves teachers feeling unsupported and frustrated and less likely to reach out for help when future student challenges arise. Instead, COST members must team up with classroom teachers to implement integrated interventions. At first, specialists are responsible for the entirety of the intervention, modeling its implementation so that the teacher can see it in action. As the teacher comes to enjoy the success of the intervention and fully understand its utility and application in the classroom, the specialist can begin to slowly transfer the onus of responsibility for its implementation to the teacher. With each successful joint implementation of each new intervention, the teacher adds one new tool to their belt, which can then be used when similar student needs arise in the future.

Immediate Actionable Interventions

Individual student meetings are primarily focused on developing modifications for the classroom environment, developing individualized special plans outside of an existing menu of interventions to be supported by both the teacher and COST members, and/or identifying needed out-of-school supports and action plans to leverage external resources. In addition, most COST action plans result in an activity related to caregiver engagement, ensuring that a clear continuum of supports exists between both the home and school environments.

In efforts to maximize the use of intervention resources, a common pitfall is to schedule every minute of specialists' time in direct work with students. While practical at first glance, in the long term, this strategy limits the ability of the specialist team to respond with on-demand support. While it can be tempting to assign all available resources during the intervention assignment phase, it is important to remember that it is often unforeseen needs that can become most critical. To ensure that resources and supports are available when these unforeseen needs arise throughout the year, the day-to-day responsibilities of members of the COST must be structured such that they have capacity to deploy on-demand support for teachers as needs arise.

Thematic Analysis

While COST referrals are submitted for individual students, teams can increase efficiency by identifying and addressing themes on the school level that affect multiple students and are related to academic or non-academic barriers to student success. When reviewing COST forms, chatting with school staff informally, or attending school meetings, COST coordinators will likely see themes emerging. Have multiple students been referred for similar issues in the past month? Are there multiple referrals coming from the same class or grade level? For example, if numerous third-grade students are consistently struggling with similar behavior issues, it may be necessary to review behavior policies that apply to all students and analyze how those policies are being implemented in specific classrooms or grades. Some samples of thematic discussions include retention, bullying, family systems, siblings, or parents who are struggling, responding to a large campus change or community crisis, and staff culture and morale. In these situations, a COST meeting is scheduled around this specific theme or issue. These meetings take the place of an individual student meeting and are an opportunity to delve into themes and identify broader interventions needed schoolwide or for subgroup interventions. The UE coach may choose to schedule students in the same weekly meeting who are having similar challenges or are from the same family system or in the same grade, for example. If the issue is around a specific subject matter (i.e., math or English language arts), it is common for an instructional coach or experienced teacher in that subject to also join the discussion. As schools become more effective in their use of data for the identification and assignment of interventions, thematic analysis become a larger part of the COST process, signaling a shift in focus and resources toward more proactive, early intervention planning.

CONCLUSION

Together, these three roles of the COST—(1) intervention assignment and monitoring, (2) individual student review and plan development, and (3) thematic reviews—ensure that schools have a structured, proactive, and efficient approach to providing tiered intervention (see Appendix 6.2 for a COST fidelity tool). The alternative is the all-too-familiar story of Ms. Reyes and Simon where schools inequitably assign interventions to students with the strongest teachers (no universal screening systems to identify needs schoolwide and strategically plan interventions), teachers can only access specialist expertise through haphazard means and receive little support with implementation (no universal referral and student review process), and principals are unaware of arising themes of need that could be efficiently addressed schoolwide before they reach crisis levels (no thematic reviews). These processes of coordination and the development of implementation fidelity will be explored more fully in Chapter 7.

APPENDIX 6.1
COORDINATION OF SERVICES TEAM (COST) REFERRAL

STUDENT INFORMATION

Student Name:		Age:	Date of Birth:	Grade Level:
Classroom Teacher:	Referred By:	Priority Rating (1 = low, 3 = highest): X 1 X 2 X 3	Special Ed. IEP?: If yes, please see case manager with these concerns. X yes X no	
Parent/Guardian:		Phone # [or other contact information]:		
E.L.L.?: X YES X NO HOME LANGUAGE?:		Referral Date:		*OFFICE USE:* C.O.S. Team Meeting Date:

HOME/LIFE INFORMATION

List any relevant information/history: (i.e. – siblings, custodial parent, other adult[s] living in the home)

Who did you speak with at home to gather this information?

Who at home was notified of this COST referral?

STRENGTHS

CURRENT INTERVENTIONS & SERVICES

School-Based	Community-Based
X SMALL-GROUP INSTRUCTION	X COUNSELING SERVICES
X READING INTERVENTION	___ SCHOOL/INDIVIDUAL ___ SCHOOL/GROUP
X INDIVIDUAL TUTORING/ONE-TO-ONE INSTRUCTION	___ OUTSIDE AGENCY ___
X MODIFIED ASSIGNMENTS	X FOSTER CARE
X OTHER: ___	X CHILD PROTECTIVE SERVICES
X BEHAVIOR CONTRACT/PLAN	X OTHER: ___
X OTHER: ___	
X COUNSELING	
X OTHER: ___	
X MENTORING	
X OTHER: ___	

ACADEMIC CONCERNS

X READING DECODING/FLUENCY	X TIME MANAGEMENT
X READING COMPREHENSION	X DOES NOT COMPLETE ASSIGNMENTS
X POOR ORGANIZATIONAL SKILLS	X POOR HANDWRITING
X MATH COMPUTATION	X CARELESS WITH WORK
X ATTENTION	X MEMORY DIFFICULTIES
X MATH REASONING	
X FINE MOTOR DIFFICULTIES	
X WRITING	
X GROSS MOTOR DIFFICULTIES	

X OTHER/COMMENTS:

SOCIAL • EMOTIONAL • BEHAVIORAL CONCERNS

X INATTENTION	X NONCOMPLIANT	X STEALING
X DISTRACTABILITY	X AGGRESSION/FIGHTING	X ANXIETY
X UNMOTIVATED	X BULLYING/TEASING/THREATENING	X GRIEF
X DIFFICULTY W/ PEER INTERACTIONS	X CHRONICALLY DISRUPTIVE	X SELF-ESTEEM/SELF-WORTH
X ANGER MANAGEMENT (IRRITABLE, LOW	X SEXUALIZED BEHAVIOR	X APPEARS DEPRESSED, SAD, WITHDRAWN
FRUSTRATION TOLERANCE)	X SEXUAL HARASSMENT	X GANG INVOLVEMENT
X DOES NOT/CANNOT FOLLOW DIRECTIONS	X ENGAGES IN DANGEROUS BEHAVIOR	X GENDER IDENTITY

X INSURANCE INFORMATION: _____

X OTHER/COMMENTS:

SPEECH & LANGUAGE CONCERNS

X RECEPTIVE LANGUAGE	X STUTTERING	X VOICE
X EXPRESSIVE LANGUAGE	X AUDITORY PROCESSING	X PRAGMATICS (SOCIAL CONVERSATION SKILLS)
X LISP	X ARTICULATION	X HEARING

X OTHER/COMMENTS:

HEALTH CONCERNS

✗ HEADACHES	✗ GLASSES ___ NEEDS ___ HAS ___ WEARS	✗ MEDICATIONS
✗ EARACHES	✗ ASTHMA	✗ HYGIENE
✗ STOMACH COMPLAINTS	✗ FATIGUE	✗ PHYSICAL DISABILITY/ONGOING ILLNESS
✗ OTHER/COMMENTS:		

SENECA
FAMILY OF AGENCIES | UNCONDITIONAL CARE

APPENDIX 6.2
COST IMPLEMENTATION FIDELITY TOOL

0 = not observed, 1 = partially observed, 2 = fully observed

Structure and Process			
a. COST team present includes representation from administration, general education, and intervention staff	0	1	2
b. Meeting has a structured agenda that can be visually referenced by all members of the team	0	1	2
c. The meeting closely follows the set agenda	0	1	2
d. A designated team member acts as time-keeper for the duration of the meeting	0	1	2
e. A designated team member acts as note-taker for the duration of the meeting	0	1	2
f. Meeting includes opening ritual that includes an element of community building	0	1	2
g. Team norms are posted and/or reviewed at the start of the meeting	0	1	2
h. Meeting agenda includes time for one or more of the discussion types (Individual Student, Thematic Intervention, Data Analysis)	0	1	2
i. Meeting agenda includes time for follow-up on previous action steps	0	1	2
Individual Student Discussion			
Protocol:			
• *5 minutes: Teacher presents background, strengths, existing interventions, and areas of concern*			
• *20 minutes: Team asks questions and discusses possible interventions*			
• *5 minute: Team makes action commitments*			
a. Referral/meeting information for student discussed is entered into the database	0	1	2
b. For each student presented, referral information is provided to the team in a visual format	0	1	2
c. Discussion follows the student meeting discussion protocol	0	1	2
d. Measureable goals are identified	0	1	2
e. COST team point person is assigned	0	1	2
f. Action steps are developed and assigned	0	1	2
g. Date of follow-up meeting is set	0	1	2
h. Presenting teacher leaves meeting with an intervention plan, which includes a summary of presented information, existing interventions, and action steps, or one is emailed within 24 hours	0	1	2

Thematic Intervention Discussion			
Protocol:			
• *10 minutes: Team defines the need/dilemma*			
• *15 minutes: Team discusses potential group or schoolwide interventions*			
• *5 minutes: Team makes action commitments*			
a. Discussion follows the thematic intervention protocol	0	1	2
b. Measurable goals are identified	0	1	2
c. Action steps are developed and assigned	0	1	2
Data Analysis			
Protocol:			
• *10 minutes: Team explores new data*			
• *10 minutes: Team analyzes data, celebrating successes, identifying areas of challenge and questions that still exist*			
• *10 minutes: Team brainstorms actions to address areas of challenge and makes action commitments*			
a. Discussion follows the thematic intervention protocol	0	1	2
b. Measurable goals are identified	0	1	2
c. Action steps are developed and assigned	0	1	2
Team Dynamics and Facilitation			
In what ways did the team include elements of celebration and team-building into the meeting? In what ways did the facilitator bring joy to the group?			
In what ways did team members adhere to/not adhere to identified norms? How did the facilitator reinforce norms during the meeting?			
In what ways did the team stay on track and demonstrate a sense of shared purpose? Were there times when they got off track? If so, how were they able to find their way back? What was the facilitator's role in this process?			

What was the participation/engagement of various members? Did any members dominate the discussion or participate very little? In what ways was the facilitator able to ensure equitable contributions by all members?	
How did the team respond to opinions of others with which they didn't agree? Did any disagreements or conflicts arise? How was the facilitator able to help resolve them?	

7 Assessment

By now it should be apparent that unconditional education (UE) is both comprehensive in its scope and ambitious in its goals. This chapter will help outline the formative assessment process that has been created as a means to inform high-quality program planning and implementation and summative assessments used to measure the extent to which the model promotes positive outcomes for students and schools. The two overarching goals of implementing this model are (1) to increase the academic performance and social-emotional well-being of the most struggling students and (2) to increase the capacity of schools serving highly stressed communities to deliver effective interventions through the implementation of a transdisciplinary multi-tiered framework. The second goal relates to capacity building and systems change within the school community itself; while the first relates to the outcomes these changes bring about. More information about the model's overall theory of action can be found in the logic model in Appendix 7.1.

The logic model also highlights the four key components of UE and the implementation strategies related to them. These key components are as follows:

- *System efficiency*, resources match the level of identified student need and schools are able to leverage braided funding, including general education, special education, and mental health dollars.
- *Coordination of services*, a transdisciplinary team reviews data, assigns students to intervention, and monitors their progress.
- *Universal supports/Tier 1*, a culture and climate team engages in a schoolwide assessment and planning process explained in great detail later in this chapter.
- *Targeted and intensive supports,* data-informed, high-quality interventions are implemented with fidelity and monitored for effectiveness.

SUMMATIVE ASSESSMENT
Long-Term Outcomes

The strategies related to these four key components are expected to influence a set of comprehensive, long-term outcomes. These outcomes measure the extent to which the model has improved school culture and climate (as measured by the School Climate Assessment Instrument), increased academic achievement (as measure by standardized tests), improved behavior outcomes (as measured by suspension rates), and increased attendance. While data are reviewed at the end of every school year, it is not until the third year that a substantial impact on these long-term measures is expected. As with the introduction of most systems initiatives, it is expected that schools will take 2 to 3 years to fully implement key components with fidelity.

Fidelity and Adaptive Integration

To complement the review of program outcomes, it is important to measure the extent to which the model was implemented with fidelity. A review of fidelity provides additional context and allows schools to draw connections between the level at which they have implemented each key component and the extent to which they are achieving improved outcomes. However, the measurement of fidelity across a broad range of contexts is complex. Interventions such as UE confront a wide range of local organizational conditions. With this in mind, Byrk and colleagues at the Carnegie Foundation for the Advancement of Teaching encourage a shift from the mindset of *fidelity* of implementation toward that of *adaptive integration*. This new mindset acknowledges that, to effectively adopt the intervention, modifications will most likely be required and prompt implementors to ask: "Are changes consistent with the original design principles that undergird the intervention?"

The Unconditional Education Implementation Fidelity Tool (see Appendix 7.2), created in partnership with SRI, specifically incorporates direct fidelity measures alongside parameters for adaptive integration. This combination has led to a tool that focuses primarily on structures, processes, and routines that create a functioning framework within which relevant and responsive content and tools (curricula, assessments, progress-monitoring tools, database systems, etc.) can be organized. In this way, the tool, paired with the comprehensive assessment process outlined in the next sections, ensures that a school community can approach the implementation of UE with an "adaptive integration" mindset.

FORMATIVE ASSESSMENT FOR PROGRAM PLANNING AND IMPROVEMENT: TIER 1

The short-term outcomes listed on the logic model (Appendix 7.1) lay the foundation for UE's cyclical process of assessment, planning, implementation, and progress monitoring as it relates to schoolwide culture and climate and targeted and intensive student interventions. These short-term outcomes are important indicators that guide program planning and improvement. Schools use an iterative approach to work towards implementation. As implementation is achieved meaningful long-term outcomes for students and schools are expected. The theory of action is as follows: If students' needs are identified early and often and students are assigned to responsive interventions where high-quality services are provided, then these students will make progress on their identified challenges (a short-term outcome) which will in turn influence the school's ability to promote increased achievement for all students (a long-term outcome). In addition to providing this cyclical structure to support student intervention, the UE model also provides a process by which schools can structure their efforts to assess, plan, and monitor their schoolwide culture and climate.

Schoolwide Assessment: Tier 1 Culture and Climate

In UE, lessons learned from work supporting individual youth are specifically applied to the work of supporting individual school communities. Just like each student, every school has its own history, challenges, strengths, and aspirations. Many current change efforts stall when they fail to recognize and systematically address the unique nature of each school. In UE implementation the individual nature of each school community is honored, by using a comprehensive, school site–level assessment and planning process capable of exploring the existing school culture, building trusting relationships with community stakeholders, and moving toward the collaborative creation of shared goals and strategies. Once UE has been adopted, most components of the assessment process are then repeated each spring, in order to gather data on previous goals and to inform new goals and strategies for the next school year. These goals and strategies are formalized in a document called the annual implementation plan (AIP).

The spring assessment is broken down into four major components. The information gathered from these four activities is used to identify top areas of need and develop responsive goals and strategies to address those needs in the coming school year. The first component, which consists of in-person interviews with all staff on campus, is traditionally carried out only once during the spring before the UE framework is to be adopted. The next three components are carried out at least annually and include (1) the School Climate Assessment Instrument (SCAI), (2) the Schoolwide Positive Behavioral Interventions and Supports (SWPBS) Tiered Fidelity Index (TFI), and (3) the Trauma Index. Each of these components will be described in more detail later in the chapter.

The National School Climate Center[1] serves as a useful resource for those interested in learning more about the impact of school culture and climate on student achievement and its critical role in any school transformation effort. In a recent research summary, the Center highlights the ever-growing body of research on school climate that continuously attests to its importance, including its impact on social, emotional, intellectual, and physical safety; mental health and healthy relationships; school connectedness and engagement; academic achievement; and teacher retention (Thapa, Cohen, Higgins-D'Alessandro, & Guffy, 2012). Intentional development of a safe and inclusive school climate is particularly vital in schools that serve

[1] https://www.schoolclimate.org

students living in communities of concentrated poverty, who may experience cumulative trauma resulting from the daily stressors of poverty and community violence, as well as from historic and structural conditions of racism and disenfranchisement (Collins et al., 2010). In order for students to learn and grow, both they and their families *must* experience school as a safe and welcoming place. An inclusive school climate can build and rebuild trust between students, families, and the institution of school.

Continuous improvement of schoolwide climate is a vital part of UE, and as discussed in Chapter 4, efforts for improvement must always begin with an engaging strengths-based assessment. In the schoolwide climate assessment, which is primarily about the human experience within the institution, stakeholder input is gathered from all perspectives in order to more fully understand the level at which families, staff, and students feel supported and engaged in the school community. This process requires the participation of all stakeholders within the community and is an opportunity in and of itself to build relationships and reaffirm a unified vision for the school.

Initial School Staff Interviews

The first component of the schoolwide assessment is an in-person interview (see Box 7.1) with every adult who works on campus, from the principal to the after-school reading tutor, from the front office administrator to the security guard. Since the goal of UE's assessment process is to uncover a common understanding about the school's overall well-being, the inclusion of multiple perspectives is important for developing a complete picture. It can be helpful to have an impartial third party complete the interviews and compile the results so that participants can remain anonymous and contributing voices and ideas are integrated without internal bias. These 30-60 minute interviews most often take place in small groups of three to five staff members, intentionally developed to promote a safe environment for sharing critical feedback. The interview is intended to provoke reflection and generate ideas for the improvement of school culture and climate and student services.

This process parallels the process of comprehensive assessment and planning that is carried out with students receiving special education or mental health services, and it is a crucial first step for schools that decide to implement the UE framework. In the provision of individual services, the assessment phase provides a meaningful opportunity to engage in relational building. These early encounters send an important message about relational trust, and a sensitive and meaningful assessment process can establish trust while gathering information that will be used to sustain it. The potential for this assessment process to serve as a relational intervention in and of itself is often felt in staff's reactions to participating in the interviews. Upon conclusion of the interview staff inevitably take a deep breath and make a comment like, "We never have the time and space to talk about these things. It felt so good to share

---

Box 7.1 Sample Questions for a School Staff Interview

Role

1. Describe your role and how long you have worked here.
2. How is your role connected to the larger goals of the school?
3. How effective do you feel you are able to be in this role?
4. What do you think would make your role more effective?
5. What kind of support do you get in your role (including from leadership, supervisor, PD, etc.)? Is it enough?

Referral Process and Student Services

6. How do you determine that a student is struggling academically, and how do you refer him or her for support?
7. How do you determine that a student is struggling emotionally or behaviorally, and how do you refer him or her for support?
8. How do you tell whether interventions are effective (for academics, behavior, and social-emotional issues)?

Discipline/School Culture

9. How is behavior handled at this school?
10. Do you feel that it is effective? If not, how do you feel it could be more effective?
11. How would you describe the school culture? What improvements, if any, do you think could be made? (This includes relationships between students, between students and staff, between staff, and between the school and the outer community.)

---

that." While staff admit that it feels good to share with someone their experiences and suggestions, they are also equally curious about with what will actually come as a result of their sharing. A few common questions include "Will we be able to see the results?" or "Is anything really going to change?"

Beyond the initial sharing, it is what happens next that is essential. Responses from all of the staff interviews are reviewed by the assessment team in order to identify themes of both strengths and areas for growth. The top themes are summarized and supplemented by direct quotes from the interviews, as well as by a set of initial recommendations for addressing the identified areas for growth. This report is shared with school leaders, who begin to identify their top priorities for transformation as they share the content of the report and their planned next steps with the larger school community. With this, staff understand that their thoughts and suggestions have not only been solicited but are in turn being used to make concrete decisions about school improvement.

The School Climate Assessment Instrument (SCAI)

Another major component of the initial and ongoing school assessment process is a formal survey of students, parents, and staff regarding the health of the school climate. The National Center on Safe Supportive Learning Environments (NCSSLE), funded by the US Department of Education, maintains a compendium of valid and reliable surveys, assessments, and scales of school climate[2] that can assist educators in their efforts to formally assess school culture and climate. The SCAI, a validated tool developed by Dr. John Shindler and his team at Alliance for the Study of School Climate, measures eight original dimensions of school culture and climate: physical environment, leadership and decision-making, faculty relations, student interactions, discipline, learning and assessment, attitude and culture, and community relations (Shindler, Jones, Williams, Taylor, & Cadenas, 2011). In collaboration with Shindler and his team, the developers of UE added a ninth dimension—special education—to include in the surveying process. The SCAI includes a survey for staff, parents, and students (grades 3–12) and, most importantly, has a strong theoretical framework connecting culture and climate to the "psychology of success" (POS) that pervades every aspect of the school. The POS includes three main variables:

- *Internal locus of control (LOC).* This factor is defined by our sense of internal causality and orientation toward personal responsibility. The more internal our LOC, the more we feel that our destiny is in our own hands.
- *Belonging and acceptance.* This factor reflects how much we feel wanted and a part of the group, and how much we like and accept ourselves as we are. The more we feel accepted and acceptable, the more we are able to express ourselves, act authentically, and be fully present to others.
- *Growth mindset.* This factor reflects our ability to view a challenge as an opportunity to learn and grow. Those with a strong growth mindset do not see their performance within a situation as a measure of their innate ability so much as a measure of their investment—better results require more practice.

When these three interdependent variables are woven into the fabric of school practice, policy, and process they influence students' growth in all aspects of their lives, traversing the boundaries of academic, social, and emotional development. These concepts are equally important in affecting the experience of staff and parents as well. Throughout the process of measuring culture and climate the aim is to assess the presence and vitality of these three variables for *all stakeholders* within the school community.

While the SCAI includes about 60 questions organized into the nine dimensions just mentioned, the underlying framework of each question is based on measuring

---

[2] https://safesupportivelearning.ed.gov/topic-research/school-climate-measurement/school-climate-survey-compendium

the extent to which the school promotes these three variables within its policies and practices. Questions are organized in an analytic trait scale with a score of 5 representing a strong POS. The long-term goal for schools implementing the UE model is to accomplish a summative score of at least 4, which represents a school with a sound culture and climate and, in turn, one that provides a foundation for social and academic success.

The SWPBS Tiered Fidelity Index

As discussed previously, one major tenant of the UE framework is to move schools away from "zero-tolerance," punitive discipline systems and toward one that is more positive, instructional, and restorative in nature. The approach of SWPBS guides this work in the behavioral strand and is highly aligned with the core tenants of a strong POS. SWPBS provides a multi-tiered behavioral framework that builds a positive school culture and climate by creating clear and consistent expectations for behavior and a continuum of interventions for students in need of support in meeting those expectations. The SWPBS TFI was created by Dr. Rob Horner and his colleagues at the national Technical Assistance Center on PBIS.[3] The purpose of this tool is to provide a valid and reliable measure of the extent to which a school is implementing the core features of SWPBS.[4] A score of 80% implementation lays the foundation for improved student outcomes. Each administration of the TFI provides information about which core components are "in place" or "not yet in place" and informs further improvement of the schoolwide behavioral support system.

The Trauma Index

For schools in communities of concentrated poverty, it is imperative that school leaders and staff are trained in trauma-informed education and dedicated to the implementation of its core principles. To accomplish this, UE schools use the Trauma Index (TI) which builds on the work of the American Institutes for Research (AIR) and is a tool that outlines the key domains that constitute a trauma-informed school: supporting staff development, creating a safe and supportive environment, adapting policies, involving children and families, and assessing and planning services and building skills (see Appendix 3.3). Many measures in this tool overlap with those in both the SCAI and SWPBS, since many trauma-informed practices not only benefit students who have experienced trauma but also improve the education experience for all members of the community. By using this tool, schools can identify which practices are already in place and what next steps still need to be taken to fully implement a trauma-informed approach.

---

[3] https://www.pbis.org/
[4] https://www.pbis.org/Common/Cms/files/pbisresources/2015_10_7_SWPBIS_Tiered_Fidelity_Inventory.pdf

Data Analysis and Development of the Annual Implementation Plan (AIP) for Tier 1

Previously in this book we noted the importance of providing genuine, meaningful opportunities for staff, parents, and students to contribute to the school community. Perhaps one of the most exciting ways in which UE promotes such contributions is through the culture and climate committee (C3). C3 members are responsible for reviewing the data from all of the previously mentioned tools and surveys to identify measurable goals for schoolwide improvement. Again, culture and climate is influenced by and, in turn, influences every member of the school community. Thus it is important that every member not only contribute their perspective when *assessing* the culture and climate but also that a representative group is responsible for *carrying out the work* to improve the culture and climate. For this reason, the C3 includes an administrator as well as representation from general education, special education, classified staff, the parent community, and, when appropriate (i.e., middle and high school), students.

The C3 sets aside time in the summer to dive into the results of the staff interviews, the SCAI, the SWPBS TFI, and the TI and to organize the data into areas of strength and areas for growth. While each of these tools helps to examine the health of the school through the different lens, there is great overlap in the practices and values they promote. As a result, members of C3 will begin to find common themes as they explore data from these different tools—and it is these more universal themes that help them to identify essential areas for growth and develop goals for schoolwide improvement (see Box 7.2).

Following the identification of goals, teams work to identify action steps. While there were many action steps taken related to the goal highlighted in Box 7.2, one key change this school made was in the use of space, by introducing safe areas for students to use when they are feeling overwhelmed. In classrooms for younger students peace corners were introduced and each was outfitted with a beanbag chair, a box of kinesthetic tools (putty, small hand puzzles, fidget toys, etc.), a visual timer, and a poster with guidelines for using the space. When students felt overwhelmed during class, they could go to the peace corner, set the timer, and engage in calming activity for 5 minutes. When the time was up, the student would complete a short, age-appropriate reflection slip and return to the class activity. At first teachers feared that students would simply use this space as a means of avoiding other demands in the classroom and missing instructional time. However, with a bit of pre-teaching about the purpose and expectations for use of the space, most students were able to use it proactively to manage frustration, and teachers saw a reduction in the number of behaviors that needed redirection. While relatively simple in preparation, this strategy shifts responsibility and a sense of control to the student, providing a more preventative and restorative approach to classroom discipline.

Box 7.2 Sample Annual Implementation Plan (AIP) Goals and Measures

Following is a sample of one goal on the AIP that was informed by the results of multiple tools. The measures listed indicate items within each tool that revealed areas for growth and where the team believes they are likely to see improvement if progress is achieved on their stated goal. Each of these items will be used to measure progress on this goal at the end of the school year by comparing baseline and end-of-year scores.

Goal

By the end of the school year, we will improve our current discipline policies to make them more restorative in nature and build in more structured time for fostering a sense of community among students.

Measures
SCAI

- Student Interactions Dimension: **Sense of Safety**
- Attitude and Culture Dimension: **Student Responsibility for Others' Behavior**
- Attitude and Culture Dimension: **Sense of Connection among Students**

Tier 1: Universal SWPBIS Features

- **Problem Behavior Definitions**: School has clear definitions for behaviors that interfere with academic and social success and a clear policy and procedure

Discipline Policies

School policies and procedures describe and emphasize proactive, instructive, and/or restorative approaches to student behavior that are implemented consistently.

Trauma-Informed School Index

- **Designated safe spaces** for children to go to when feeling overwhelmed or triggered
- **School regularly examines and adjusts policies and procedure** in light of trauma principles (e.g., understanding safety, choice, control, and empowerment)

Feedback Loops and Program Improvement

The processes for formal assessment and plan development described thus far are essential first steps. However, transformative change requires an iterative process, and the ongoing collection and analysis of data is an essential component of ongoing continuous improvement. Processes within UE include tools and recommended practices for soliciting such feedback from students, families, school staff, and leaders as follows:

- *Tier 3 student and family survey:* In addition to the annual School Climate Assessment Survey that is completed by both students and caregivers each spring, UE schools need more specific feedback from students who receive intensive (Tier 3) interventions and their families. Parents and students are asked about their satisfaction with services provided and their impact. (See sample questions for caregivers and students in Box 7.3.)
- *Staff experience survey:* A formal, annual survey is also conducted with all staff collecting information about staff's perception of the quality and impact of the

---

Box 7.3 Sample Student and Caregiver Satisfaction Survey Questions

For students who are 8 years old and older (or developmentally equivalent), we ask a simple set of questions and ask students to rate their response on a four-point Likert scale:

- My service provider, (name), appreciates my individual strengths, talents, and accomplishments.
- My service provider, (name), provides opportunities for me to share my ideas about my experiences and who I am.
- My service provider, (name), is interested in my culture, values, and beliefs and asks me questions about them.
- My service provider, (name), believes in me and my ability to reach my goals.
- My service provider, (name), believes I can succeed through difficult times.
- My service provider, (name), makes time to have fun with me.

For parents and caregivers, we conduct phone-based surveys and ask a combination of Likert scale questions as well as open-ended response questions. The Likert scale questions include the following:

- Service providers are skillful and knowledgeable in their work with my child.
- I am well informed about what my child is working on and how they are progressing.
- I feel supported in meeting the needs of my child.
- My child made progress as a result of their work with their service provider.

Open-ended response questions include the following:

- In working with your child, is there anything specific that service providers did that you found most helpful?
- Do you have any suggestion for how service providers could better support your child?
- Do you have any other thoughts to share?

school's system of supports (see Appendix 7.3). The survey includes questions regarding the overall coordination of student support services, the quality of support for teachers in meeting the needs of their students, the knowledge and quality of service providers on campus, and the impact of Tier 2 and Tier 3 interventions on the achievement and well-being of students.

- *Leadership reflection:* While all staff are included in the anonymous staff survey just described, a formal leadership reflection identifies implementation strengths and challenges as seen from the unique perspective of the school leader. In particular, leaders are prompted to consider relationships between general education and intervention staff, staff buy-in, messaging of a unified vision, existence of trusting relationships, and communication of roles and responsibilities. (See sample leadership reflection questions in Box 7.4.)

Box 7.4 Sample Leadership Reflection Questions

The following questions help to initiate a meaningful, reflective conversation between school-based partners and school leaders:

- Was the unconditional education (UE) model clearly articulated to the school community? What was done to help the school community understand the model? What could be done next year to make sure that staff and parents are familiar with the model?
- Was the role of the UE coach clearly articulated to the school community? What was done to help promote an understanding of the coach's role? What could be done next year to better articulate the role and responsibilities of the coach to administration, staff, and parents?
- How effective was communication between intervention providers and community-based partners and administrators, school staff, and the parent community? How could communication be improved?
- How well do intervention providers and community-based partners understand the local school context? How well did providers customize their services and supports based on your school's strengths, needs, and goals?
- Were sufficient processes in place for parents, staff, and school administrators to provide feedback to intervention providers, community-based partners, and the UE coach? How could feedback processes be improved?
- How responsive were intervention providers and community-based partners to challenges that arose throughout the year?
- How well did intervention providers and community-based partners share data, results, and outcomes related to UE? What information would you like to have more of next year?
- Have there been any other barriers this year? How might those barriers be addressed next year?

After each phase, results along with plans for future program improvement efforts are shared with relevant stakeholders. When stakeholders see that their input is reviewed and acted on, they are more willing to provide feedback via surveys and interviews going forward.

CONCLUSION

Data-driven analysis is an essential component at all levels of the UE practice. The series of formative and summative assessment practices described here aim to set the structure for continued improvement while allowing schools to account for the priorities of their local context. The tools prompt teams to engage in systematic review, focus their efforts on areas of greatest need, and engage in action planning that builds on existing efforts. This framework supports schools and their leaders to engage in steady, yet incremental, processes of transformation aimed at the system itself and, even more importantly, to focus on outcomes for their most vulnerable students.

APPENDIX 7.1
UNCONDITIONAL EDUCATION LOGIC MODEL

Goals

1. To increase the academic performance and social-emotional well-being of the *most struggling students*
2. To increase capacity of schools serving high poverty communities to deliver effective interventions through the implementation of a multi-tiered framework

Input	Strategies	Short-Term Outcomes	Long-Term Outcomes
Multi-Service lead agency • Strong belief in collaboration and partnership • A continuum of services and expertise including established partnerships with systems of care (social services, child welfare, mental health, behavioral health, probation, etc.) • Training capacity and expertise	**KEY COMPONENT: System Efficiency** • Assess the current system of student supports and to create a responsive intervention plan • Create a customized braided funding structure	• Resource allocation at each tier is aligned with demonstrated need	• Improved school climate as demonstrated by an increase in School Climate Assessment Instrument (SCAI) scores • Increase in academic achievement as measured by progress assessments and standardized tests • Improved behavior outcomes as demonstrated by a decrease in disciplinary referrals and suspensions • Increased time in school as demonstrated by increased attendance rates • Services are more cost efficient, as demonstrated by cost per pupil rates and an analysis of special education local contribution
	KEY COMPONENT: Coordination of Services • Coordinate support services through the creation of a multi-disciplinary coordination of services team (COST) and the use of data management and analysis • Facilitate collaboration with county mental health, child welfare and probation • Establish a protocol for parental engagement during the referral process	• Staff report that services are more coordinated, responsive, integrated, individualized, effective, and data driven	
Educational organization • Strong belief in collaboration and partnership • System-wide commitment to providing Unconditional Education for all students • Organizational sustainability and commitment to the process of school transformation • Leadership capacity including the ability to develop a shared vision, and to promote relational trust and stakeholder investment	**KEY COMPONENT: Universal Supports/Tier One** • Provide staff with a set of tools including differentiated instruction, School Wide Positive Behavioral Interventions and Supports, and trauma-informed practices, to address the general variance of needs of all students. • Provide responsive professional development for staff that will enable them to better support students within the classroom setting • Promote active involvement amongst family and provide training and workshops for parents and caregivers	• Schools are more responsive to students who have experienced trauma • School has a consistent system of PBIS • School has a differentiated approach to classroom instruction • Staff and parents report increased knowledge and skills in their ability to support the diverse needs of their students	
	KEY COMPONENT: Targeted and Intensive Supports/Tier Two and Three • Provide high quality intervention services by credentialed and licensed professionals • Provide responsive and specialized training for academic, behavioral and/or mental health support staff • Provide responsive training for targeted parent groups experiencing similar challenges/needs	• Students in T2 and T3 interventions experience growth on social emotional and behavioral benchmark measures • Students in T2 and T3 interventions experience growth on academic benchmark measures • Students in T2 and T3 interventions experience a reduction in discipline incidents • Staff and parents report increased knowledge and skills in their ability to support the diverse needs of their students	

APPENDIX 7.2
UNCONDITIONAL EDUCATION IMPLEMENTATION FIDELITY TOOL

Key Indicators	Operational Definition for Indicator	Fidelity Data Source(s) for Indicator	Fidelity Score	Weight
		SYSTEM EFFICIENCY		
		SYSTEMS AND LEADERSHIP		
Initial/Annual Assessment	School will complete an initial/annual analysis of the allocation of student caseloads across the three tiers	Initial partnership assessment report, end-of-year report	0 = Quantitative analysis of student distribution across tiers of academic, behavioral, and social-emotional services has not been completed or shared with school leadership 1 = Quantitative analysis of student distribution has been completed and shared with school leadership	2
Braided Funding	School will develop a braided funding model for special education (SPED) and non-SPED services, including a source of funding for mental health services	Budget worksheet	Budgets will be coded by members of the program evaluation team to determine whether budget: 0 = does not include mental health funding 1 = includes mental health funding	5
"Blended Positions"	School will have "blended positions"	Fiscal team survey	0 = Does not use blended positions as a component of funding model 1 = Uses blended positions as a component of funding model 2 = Does it for both mental health and instructional staff	5

Score range for "system efficiency" at school level	0–12	12
Categories of "system efficiency" at school level	Low: 0–4.5; Medium: 5–8.5; High: 9–12	
Threshold for adequate fidelity of "system efficiency" at school level	Adequate fidelity = score of "High" (9–12)	

COORDINATION OF SERVICES TEAM (COST)				
Key Indicators	Operational Definition for Indicator	Fidelity Data Source(s) for Indicator	Fidelity Scores	Weight
SYSTEMS AND LEADERSHIP				
New COST Facilitator Training	New COST facilitators will complete the training checklist	Training checklist	0 = Less than 80% of activities are completed 1 = At least 80% of activities are completed (if the COST facilitator is not new, mark this as "1")	4
COST Team Composition	COST team will include representation from administration, general education, and intervention staff, as reflected by regular COST meeting attendance	Annual implementation plan (AIP)	0 = COST team not indicated on AIP or does not include the appropriate representation 1 = COST team indicated on AIP and includes the appropriate representation	2
Community Partner Connections	Lead service provider will develop relationships with the appropriate child welfare, probation, and community service providers	AIP (Addendum)	0 = AIP does not identify key community partners 1 = AIP identifies key community partners	1

			1
Regular COST Meeting Time	School will identify a regular COST meeting time that facilitates regular attendance from all team members	AIP and meeting notes	0 = Less than two meetings a month are scheduled and/or occur 1 = At least two meetings a month are scheduled and occur 2 = At least three meetings a month are scheduled and occur (excluding months with 1 or more weeks of vacation)
COST Orientation	COST team will complete initial orientation meeting	COST meeting notes	0 = Orientation meeting has not been completed 1 = Orientation meeting has been completed
COST Protocol	COST teams will develop a standard protocol that guides the structure of meetings	COST master file	0 = COST team has no standardized agenda developed 1 = COST team has created a standard agenda for regular meetings
Screeners	School wide academic, behavioral, and social emotional screeners and data sources will be identified	AIP (Addendum)	0 = Schoolwide academic, behavioral, and social emotional screeners and data sources are not identified on AIP 1 = Schoolwide academic OR behavioral/social emotional screeners are identified on AIP, but not both 2 = Schoolwide academic AND behavioral/social emotional screeners and data sources are identified on AIP

			1
Master Calendar	A master calendar is created that identifies timing of universal screeners, school wide cycles of intervention and progress monitoring for tier two and tier three services, and meetings to regularly review student progress data	COST master file	0 = Master calendar is not created 1 = Master calendar is created and includes some of the elements listed 2 = Master calendar is created and includes all elements listed
COST Database	COST will utilize a database to track referrals and whether or not action steps are completed in a timely manner	COST database	0 = Action steps are not tracked in database 1 = Actions steps are tracked but less than 75% of action steps are completed on time 2 = Action steps are tracked and more than 75% of action steps are completed on time
		PARENT AND FAMILY	
Parent Engagement	Parents and caregivers will be engaged when their students are identified as needing additional interventions and/or support	COST database	0 = Less than 75% of COST referrals in the database include a completed parent engagement action item 1 = At least 75% of COST referrals in the database include a completed parent engagement action item 2 = At least 90% of COST referrals in the database include a completed parent engagement action item

TEACHERS			
Universal Referral Form	Referral will be collaboratively created and made accessible to all staff	COST master file	0 = No universal referral form or not accessible to all staff 1 = Universal referral form accessible to all staff	1
Referral Form Training	A formal training/introduction on the use of the referral form and the teacher's roles in the referral and COST process will be completed	PD and/or staff meeting notes	0 = Formal training has not occurred 1 = Formal training provided to some teachers and school staff 2 = Formal training provided to all teachers and school staff	2
Referral Use by Teachers	Teachers report that they know how to refer a student to COST	End-of-year teacher survey	0 = Less than 50% of teachers report that they know how to make a referral when a student is in need of additional support 1 = 50–75% of teachers report that they know how to make a referral 2 = More than 75% of teachers report that they know how to make a referral	2
Score range for "COST" at school level			0–19	19
Categories of "COST" at school level			Low: 0–8.5; Medium: 9–13.5; High: 14–19	
Threshold for adequate fidelity of "COST" at school level			Adequate fidelity = score of "High" (14–19)	

UNIVERSAL SUPPORTS/TIER 1

Key Indicators	Operational Definition for Indicator	Fidelity Data Source(s) for Indicator	Fidelity Scores	Weight
SYSTEMS AND LEADERSHIP				
SWPBS Fidelity Assessment and Goals	SWPBS implementation inventory will be completed and results will be integrated into the annual implementation plan (AIP)	AIP	0 = SWPBS implementation inventory not completed and goals/objectives are not integrated into AIP 1 = SWPBS implementation inventory completed but results and goals/objectives are not integrated into the AIP 2 = SWPBS implementation inventory completed and results and goals/objectives integrated into AIP	2
School Culture Assessment Instrument Implementation (SCAI) Assessment and Goals	SCAI will be completed and results will be integrated into AIP	AIP	0 = SCAI not completed and tier one culture and climate goals/objectives are not integrated into AIP 1 = SCAI completed but results and culture and climate goals/objectives are not integrated into AIP 2 = SCAI completed and results and goals/objectives integrated into AIP	2

Trauma-Informed Index Assessment and Goals	Trauma-Informed Index will be completed and results will be integrated into AIP	AIP	0 = Trauma-Informed Index not completed and trauma-informed goals/objectives are not integrated into AIP 1 = Trauma-Informed Index completed but results and trauma-informed goals/objectives are not integrated into AIP 2 = Trauma-Informed Index completed and results and trauma-informed goals/objectives are integrated into AIP	2
Annual Implementation Plan (AIP) Review	Team will review progress made toward AIP goals, adjust action steps as necessary, and report progress in measurable terms in line with timetable identified in AIP	AIP and C3 meeting notes	0 = AIP does not contain measurable objectives with clear timelines for each annual goal and/or does not contain a clear plan for review 1 = AIP contains measurable objectives with clear timelines for each annual goal and contains a clear plan for review, but not all review cycles are documented through meeting notes 2 = AIP contains measurable objectives with clear timelines for each annual goal and contains a clear plan for review, and all review cycles are clearly documented in meeting notes	6

PARENT AND FAMILY				
Parent Engagement Assessment and Goals	Annual assessment will be completed and parenting events, trainings, and workshops will be identified in AIP	AIP	0 = Parent engagement goals/objectives not identified in AIP 1 = Parent engagement goals/objectives identified in AIP	1
Attendance at Schoolwide Parent Trainings	Schoolwide parent events, workshops/trainings will be well attended	Attendance logs and AIP (addendum)	0 = Schoolwide trainings and/or events reached attendance goals less than 50% of the time 1 = Schoolwide trainings and/or events reached attendance goals at least 50% of the time 2 = Schoolwide trainings and/or events reached attendance goals at least 80% of the time (Note: if no trainings occurred, mark as "0")	1
TEACHERS				
Professional Development Assessment and Goals	Annual assessment completed and schoolwide professional development goals are identified in AIP	AIP	0 = Professional development goals/objectives not identified in AIP 1 = Professional development goals/objectives identified in AIP	1
Attendance at Schoolwide Professional Development	Schoolwide professional development will be well attended	Attendance logs and AIP (addendum)	0 = Schoolwide trainings reached attendance goals less than 50% of the time 1 = Schoolwide trainings reached attendance goals at least 50% of the time 2 = Schoolwide trainings reached attendance goals at least 80% of the time (Note: if no trainings occurred, mark as "0")	1

Score range for "Universal/Tier 1 Supports" at school level	0–16	16
Categories of "Universal/Tier 1 Supports" at school level	Low: 0–5.5; Medium: 6–10.5; High: 11–16	
Threshold for adequate fidelity of "Universal/Tier 1 Supports" at school level	Adequate fidelity = score of "High" (11–16)	

		TIER 2 AND TIER 3		Weight
Key Indicators	Operational Definition for Indicator	Fidelity Data Source(s) for Indicator	Fidelity Scores	
		SYSTEMS AND LEADERSHIP		
Adequate Levels of Academic Intervention Services	Responsive evidence-based and promising practice academic interventions will be delivered to meet the identified student needs	Database and participation information from partner organizations	0 = There are no Tier 2 or Tier 3 academic interventions provided 1 = There are some Tier 2 and Tier 3 academic interventions provided, but below the minimum level of service recommended by response to intervention (RtI) (at least 15% Tier 2, and at least 5% Tier 3) 2 = Tier 2 and Tier 3 academic interventions meet the minimum level of service recommended by RtI	8

				Points
Adequate Levels of Behavioral Intervention Services	Responsive evidence-based and promising practice behavioral interventions will be delivered to meet the identified student needs	Database and participation information from partner organizations	0 = There are no Tier 2 or Tier 3 behavioral interventions provided 1 = There are some Tier 2 and Tier 3 behavioral interventions provided, but below the minimum level of service recommended by RtI (at least 15% Tier 2, and at least 5% Tier 3) 2 = Tier 2 and Tier 3 behavioral interventions meet the minimum level of service recommended by RtI	8
Adequate Levels of Clinical Intervention Services	Responsive evidence-based and promising practice clinical interventions will be delivered to meet the identified student needs	Database and participation information from partner organizations	0 = There are no Tier 2 or Tier 3 clinical interventions provided 1 = There are some Tier 2 and Tier 3 clinical interventions provided, but below the minimum level of service recommended by RtI (at least 15% Tier 2, and at least 5% Tier 3) 2 = Tier 2 and Tier 3 clinical interventions meet the minimum level of service recommended by RtI	8
Progress Monitoring tools	Progress-monitoring tools that correspond to each intervention will be developed	AIP (addendum) and database	0 = Goal progress monitored for less than 50% of Tier 2 and Tier 3 interventions in database 1 = Goal progress monitored for at least 50% of Tier 2 and Tier 3 interventions in database 2 = Goal progress monitored for at least 80% of Tier 2 and Tier 3 interventions in database	6

			10
Highly Qualified Staff	Highly qualified and credentialed staff will be in place to implement identified intervention services	AIP (addendum)	0 = Less than 80% of positions are filled for entire school year or less than 80% of staff have proper qualifications for the services they are providing 1 = At least 80% of positions are filled for entire school year and 80% of staff have proper qualifications for the services they are providing 2 = All positions are filled for entire school year with staff that have proper qualifications for the services they are providing
		PARENT AND FAMILY	
Targeted Trainings	Targeted parent groups and/or trainings will be identified and trainings will be well attended	AIP (addendum) and attendance logs	1
			0 = Targeted groups and/or trainings reached attendance goals less than 50% of the time 1 = Targeted groups and/or trainings reached attendance goals at least 50% of the time 2 = Targeted groups and/or trainings met attendance goals at least 80% of the time (if no trainings are necessary, mark as "2")

TEACHERS			
Targeted Trainings	All staff receive at least 4 hours a month of professional development and training related to improved job performance	Intervention staff professional development syllabus	0 = All intervention staff do not receive at least 4 hours a month of training 1 = All intervention staff receive at least 4 hours a month of training related to improved job performance	6
Score range for "Tier 2 and Tier 3" at school level			0–47	47
Categories of "Tier 2 and Tier 3" at school level			Low: 0–16.5; Medium: 17–31.5; High: 32–47	
Threshold for adequate fidelity of "Tier 2 and Tier 3" at school level			Adequate fidelity = score of "High" (32–47)	

APPENDIX 7.3

Unconditional Education End-of-Year Teacher Survey

You are invited to participate in this survey about the academic, behavioral, and social-emotional support services provided in your school. The results of this survey will be used to better understand the strengths of support services provided as well as areas for growth. Your responses are valuable and will help to improve the coordination and quality of services provided for the next school year. This survey should take about 20 minutes to complete.

Voluntary Participation. Your agreement to participate is entirely voluntary. At any time for any reason, you can decide not to participate in the survey. Participating or declining to participate will have no effect on your current or future employment. You can skip any question that you do not want to answer. If you do not complete this survey, nothing will happen. If you agree to participate in the survey now, you can always change your mind and have your information erased. To do this, send a written request to the contact person listed below.

Risks. There are no known risks to completing this survey.

Benefits. We are offering a $5 gift certificate as a token of appreciation for your time. To obtain the gift certificate, you must submit your email to us in the following section.

Confidentiality. No identifiable information about you or your school will ever be in any reports, publications, or presentations on this research.

INTRODUCTION AND CONSENT

Contact Person. If you have any questions about this survey, you may contact _____ at (XXX) XXX–XXXX.

1. By checking one of the boxes below, I verify that the box checked expresses my consent to participate or not participate in this survey.

   ○ Yes, I consent to complete this survey and share my information.

   ○ No, I do not want to complete this survey.

2. Please indicate your preferred gift certificate:

   ○ Caffeine boost

   ○ Summer tunes and entertainment

3. Please provide an email address where you would like the gift certificate sent:

   _____

Unconditional Education End-of-Year Teacher Survey

BACKGROUND INFORMATION

4. Which school do you work at?

   ○ School A

   ○ School B

   ○ School C

5. Which of the following best describes your current position?

   ○ Classroom teacher   ○ Administrator

   ○ Other teacher   ○ Support specialist

   ○ Coach   ○ Other (please specify)

   [   ]

6. Experience

	Less than 1	1–2	3–4	5–7	8–10	More than 10
Number of years working in schools	○	○	○	○	○	○
Number of years at your current school	○	○	○	○	○	○

OVERALL QUALITY OF STUDENT SUPPORT SYSTEMS

7. How COORDINATED are student supports?

"Coordinated" means: Teachers, administrators, and support providers work together to create a common understanding of students' needs, to connect students to appropriate services, and to set goals and track outcomes. Each do their part, avoiding redundancies and gaps in service.

Very coordinated	Coordinated	Slightly coordinated	Not coordinated
○	○	○	○

8. How INTEGRATED are student supports?

"Integrated" means: The content and timing of students' support services complement their general education program. Experts in general education, special education, and mental health work collaboratively to share knowledge and provide interdisciplinary supports.

Very integrated	Integrated	Slightly integrated	Not integrated
○	○	○	○

Unconditional Education End-of-Year Teacher Survey

9. How RESPONSIVE are student supports?

"Responsive" means: Student services are flexible and agile. School teams are able to address individual student needs and respond to changes in those needs.

Very responsive	Responsive	Slightly responsive	Not responsive
○	○	○	○

10. How INDIVIDUALIZED are student supports?

"Individualized" means: Services meet students where they're at and take into account their individual strengths and challenges.

Very Individualized	Individualized	Slightly individualized	Not individualized
○	○	○	○

11. How EFFECTIVE are student supports?

"Effective" means: Services support students to make progress on their academic, behavioral, and/or social-emotional goals.

Very effective	Effective	Slightly effective	Not effective
○	○	○	○

12. Please rate the following statements about the student support team at your school (e.g. COST, CARE, SAP, SST)

Teachers, administrators, and student support providers . . .	Strongly agree	Agree	Slightly agree	Disagree
. . . strive to establish shared values and vision	○	○	○	○
. . . are creative and think outside the box for solutions	○	○	○	○
. . . demonstrate perseverance in the face of adversity in their efforts to meet students' needs	○	○	○	○

Unconditional Education End-of-Year Teacher Survey

WHOLE-CLASS/WHOLE-SCHOOL ACADEMIC SUPPORTS

13. Please rate the following statements as they relate to academic support at your school.

	Strongly agree	Agree	Slightly agree	Disagree
If I have a student who needs academic support, I know the process for seeking that support.	○	○	○	○
When I seek additional academic support, I receive a response from those responsible for coordinating student services.	○	○	○	○
My school offers the training and resources I need to effectively provide differentiated instruction in my classroom.	○	○	○	○

WHOLE-CLASS/WHOLE-SCHOOL BEHAVIOR SUPPORTS

14. Please rate the following statements as they relate to behavior support at your school.

	Strongly agree	Agree	Slightly agree	Disagree
If I have a student who needs behavior support, I know the process for seeking that support.	○	○	○	○
When I seek additional behavior management support, I receive a response from those responsible for coordinating student services.	○	○	○	○
My school offers the training and resources I need to effectively provide behavior management strategies that promote a learning environment.	○	○	○	○

Unconditional Education End-of-Year Teacher Survey

15. Please rate the following statements as they relate to social-emotional support at your school.

	Strongly agree	Agree	Slightly agree	Disagree
If I have a student who needs social-emotional support, I know the process for seeking that support.	○	○	○	○
When I seek additional social-emotional support, I receive a response from those responsible for coordinating student services.	○	○	○	○
My school offers the training and resources I need to effectively provide social-emotional supports that promote healthy relationships.	○	○	○	○

16. Please feel free to share any additional thoughts or feedback about class-wide/schoolwide intervention supports and services.

17. Are you a classroom teacher or teaching assistant?

○ Yes   ○ No

18. Did any students in your classroom receive any academic Tier 2 and Tier 3 services this year (i.e., special education services and/or push-in/pull-out academic groups)

○ Yes   ○ No

Unconditional Education End-of-Year Teacher Survey

ACADEMIC TIER 2 AND TIER 3 INTERVENTION SERVICES

19. Please rate the Tier 2 and Tier 3 academic services according to the statements below.

	Strongly agree	Agree	Slightly agree	Disagree
I found the provider(s) of this intervention to be professional and collaborative.	○	○	○	○
Providers were knowledgeable and skillful in helping me implement classroom interventions to support students receiving this service.	○	○	○	○
Students demonstrated growth as a result of this intervention.	○	○	○	○
I was well informed about what my students were working on and what growth they made with this intervention provider.	○	○	○	○
I feel that students' intervention time is a seamless part of their overall program.	○	○	○	○

20. Please feel free to share any additional thoughts or feedback about your experience with this intervention.

Unconditional Education End-of-Year Teacher Survey

TIER 2 AND TIER 3 INTERVENTION SERVICES

21. Did any students in your classroom receive any behavior management Tier 2 and Tier 3 services this year? (i.e., development of an individual behavior support plan or behavior intervention map, behavior contract, check-in check-out (CICO), one-to-one behavior support services, individual incentive system, etc.)

    ○ Yes   ○ No

BEHAVIOR MANAGEMENT TIER 2 AND TIER 3 INTERVENTION SERVICES

22. Please rate the Tier 2 and Tier 3 behavior management services according to the statements below.

	Strongly agree	Agree	Slightly agree	Disagree
I found the provider(s) of this intervention to be professional and collaborative.	○	○	○	○
Providers were knowledgeable and skillful in helping implement classroom interventions to support students receiving this service.	○	○	○	○
Students demonstrated growth as a result of this intervention.	○	○	○	○
I was well informed about what my students were working on and what growth they made with this intervention provider.	○	○	○	○
I feel that students' intervention time is a seamless part of their overall school program.	○	○	○	○

23. Please feel free to share any additional thoughts or feedback about your experience with this intervention.

Unconditional Education End-of-Year Teacher Survey

TIER 2 AND TIER 3 INTERVENTION SERVICES

24. Did any students in your classroom receive any *social-emotional* Tier 2 and Tier 3 services this year? (i.e., individual or family counseling, group therapy or social skills group, social work services/case management)

○ Yes   ○ No

SOCIAL-EMOTIONAL TIER 2 AND TIER 3 INTERVENTION SERVICES

25. Please rate the social-emotional Tier 2 and Tier 3 services according to the statements below.

	Strongly agree	Agree	Slightly agree	Disagree
I found the provider(s) of this intervention to be professional and collaborative.	○	○	○	○
Providers were knowledgeable and skillful in helping implement classroom interventions to support students receiving this service.	○	○	○	○
Students demonstrated growth as a result of this intervention.	○	○	○	○
I was well informed about what my students were working on and what growth they made with this intervention provider.	○	○	○	○
I feel that students' intervention time is a seamless part of their overall school program.	○	○	○	○

26. Please feel free to share any additional thoughts or feedback about your experience with this intervention.

Unconditional Education End-of-Year Teacher Survey

27. Please rate the following statements about accessing and using data from intervention services.

	Strongly agree	Agree	Slightly agree	Disagree
Progress and outcome reports from all additional supports my students received were available to me.	○	○	○	○
Progress and outcome reports were shared and used for collaboration and during service meetings.	○	○	○	○
I used the progress and outcome reports from the additional supports that my students received to tailor instruction and support for them.	○	○	○	○

THANK YOU for participating in this survey! Please know that your feedback is valuable to us and will directly affect the services your school offers. Please click the "Done" button to officially complete the survey. We hope you have a fabulous summer!

[Done]

8 Leadership and Strategic Planning

Researchers within the field of organizational development have made a concerted effort to distinguish between two types of change organizations experience: first-order change, in which individual parameters shift but the system itself stays firmly in its place, and second-order change, in which the system itself undergoes meaningful transformation (Watzlawick, Weakland, & Fisch, 1974). The unconditional education (UE) approach shares the four common features of complex, or second-order, change:

- *change that involves multiple processes and tools being introduced to multifaceted human service systems*, thereby requiring a certain level of trial and error to determine how the intervention best "fits" within each adoptive organization;
- *change that involves a shift in stakeholders' work roles and responsibilities*, including how individuals coordinate and communicate;
- *change that introduces new skills and knowledge*; and
- *change that requires a fundamental paradigm shift that may conflict with prevailing values and norms*, including shifts in how participants are supposed understand and think about their work (Bryk, 2016; Waters & Grubb, 2004).

Acknowledging the complexity that exists in change initiatives is often the first step in understanding how to promote their successful implementation (Bryk, 2016; Waters & Grubb, 2004). Chapters 5, 6, and 7 have introduced the framework behind the UE model and its core principles of practice. This chapter will explore some of the essential strategies that promote successful implementation within a wide range of school and district settings, including (1) the role of leadership in initiating complex change, (2) the common developmental stages that begin UE transformation, and (3) the financial drivers capable of sustaining change over time.

THE ROLE OF LEADERSHIP IN GUIDING IMPLEMENTATION

Initiating a complex change process requires an intentional approach. Successful implementation of UE hinges on the ability of leaders to inspire a unified vision across all stakeholders while simultaneously connecting this vision to concrete actions that create a clear path forward. Rather than assuming an overwhelmingly positive response, successful UE leaders anticipate skepticism and resistance. They celebrate early adopters, but also make plans to ensure the voices of dissenters are included in decision-making. Rather than ignore the feedback of certain members of their team, they adopt their concerns as their own and work to address them. Successful implementation efforts begin with leaders who connect their teams to the core commitments of UE, particularly the beliefs that:

- All students can learn and thrive when given the appropriate level of support.
- Students' unbound potential is best realized when all students feel connected, safe, and welcomed within their schools, homes, and communities.
- Students are most effectively served when leaders, staff, families, youth, and community partners work hand in hand and learn from each other's experience and expertise.

What's more, successful leaders tie these core commitments back to the overall vision of the school itself, so that staff, parents, and students make connections between new practices and the school's existing mission. The specific stages of UE implementation where this alignment is built are described in more detail in the next section.

By the time schools begin actively looking for more holistic solutions to meet the needs of their students, they are often feeling a great sense of urgency for change. In these moments it can be all too easy to jump to reactive solutions that may provide short term relief, but lack sustainability. Inevitably, schools that attempt to skip any of the crucial stages described next will spend precious time back-peddling. Instead, engaging in complex change requires teams to be grounded in their vision, soliciting input from and cultivating alignment of all members. Doing so allows individual school communities to engage in the complex change that results in long-term success.

STAGES OF IMPLEMENTATION

Change takes time, especially within complex organizations like urban schools. To mark progress and success amidst this difficult process it can be useful to turn to change experts, such as the National Implementation Research Network, to understand typical mile markers and stages of successful organizational transformation.[1] Although these stages are presented here in a linear fashion, it is important to remember that they are dynamic in nature, with schools moving back and forth among stages as circumstances within the community develop and change. This

[1] See http://nirn.fpg.unc.edu/learn-implementation/implementation-stages

reality requires a sense of flexibility and responsiveness from leaders, who must recognize dynamic changes and shift their approach accordingly.

Breaking apart long-term change efforts into short-term, attainable goals throughout each stage of the process enables school communities to participate in ongoing reflection and celebrate the small, incremental accomplishments that together lead to the larger victory (DuFour, 2002; Schmoker, 1996, 2004). This approach, further explored in Chapter 4 within the discussion of learning theory, is promoted by numerous experts in the field, who encourage school leaders to create professional learning communities that focus on incremental change by "creating conditions for teams... to continuously achieve short-term wins" (Schmoker, 2004, p. 427). Schmoker (1996) further notes that while many schools are working on massive system-wide plans to implement the sort of change this book describes, most of these plans never move beyond philosophical discussions. Instead, Schmoker (1996) calls for immediate responsiveness to issues that have been formally identified and supports the call for incremental change analysis, even if seen as baby steps or "small wins." In the sections that follow, we outline the "small wins" that make up each developmental stage.

Stabilization

Too often, the impetus for change comes once a school community has reached a state of crisis. In many cases, the inability to meet the intense needs of a small number of students spirals into a deterioration in the overall school climate, thereby adversely impacting a much larger group of students, as well as the adults who are tasked with their learning. When embarking on the journey to serve students unconditionally, schools experiencing elevated levels of crisis must first work to reinstate a calm, safe, and predictable school environment. Only then are they fully equipped to institute systems-level change.

When schools begin to think through and invest in de-escalating acute crises, they must first prioritize targeted areas likely to have a major positive impact on the trajectory of healing a school community (see Box 8.1). For example, if data analysis readily shows that office referrals spike after recess, a school principal may wisely consider strategies particular to that period of time. Meanwhile, if it is noted that most challenges arise from four classrooms with relatively new teachers, immediate supports in those particular pockets may be warranted. Leaders are encouraged to make the most efficient use of existing resources, supplementing strategically with temporary, outside resources only when absolutely necessary.

Reflective Assessment

Once safety and order are restored, the school community is well positioned to embark on the path of reflective assessment. This marks the formal beginning of the transformation process. During this time, school leaders and key stakeholders have

Box 8.1 Stabilization Stage Milestones

- Trends related to schoolwide behavioral challenges are analyzed (time of day, individuals involved, location, etc.) and key strategies are identified to help reinstate a safe and predictable school climate

- Trends related to high staff turnover, disengaged or highly dissatisfied parents, or other problematic relational challenges that impede collaborative visioning and planning toward transformational change are analyzed.

- Individualized plans are developed for students demonstrating acute behavioral needs.

- A joint understanding is developed among teachers as to which kinds of behaviors should be addressed in the classroom and which behaviors warrant a referral for additional levels of support, and clear systems for referring students are established and widely understood and utilized across the school community.

- A consistent and safe space within the school is established where students go to receive additional behavioral support from identified staff; the front office is calm and orderly.

- Procedures are developed to promote safe and structured transition periods (e.g., use of bells and clear expectations for behavior during transitions) with adequate supervision, based on the developmental level of students.

- Procedures are developed to assist staff overseeing lunch, recess, elective classes, and before- and after-school programs in responding to students who are demonstrating behavioral and/or social challenges.

- A unified crisis-response and notifications procedure is implemented, including a clear understanding of who participates in crisis decision-making and processes for communication with parents and caregivers.

- Schoolwide, classroom-specific, and individual-student positive incentive systems are implemented.

- Practices are instituted that help develop intentional relationships, engage in practices of mattering, and address barriers to self-care.

- All staff engage in training and coaching on understanding the effects of trauma, identifying a student's internal working model, intervening with a disconfirming stance, employing specific behavioral interventions matched to behavioral function, and practicing of self-care and self-control.

the opportunity to evaluate both the readiness and capacity for change within the organization, as well as the current strengths and areas for growth in terms of instruction, school climate, and multi-tiered systems of academic, behavioral, and social-emotional support. Taking time to complete a thorough assessment helps ensure that the highest priorities are identified and addressed and that the change

Box 8.2 Reflective Assessment Stage Milestones

- Qualitative and quantitative feedback is solicited from the entire school community (students, parents, and faculty/staff) to assess
  - The extent to which their school community operates as a learning organization
  - Quality of existing school culture and climate
  - Effectiveness of behavioral intervention and response processes
  - Implementation of trauma-informed practices across the school
- Existing multi-tiered supports are mapped out, including
  - Screening tools used schoolwide to identify students with academic, behavioral, social-emotional, and health needs
  - Data systems and progress monitoring tools utilized by school staff and partners
  - Coordination of services processes, team members, and meeting structures and protocols to ensure student needs are identified and addressed
  - Academic, behavioral, and social-emotional interventions available at each tier
  - Roles and responsibilities of each school staff member and their relationships to one another
- Distribution of student needs, corresponding caseloads, and staff hours across the three tiers of service are mapped out
- Assessment results are shared with staff and other relevant stakeholders (parents, district leadership, community members, etc.)

process builds upon existing strengths and resources (see Box 8.2). This intentional approach promotes a transformation process that is both efficient and effective. When leveraged as a collaborative opportunity to gather insight and input, the assessment process can increase investment from staff, families, students, and community stakeholders alike. UE's current reflective assessment practices are further outlined in Chapter 7.

Coordination of Existing Resources and Services

With the results of the comprehensive assessment process in hand, school leaders are ready to engage in strategic identification of existing strengths and resource gaps. An effective understanding and reallocation of current resources is a crucial step that must precede any efforts to introduce additional supports (see Box 8.3). While it can be tempting to skip directly to the introduction of new resources, coordination is a necessary prior step. Adding supports before determining what strategic gaps they are intended to fill may provide some short-term relief but will ultimately perpetuate an unbalanced and incoherent system unable to meet the current or future needs of the community it serves.

Box 8.3 Coordination of Existing Resources Stage Milestones

- Current strengths, redundancies, gaps, and priorities in school culture and climate and intervention systems are identified
- Annual implementation plan is created
- Coordination of services team (COST) is established and universal student referral form is created
- Roles and responsibilities of each school staff member are articulated and community partners align behind a shared vision and goals;
- Joint accountability toward the success of intervention systems and plans is established amongst team members
- Processes for the continuous review of data and for responding to areas of unmet need are identified

Strategic Identification of New Resources

Once existing assets have been strategically realigned, implementation teams may begin to research the resources they will need to complete a comprehensive and coordinated service delivery system. Potential tools, programs and partners should be vetted to identify those that are best suited to for the local context of the school community (see Box 8.4).

Box 8.4 Strategic Identification Stage Milestones

- Appropriate resources to meet remaining needs are identified, including
  - Data tools that help to track and monitor indicators needed for decision-making
  - Curricula/interventions that are culturally relevant and target areas of identified student need
  - Community providers aligned with the school's vision, mission, and goals and who have a track record of high-quality services
- A plan to monitor ongoing effectiveness of interventions and UE implementation fidelity is developed
- School community remains engaged in meaningful and productive collaboration and relationship building, consistently challenging the limits of the school's capacity to serve all students exceptionally

FINANCING CHANGE

The aim of the four developmental stages just outlined is to create improved systems for schools and better outcomes for students. But how can a school with limited funding possibly fill the existing gaps? How can this lead to sustainability? On the surface, the financial premise of UE is simple: create cost savings by building more efficient systems, then reinvest these savings into prevention and early intervention efforts. Over time, an investment in prevention and early intervention translates into fewer students reaching higher levels of need. Resources that are no longer being spent on intensive services can then be freed up for other means. First, they can be used to ensure that students who truly do have specialized needs can receive comprehensive supports. Beyond that, these newly available resources can be further invested into early interventions and preventative care.

Investing in Wellness

Helping schools develop a self-sustaining system that promotes prevention and early intervention requires an initial 3- to 5-year investment per school. This investment supports the scope of services typically held by the UE coach. This role is dedicated to enacting such systems as the school's culture and climate committee (C3) and the coordination of services team (COST), as well as the identification and implementation of the various databases, tools, and systems each will use in their work. Once cost savings from the reduction of higher-level placements is realized, these savings can be reinvested as the sustainable funding source needed for continuity in school culture, climate, and coordination improvements. This reduction of student placements within isolated and restrictive settings curtails unsustainable spending by districts. Equally important, it also has an increasingly positive impact on the educational opportunities of high-needs youth.

While simple in theory, the integration and coordination of the diverse set of funding streams required to implement this systems transformation can prove slightly more complex in its execution. In identifying a starting point for the reconfiguration of resources, districts and schools should consider that the highest payoff generally comes from streamlining budget areas that are simultaneously resource intensive and highly inefficient. Special education and mental health placements often fit the bill. This is especially true for under-resourced districts, where these placements occur at disproportionately high rates. It is estimated that for many urban schools that serve students who regularly experience stressors such as poverty and exposure to violence, over 50% of youth manifest significant behavioral, learning, and emotional challenges (Center for Mental Health in Schools, 2003).

These same students are in turn more frequently referred for disciplinary action or to the highest level of intervention. Those with the greatest needs are often assigned to restrictive and costly environments that, while meant to provide short-term help, often exacerbate educational disparities.

In the state of California, more than 60% of special education expenditures are allocated for non-public schools and separate classrooms, with some districts allocating as much as 80% of their special education expenditures to these isolating settings (Ed-Data, n.d.; Steward, Steward, Blair, Jo, & Hill, 2008). Similarly, Massachusetts, completed a survey of districts and found that, on average, 6% of its overall budget and 33% of its special education expenditure were funneled to 1% of its students for placement in these intensive settings (Deninger & O'Donnell, 2009). In this survey, placement costs were reported from $26,000 to $149,000 per student for day programs and up to $292,000 per student for residential programs. In some states, such as California and Massachusetts, this financial lift is shared among different entities, as county mental health departments and schools collaborate to fund placements that address both educational and health-related needs. In others, this collaborative architecture is missing, putting the onus for funding these cost-intensive programs squarely on districts and schools. Additionally, because of the specialized nature of these programs, it is not uncommon for students to have to travel great distances to attend them, and for schools to have to fund their individualized transportation arrangements. One district special education director began exploring UE after tiring of the line item on his budget for cabs to transport students long distances to the only available placements, sometimes up to 60 miles each way. Not only is spending several hours in a cab a miserable way for a child to start and end a school day, this arrangement required substantial resources that could have been leveraged elsewhere in this multi-stressed district. The whole of these expenditures is extensive, particularly when dedicated to a single seat, for a single student, for a single year. Instead, advocates of UE propose that the resources currently dedicated to these restrictive settings can be more impactful to the overall system when students with substantial needs are served within their community schools.

It is imperative to underscore one particular aspect of this fiscal plan before continuing: merely transitioning to inclusive rather than exclusionary practices is not in and of itself a cost-saving endeavor. In fact, many efforts at inclusion are ineffective when districts attempt this transition with cost-savings expectations. When initiatives are enacted in the name of inclusion that simply move high-needs students back to their neighborhood schools and expect teachers and administrators to do more, they will undoubtedly fail. Successfully transitioning to a model where students are served in their community schools requires a fundamental change in the flow of resources, but not in overall expenditure. UE only works when the resources dedicated to the provision of intensive student services follow the individual students they were designated to serve. In this case, these resources accompany students in the transition back to community school sites, where decisions around how they are to be deployed to support remains within the purview of the site based team, while the district maintains mechanisms for oversight to ensure identified students receive needed support through the identified resource allocations.

If cost savings to the district don't come through cost reductions in the provision of services themselves, how are the savings required for sustainable funding of prevention and early intervention efforts realized? The answer is threefold:

- *Reduction in duration of high-intensity services.* Inclusive settings provide the opportunity to reduce the duration of intensive services. In contrast to a student having to be ready to transition from the highest levels of care in a specialized setting back to a neighborhood school where little to no specialized support is offered, embedded programs have greater flexibility to taper services as a student demonstrates readiness, thus curtailing multi-year costs for individual students.
- *Reduction in student pipeline to high-intensity services.* Schools with strong climates and cultures of inclusion will reduce future referrals to costly external services by increasing the capacity of the school community to prevent intensive mental health and behavioral challenges. In turn, this brings added benefit and service capacity to the entire school population.
- *Maximizing available public funding streams for high-intensity services.* Education funding in and of itself is insufficient to support students with intensive, cross-sector needs, including those who have experienced trauma. At the same time, youth with the most intensive educational needs frequently qualify for public benefit programs beyond education services. Partnerships between education and public service agencies can dramatically increase educational opportunity by bringing publicly available funding to bear within the school setting. The remainder of this chapter is dedicated to exploring the critical role these partnerships play in the implementation of the UE framework.

FUNDING STREAMS

UE's intentional focus on the power of relationships to transform outcomes is behind its emphasis on localized decision-making—those individuals closest to young people and families are also the best positioned to identify and implement successful interventions to support them. The application of this principle requires school leaders to consider not only the holistic needs of children and youth but also the cross-sector funding streams available to provide for these needs. This is a heavy lift. Before exploring more specific strategies for blending or braiding funds together, let us first review the relevant funding streams, including the role each can play in the implementation of UE, and existing barriers that must be resolved for seamless integration (see Table 8.1).

Table 8.1 Funding Streams by Tier and Strand

	Academic	Behavioral	Social-Emotional
Tier 3	Special education	Special education Medicaid (EPSDT) Child welfare	
Tier 2		General funds Medicaid (EPSDT)	
Tier 1	General funds	There are few available public sources of funding. Philanthropic or other private dollars can be used to fill the gap, but additional policy shifts are needed to prioritize funds for prevention and early intervention.	

EPSDT, Early Periodic Screening, Diagnostic and Treatment.

Schools' General Fund

The largest proportion of schools' revenue comes through an allocation of state funds. According to Cornman (2014) and the National Center for Educational Statistics (NCES), in 2012, state dollars accounted for an average of 45.1% of school funding. Local funding made up an additional 44.8%, with federal funding filling out the remaining 10.1%. While exact strategies vary across states, 46 states in some way tie the distribution of funding to per-pupil count (Verstegen, 2016). Within these general funds, school boards and executive leaders have relative flexibility to deploy resources in a manner that best meets the needs of their community. In such per-pupil systems, each student in each school receives an equal dollar amount. The amount is equal but hardly equitable, since the amount is largely insufficient to tackle the scope of services needed in high-poverty schools. Many states have programs built to remedy these gaps by designating specific funding streams to traditionally underserved groups. Thirty-seven states have programs for low-income or more broadly "at-risk" students, while 42 dedicate funds for students who are English-language learners. Still, when students begin school further behind and are exposed to higher rates of chronic stress and trauma, this allotment is not enough. In addition, these categorical programs create a complex and fractured web of funding that imposes a huge administrative burden on school leaders, who must learn to navigate the implementation of these resources on the local level.

Special Education

The largest, and perhaps most contested, protected program in school budgets is special education. Federal protections for students with disabilities, first established in 1975 and now enacted under the Individuals with Disabilities Education Act (IDEA), require that students with disabilities receive a "free and appropriate public education," which must be provided regardless of cost to the school or district. The federal government has yet to fully fund this mandate, providing only about one-third of the funds committed in the original legislation (Griffith, 2015). This funding gap has placed tremendous financial pressure on states, districts, and schools. Moreover, the distribution formulas for special education dollars at the federal level, and in most states, rely in part on the number or severity of qualification or placement (McCann, 2014; Millard & Aragon, 2015; Verstegen, 2016). These very funding mechanisms both create and perpetuate disabilities, and the separation of special education and general education funding creates an unintended and perverse incentive for the qualification of students and/or their placement in restrictive settings (Greene & Forster, 2002).

Take, for example, Alpha School and its counterpart two blocks over, Beta Academy. Both schools belong to the same district and serve a similar demographic, and both are run by intelligent and passionate principals. Alpha School follows a traditional approach, whereas Beta's principal has invested heavily in prevention and early strategies and service coordination efforts. Students receive extra support when they need it at Beta and, as a result, teachers are going above and beyond, and special education referrals have dropped. Meanwhile, over at the district office, the special education budgeting team is meeting to create next year's allocation plans. They look at a spreadsheet and tally up the number of students who qualify for special education at Alpha and Beta. Quite logically, they portion out supports based on those realities. As a result, Alpha School will be allocated more staff and resources and Beta Academy's extra efforts will go unrewarded, likely becoming unsustainable.

Alpha and Beta may be imaginary schools but the scenario is very real. Because of the critical protections provided to students with disabilities, when more students qualify, the obligation of the school and district to serve them grows. As the mandate to serve grows, the overall funding amount remains stable. As funds previously marked for the general fund are redistributed specifically to special education, less money remains for schoolwide preventative services and for pre-referral early interventions. In other words, the ability to provide support for any student but one who qualifies is threatened. In many places, this translates into a stark reality: if you qualify, you will get help; if you don't, you won't. Without this critical help at the very moment students begin to struggle, they fall further and further behind. The further behind they are, the more likely they are to qualify, and the snowball effect has begun. While the federal mandates of IDEA play an important role in the protection of students with disabilities and should no doubt guide programmatic implementation, the separate funding and reporting structures designated for this class of students also provide a significant barrier to a holistic approach.

On the surface, the distinction between whether a student has a disability (and therefore should qualify) or does not have one appears unambiguous. Yet, upon closer examination, the issue becomes far more nuanced. While federal legislation requires that students meet established criteria to qualify, some disability categories are clearer than others. Blindness, deafness, orthopedic impairment, and other visible disabilities have the clearest criteria for qualification. Unsurprisingly, they also have the lowest rates of disproportionality, meaning that there is little variance across schools or student subgroups in relation to which students qualify (Skiba et al., 2008). At the other end of this continuum are invisible disabilities, including emotional and behavioral disabilities and specific learning disabilities. In these cases, qualification becomes much harder to parse out, forcing consideration of how to factor in missed educational opportunity, experiences of trauma, language acquisition status, and other factors.

Students without clear-cut disabilities qualify into the special education system because it is the only means of support. There are inherent costs of qualifying and serving a student through this system. While the day-to-day experience of a student who receives a given service will look no different if it comes through a general education or special education pathway; the cost of the service is greater when provided through the special education function, owing to the paperwork, compliance monitoring, and legal assurance related to special education functions. And since these types of services have a legal requirement for provision, this increase requires schools to make difficult choices about what other supports and services will no longer be offered.

When the initial introduction of supports is contingent upon accessing a separate and centralized set of resources, perverse incentives for referral will continue. This is particularly evident in the blatant disproportionality in referrals and qualifications for youth based on race, income level, and sex. Eliminating this disproportionality will not happen unless we can close the current perverse incentives to identify students. The way to do that is to ensure that resources and expertise are not contingent upon a special education label. Otherwise, when youth of color from low-income homes continue to struggle in schools that are ill-equipped to meet their needs, our tendency to label them with disabilities will remain high as schools employ the only tactic at their disposal for securing additional resources: special education qualification.

Medicaid

Medicaid funding plays an essential role in the UE framework in schools where poverty is a significant factor. For students who qualify for Medicaid services because of low-income status or other extenuating circumstances, funds may be used to pay for applicable health-related services, including mental health treatment. By appropriately assigning the cost of medically necessary treatment to this entitlement program, the integration of Medicaid as a foundational funding stream for school-based mental health frees up general state and federal educational revenue to fund the intended educational core (Schubel, 2017).

Medicaid is a comprehensive entitlement program consisting of multiple programs and funding streams, including several designated specifically for children. While savvy school leaders benefit from understanding several of these programs in detail, including LEA Medicaid and Medicaid Administrative Claiming, of particular interest to the UE model is one specific program: the Early Periodic Screening, Diagnostic and Treatment (EPSDT) program. EPSDT is designed to provide eligible children with comprehensive health care, including mental and behavioral health services.

While the Centers for Medicare and Medicaid Services' *Guide for States* (2014) clarifies that it is the goal of the EPSDT program "to assure that individual children get the health care they need when they need it—the right care to the right child at the right time in the right setting," a number of systemic barriers exist to the full integration of these supports in the educational arena. First and foremost, as a component of Medicaid, services are currently distributed through a medical model, requiring the identification of a singular "patient" to be treated by a specific "provider" for a condition that meets "medical necessity." Like special education qualification, medical necessity becomes another threshold to be passed in order to receive help. Only once a young person has become "sick" will the system invest in the efforts to make them "well." Thus, the current approach incentivizes the pathologizing of children who have experienced chronic stress. In addition, this label-happy approach limits flexibility in the design of treatment models promoting those that focus on symptom relief and treatment rather than prevention and wellness.

A second limitation in the existing implementation of EPSDT services is related to access. State and local agencies have a great deal of discretion in the ways in which they make services available to children. Many states rely largely on community-based providers as purveyors of EPSDT services. These providers' hours, locations, or approach may make services inaccessible to multi-stressed families whose resources are already limited. Instead, locating EPSDT services within schools can offer greater accessibility to families, since schools are locations they already visit. Meanwhile, the provision of services through the school increases opportunities for the integration and coordination of students' care. Policy and advocacy efforts are needed in many states in order to make this transformational shift.

Private Insurance Providers

While many children in high-poverty schools are eligible for the EPSDT benefits, some students may be the recipients of care through managed healthcare or other private provider plans. For those students who have access to private insurance, it can be beneficial for districts or other large networks of schools to build relationships with private health insurers. Such partnerships allows for services to be delivered in schools for youth who are not eligible for Medicaid services but still present a high level of need.

Child Welfare

While relatively small in comparison to the overall Medicaid program, funding from the child welfare system can play an important role in the provision of support in high-poverty schools. In particular, this funding stream can be brought to bear when a school system identifies that certain schools generate a high concentration of reports of abuse or neglect. Child welfare funding streams provide intervention to families when there is either a risk or substantiated case of abuse or neglect. When a family is identified as "at-risk," many jurisdictions have available pools of funds that can be used to support children to stay in their homes through various diversion programs. Co-locating these programs within schools, in coordination with local child welfare agencies, strengthens the network of early intervention supports students receive in a coordinated manner. In addition, partnerships between education and social services can be leveraged to implement alternative response systems, providing teachers with a direct access to social support services, particularly in suspected cases of neglect.

For youth with substantiated reports abuse or neglect, schools can similarly coordinate with local child welfare agencies. These funds provide wraparound supports to assist caregivers at the greatest risk of losing custody of their children and can be aligned with a child's school-based interventions. In these extreme circumstances of acute family trauma, careful school-level coordination with child welfare often opens up additional resources for schools, such as increased case management and access to supportive county services. For young people with significant behavioral challenges, the presence of wraparound-trained staff during school hours can ensure continued access to educational opportunity while stabilization at home is being realized.

There is another social services funding stream that can be of assistance to schools looking for holistic approaches. Each state is provided set-aside funding to offer ongoing training and education to service providers, county workers, foster families, and others working directly with youth who have experienced documented abuse or neglect. While the training funds do not pay for any direct services for students, they can be used to provide training and educational programs specially designed for adults working to meet the needs of youth impacted by family trauma. Contacting local child welfare offices to inquire about training opportunities can add to a school's toolkit of resources to offer practitioners.

Local or State-Specific Grants

In addition to the federally available funding streams, in some cases local or state dollars may be specifically allocated to the social and emotional well-being of children. Partnerships between school systems and the appropriate local or state agencies can help in translating these funds into meaningful impact for schools.

For example, in the state of California, the Mental Health Services Act (MHSA) is an income-based tax revenue that, among other programs, dedicates funds specifically to prevention and early intervention (PEI). Resources such as these are well positioned to provide the initial investment of resources needed for school climate and coordination efforts in the UE model.

FROM FUNDING STREAMS TO INTEGRATED SERVICES

The previous seven chapters returned time and again to the distinction between the mere co-location of services and their true coordination and integration. Paralleling this process, the identification of available funding streams must be seen as a necessary first step toward continued collaboration. Even when schools have successfully tapped into a rich array resources, it is only through meaningful coordination that that both gaps and redundancies can be eliminated. Beyond a school, this requires district, state, and federal entities to develop the necessary partnerships and structures to facilitate effective cross-sector collaboration.

To initiate integrated funding mechanisms, school systems must first and foremost engage in collaborative partnerships, solidifying objectives and mapping out strategies to achieve common goals. When forged thoughtfully, such partnerships between districts and other public agencies, including Medicaid and social services programs, provide new opportunities for all entities to carry out the missions for which they were designed. Children spend many of their waking hours at school and families are naturally connected to the schools their children attend. As such, schools become an obvious place for public service agencies to carry out their work while, in so doing, providing schools with additional capacity to meet the needs of their students. Intentional partnership in this area can dramatically improve the coherence and responsiveness of service delivery to children and families while increasing the efficiency and impact of the overall child- and family-serving system. Joseph Starr, the student described in the first part of this book, experienced this level of collaboration. His diverse team of providers came into fruition as a result of the combined efforts of school staff and a Medicaid behavioral health program orchestrated within the school setting. Alongside the obvious benefit for him and his family, each individual public system benefitted as well. The public agency did not require the upkeep of an off-site clinic in which to do their work, realigning more dollars to direct service. Meanwhile, school practitioners profited from the opportunity to see discipline experts modeling interventions in the school's classrooms and hallways, in turn growing their own confidence in attempting these both with Joseph directly and with others who had similar needs.

Like most other aspects of UE, assuring cross-sector success relies on a deep commitment to collaboration and shared responsibility. Beginning with the premise that holistic thinking must match holistic funding approaches, successful UE leaders recognize that multiple agencies hold the responsibility, and associated funds, for meeting young people's needs. They partner with cross-sector leaders who share a commitment to reducing the inefficient silos that tangle up these funds and keep them from effectively reaching youth and families.

In such an arrangement, it is the school leader's responsibility to learn and navigate resources outside the bounds of traditional education funding. It is the responsibility of public agency leaders and the system of care providers to act as guides, translating complicated funding stipulations and acronyms and finding concrete paths toward blending and braiding existing funding streams. Because different funding streams follow different funding mechanisms, some with stringent boundaries that dictate how and for whom they are used, funding integration is unique in each local context. Some funds will be easy to braid together, lending themselves nicely to deliver the "small wins" that enable ongoing commitment to change efforts (Schmoker, 1996). Other funding streams will require a more nuanced examination; in some cases braided funding—the intentional spiraling of discrete funding sources—is appropriate, whereas in others a blended, all-in-one approach may be more favorable. We explore both types further in the next section.

Benefits of Braiding and Blending Funding

Successful UE programs use a combination of braided and blended funding models. In braided funding models, cross-sector partners coordinate funding from individual sources while still maintaining distinct allocation and reporting mechanisms for each stream. Maintaining a level of distinction between funding streams can help ensure that certain traditionally underserved populations, such as students with disabilities or English-language learners, receive a protected share of the funding. Often, the trade-off is that a level of fragmentation remains in place. This fragmentation can be remedied through careful coordination efforts and a systematic approach to aligning resources. Blended-funding takes the merging of funds one step further, pooling all funding sources into a single stream. Rather than maintaining separate allocation, expenditure, and reporting guidelines for each individual source, a blended approach merges all funds into one unified pot. Doing so removes the ability to preserve particular funding for particular subgroups of students but maximizes flexibility to meet the needs of individuals and communities with consideration for the local context. This tension is further explored in Chapter 9. Building on the integration of systems discussed in Chapter 2, braided and blended funding models improve service delivery in important ways.

- *Services are coherent.* When public agencies act in concert, demonstrating cross-sector collaboration and sharing in decision-making, they improve the experiences of children and families. Rather than families having to access different supports and services from different entities, in different locations, at different times, relevant supports and services can be provided in a one-stop shop. In addition, having multi-agency participation allows for the integration of approaches, borrowing from the expertise of each individual discipline or player. Doing so leads to more holistic and innovative solutions to the multifaceted challenges young people face.

- *Services are responsive.* Braided and blended funding models allow for more local decision-making regarding services at the school-site level. Doing so means that individual plans can be tailored to meet the specific needs of students, families, schools, and communities rather than employing a one-size-fits-all approach. Braided funding also enables schools to use providers more flexibly and effectively. Walk into many public schools and ask about who provides mental health services, and in return you will receive a laundry list of providers: the counselor who can provide some social skills groups, particularly during periods when course scheduling becomes less of an urgent priority; the social work intern who is there every Tuesday and Thursday until graduation in May; the myriad of community-based therapists who hop in and out of the building to check in on individual students on their caseloads, and so forth. This is often the result of inadequate funding in any one area to pay for a full-time person. In this example, rather than having a patchwork list of providers, each able to provide only fractured supports to the school, the leader can ensure a single, qualified staff member can be more fully integrated into the fabric of the school community and responsive to its needs. Blended funding models that eliminate the individual qualification and reporting requirements related to each stream further allow site leaders to match available resources with the highest priority needs at their schools.

- *Services are more efficient.* When services are provided through strong partnerships, the delivery of services becomes more efficient. Fewer resources are lost to a duplication of efforts across multiple service agencies. Instead, when multiple agencies develop consensus around outcomes, referrals, service structure, tracking, and reporting, a greater portion of available resources is spent on the actual provision of services rather than on administrative tasks.

Implementation of Integrated Funding Models

There are endless variations in how districts and mental health departments can work together to maximize efficiency, improve coherence in service delivery, and increase flexibility in service provision to meet individual needs. Table 8.2 identifies key areas for planning and coordination between participating districts and partner agencies.

To further illustrate how various district and agency partners can use integrated funding in partnership, the following three scenarios provide configurations based on the availability of resources in California.

Table 8.2 Implementation of Braided and Blended Funding

Complex Change Processes	Activities for Implementation
Fundamental paradigm shift	• Agencies rework funding arrangements such that funding follows a child rather than an organization or service.
Roles and responsibilities	• Governance structures are redesigned to facilitate oversight and offer a single point of authorization for all needed services.
	• Agreements around joint leadership are established, including shared operation or appointment of a fiscal agent.
Processes and tools	• Resource mapping establishes existing service capacity and gaps.
	• Memorandums of Understanding (MOUs) are established to articulate shared fiscal responsibility, including operational cost-sharing and cost-allocation methods.
	• Joint planning and program reviews establish shared goals, metrics and aligned process for reporting on each agency's required outcomes.
	• Common referral and need identification methods are identified.
	• Regular touchpoints are established between school staff and their appropriate counterparts at various agencies.
	• Consent and data-sharing agreements are established.
	• IT systems are coordinated to prevent providers from dual entry of student information and maximize access to shared knowledge and insights across the provider network.
	• Shared employee management and performance review systems are established.
Skills and knowledge	• A shared understanding of the role, purpose, and service delivery capacity of partnering agencies (education, mental health, child welfare, etc.) is built at all levels of the organization (direct service providers, leadership, and those holding administrative functions).
	• Technical assistance is provided to support inter-agency collaboration and dispute resolution.
	• Staff at all levels engage in transdisciplinary training.
	• Students, parents, and families are educated about the networked nature of services.

The School Partnership Model

Many districts choose to partner with community-based organizations (CBOs) to provide mental health and special education services. Nonprofit providers with a history of serving children and families are often poised to bridge the gap between districts and publicly funded mental health services. In particular, CBOs that provide both special education and Medicaid services can translate between the technical operations of these two heavily regulated streams. These organizations bring expertise in finding effective solutions for students with specialized needs and often have the internal administrative capacity already built out to access Medicaid funding. Traditionally, CBOs are brought in through a single source of funding—perhaps the school needs a behavior analyst to fulfill their special education responsibilities, or perhaps the county has agreed to co-locate a CBO with a school site to provide Medicaid services.

In UE implementation inquiry into the appropriateness of braiding or blending funding is required. If successful, such approaches can increase flexibility and responsiveness to students' needs. For example, in a braided funding scenario– one full-time mental health therapist could be employed and the position paid for through a blend of EPSDT, state mental health early intervention dollars, and from both special education and general education funds. The flexibility this creates allows the therapist provide targeted mental health in compliance with the stringent requirements of EPSDT while spending a portion of their time on whole-school early intervention. The presence of a full-time clinical expert on the school campus strongly influences schoolwide, trauma-informed approaches. The importance of establishing an aligned vision, underscored earlier in this chapter, is particularly important when schools and districts partner with multi-service organizations. Creating a unified voice between school leaders and agency staff and projecting a singular vision based on shared values helps promote the sense of true partnership within the school community. This process is best supported when partnering entities engage in detailed, up-front conversations about how they will collaborate and communicate. To help guide these conversations, we have created a "Beginning of Year Partnership Checklist," available in Appendix 8.1.

Expanding the Federal Match

EPSDT is funded through a combination of state or local funds, matched by dollars from this federal entitlement fund. In other words, for every 50 cents a state puts into the EPSDT pool, the federal government will match their contribution to return a dollar's worth of services. The overall size of the EPSDT pool, then, is often determined by the state's funding availability. While not widely known, local public agencies, including school districts, can themselves put forth the initial match. In other words, districts are able to expand their EPSDT services by putting up additional education dollars from their general fund with which to leverage available federal dollars. These are not additional investments. Instead, by changing the mechanism by which districts fund current efforts, they may be able to bring more dollars to bear for students and schools. Say that a district currently spends $100,000 on student mental health services. By working with their county or state public health agencies to allocate $50,000 of their internal mental health budget toward the EPSDT pool, that same district could generate an additional $50,000 through the federal match. The execution of this arrangement requires a highly collaborative relationship between districts and requisite state and local mental health agencies. When done successfully, however, the end result is an increase in services through a more efficient application of initial funds.

The District as a Medicaid Provider

Through agreements with state or local mental health and child welfare agencies, the district itself has the potential to build the internal capacity to act as a provider of Medicaid services. By doing so, the district can directly employ a broad array of mental and behavioral healthcare professionals and implement a continuum of care that is integrated into its broader instructional program. The district can braid these Medicaid funds with general dollars and with those from special education to more flexibly implement tiered mental health and behavioral supports in a single unified system of care.

CONCLUSION

The UE model is inherently complex. This complexity lies both within the intervention itself and within the district and school systems the intervention is meant to transform. Successful implementation begins with mindset. Careful attention to creating and aligning to a vision precedes most other priorities. From there, charting out a developmental path from stabilization to full operationalization can assist leaders and practitioners in achieving "small wins" while making definitive progress toward a singular goal. In order to stay this course and put forth sustainable solutions independent of funding whims, implementation efforts must purposefully focus on leveraging public dollars effectively, reorganizing the ways in which individuals and agencies work together to meet the diverse needs of youth and families.

Performing any one of these steps successfully is fraught with internal conflict. These implementation challenges inherent within the UE Framework are further discussed in Chapter 9.

Beginning-of-Year Partnership Checklist

PARTNERSHIP AND COMMUNICATION

- Share phone numbers/emails of essential staff, and share leadership directory
- Discuss values of partnership
- Goal setting for the year
  - Review historical context of partnership
  - Review past goals, successes, and lessons learned
  - Set shared goals for the upcoming school year
- Review school professional development calendar, scope, and sequence
  - Establish what professional development sessions will be provided by partnering agencies, and what team members should attend different professional development opportunities throughout the year
- Review organizational charts, supervision/management structures and schedules
- Review meeting structures and agendas. Schedule as necessary
- Schedule recurring meeting for leaders of the school and its partnering agencies
  - Plan for reviewing problems that arise -- what meetings, how often, when
- Norm on feedback processes (what, when, how)
  - Plan for discussing and addressing staff performance issues, team dynamics, alignment issues among staff

Collaboration

- Identify how and when classroom teachers and intervention service providers will collaborate
- Develop a collaborations protocol and a plan for training staff to effectively engage in these collaborations

OPERATIONS

Team Planning

- Identify partnership staffing structures and budget
- Complete *Interventions Team Roles and Responsibilities Worksheet*
- Collect pictures and bios from staff and create an Intervention Team Directory
- Review caseloads and caseload calculations
- Review which intervention staff will attend which meetings (monthly team meetings, professional development, group supervisions, etc.)

Scheduling

- Schedule all meetings for the year
- Develop Master Schedule with identified times for intervention providers to be integrated into classroom instruction/provide pull-out services

- Create first month schedule/plan for each intervention provider
- Develop a scheduling system for intervention spaces

Facilities and Space

- Identify intervention and provider work spaces
- Coordinate need for renovations, furniture, set-up, etc.
- Identify a central area within the school to post information about the UE approach, information about the intervention team, COST process, resources for parents, etc.

Curriculum, Assessments, Technology and Supplies

- Decide which supplies will come through partnering agencies and which will be provided by the school
- Order curriculum, assessment tools and supplies needed to start the year

Financials and Billing

- Review comprehensive budget
  - Review related funding streams and billing expectations of staff ("productivity")
- Review billing deadlines (monthly, and yearly SPED deadlines)

DATA

Data Systems, Access, and Tools

- Discuss the "culture of data" on site (how it's used, how staff view it, how leadership values it)
- Identify all data systems to be used by the school and partnering agencies and develop a plan for integrating these various systems
  - Identify which systems partnership staff should have access to, either as contributors or reviewers
- Create data sharing agreements
- Import student information into relevant partnership databases

Expectations for Data Collection and Usage

- Discuss why data is collected on site. What are goals for data use? What decisions are you hoping to inform with data?
- Discuss when and how each type of data are collected. Create and share any assessment calendars or data cycles

Data Sharing and Collaboration

- Determine what type of data will be shared/reviewed with admin, with teachers, and with families
- Determine the timelines and forum for sharing data with those stakeholder groups and the methods used
  - Examples of data sources
    - Office discipline referrals (ODR's)

- Individualized Education Program (IEP) goals progress data
- Social skills groups progress data
- Check-In/Check-out (CICO)
- Mid-year and end-of-year staff surveys
- School Climate Assessment Instrument (SCAI) data
- Annual implementation plan (AIP) goals

ACADEMIC STRAND

School Wide Systems

- Develop an academic screening plan for all students to complete prior to the start of school or within the first two weeks of school
  - What skills will be assessed? What assessment tools will be used?
  - Who will complete the assessments? Where?
  - How will the data be compiled and reviewed?

Special Education

- Review student files for students with IEPs
- Distribute *Child-Find Letters*, or other similar language to parents of all students
- Collect IEPs for identified students and have them entered into appropriate database
- Set up IEP binders and store in a locked space
- Review IEPs and cross check with staffing/services plan
- Hold Interim IEPs with all families
- Identify and obtain any additionally needed specialized staff/services or supplies for new students
- Map existing services minutes and develop a first two-week plan for delivering identified services
- Develop month-to-month schedule of 30-day, annual, triennial IEPs and 504s

BEHAVIORAL STRAND

School Wide Systems

- Review *Positive Behavioral Interventions and Supports (PBIS) Tier One Fidelity Inventory* and identify goals for the year
- Prior to the start of school create:
  - Behavioral Expectations Matrix
  - A Plan for Teaching Expectations
  - Definitions of Problem Behaviors
  - Discipline Policies
- Develop a plan to train staff on discipline policies and strategies for addressing challenging behaviors
- Print and hang posters with stated behavioral expectations
- Discuss idea of handbook to be shared with staff and families
- Identify process for teachers to access immediate support in responding to a classroom behavioral need
  - What will the documentation (referral) process look like?
  - How will this get recorded within the designated behavior tracking system?

Targeted and Intensive Students

- Review student files to identify students who may need interventions
- Meet with families of targeted students to identify support plans and create *Behavior Intervention Maps*
- Meet with staff who worked with targeted students previously
- Introduce additional external services (e.g. WRAP)

SOCIAL-EMOTIONAL STRAND

School Wide Systems

- Review the *Trauma-Informed Schools Index* and set goals for the year
- Select a social-emotional learning curriculum and develop plan for training teachers and implementing curriculum across the school
- Discuss purpose of social emotional screener (SES), and develop a timeline/plan for completion
- If SES completed at end of last year, review results and next steps

Targeted and Intensive Students

- Review SES to identify students who may need initial interventions or are receiving outside services
- Meet with families of students with high-needs, identify best supports for school and complete release of information documents to communicate with outside providers
- Work with families to complete permission for participation in group services and complete release of information documents to communicate with outside providers
- Meet with staff who worked with targeted students previously
- Introduce behavioral screeners (i.e. Strengths and Difficulties Questionnaire) and discuss purpose, function, and plan for roll out (how teachers will complete)

COORDINATION OF SERVICES

Coordination of Services Team (COST)

- Identify members for your COST team
- Identify a weekly meeting time (1.5 hours)
- Plan team orientation to occur during first meeting
- Identify how you will introduce and train the larger school community on this process
- Identify system for tracking COST referrals, action steps, and follow-up/accountability for action steps
- Complete the *Interventions Plan* worksheet to identify intervention cycles, cut-points, and data collection and review processes

SCHOOL CULTURE AND CLIMATE

- Review School Climate Assessment Instrument (SCAI) and set goals for the year
- Develop School Climate Annual Implementation Plan (AIP) with key priorities for social emotional learning, behavioral interventions/responses, and coordination of services.
- Identify Culture and Climate Committee (C3) members and meeting times

- Identify specific school values around adult interpersonal relationships, collaboration, giving and receiving feedback, working with families, etc. and develop a plan to document and explicitly train on these with staff

CAPACITY BUILDING

Professional Development Planning

- Develop professional development plan for prior to start of school including:
  - Introduction to the unconditional education approach
  - Introduction to the intervention teams and collaboration protocols
  - Screening processes
  - Foundation Series (Trauma-informed education, crisis prevention & intervention)
  - COST members and referral process
  - PBIS and behavioral response systems
  - Specific chosen interventions
  - Expectations for adult behavior
- Develop year-long professional development plan including:
  - Re-teach on COST, interventions team roles, collaboration protocols
  - Strategies for managing challenging behaviors
  - Follow up training on PBIS and social emotional curriculum instruction

Parent Education

- Revise Parent Info Sheet to reflect partnership and send home to parents
- Identify how to educate parents about the partnership, services offered, and COST process
- Develop year-long parent workshop and family engagement schedule and preliminary topics for each session

9 Implementation Challenges

By now you are likely aware that unconditional education (UE) is a practice of optimization. That is, the aim is to provide just the right amount of intervention to get the job done, but never unnecessary excess. Chapter 1 introduced the key principles that drive UE: efficiency, intentional relationship building, cross-sector responsibility, and local decision-making. Much of the rest of this book has addressed what happens in schools when these principles are absent. However, in reviewing early UE implementation pitfalls, most, if not all, missteps can be traced back to an overzealous application of these principles without adequate consideration for a just-right approach. This chapter will explore these common missteps and trace the surprising ways in which an over-application of the principles of UE can unintentionally replicate the very practices of exclusion it was designed to address.

INTENTIONAL RELATIONSHIP BUILDING WITHOUT LIMIT SETTING

The previous chapters have proposed that healthy and trusting relationships play a central role when it comes to both personal and organizational learning. While the cultivation of relationships takes time, once established, the presence of relational trust can accelerate efforts. In schools highly impacted by trauma, an initial investment in relationship building is in fact a prerequisite for any successful transformation to take hold. The work of creating trauma-informed schools necessitates that we acknowledge these experiences and create plans to address the vicarious trauma often felt by school staff themselves. In some cases, even this is not enough. Organizational trauma—in which interactions within the entire building or district itself evidence the weight of working in resource-strapped environments—is common in public schools. It is often the case that years of unhealthy competition, inadequate funding, and failed initiatives and promises have overwhelmed an organization's protective structures and rendered it less resilient for the hard work required to bring about the exact change the organization needs in order to heal and thrive (Vickers & Kouzmin, 2001). Not all public schools operate as traumatized systems, yet the conditions within many schools, particularly those serving a high percentage of students who belong to systematically oppressed groups, are most vulnerable.

Knowing this, UE implementers have recognized that one of the most effective relational techniques is demonstrating attuned responsiveness. Adeptly meeting the most pressing needs of another sends a clear message of alliance and support. But what happens when practitioners rely primarily on responsiveness as a means of intervening across a system? When do attempts to respond to each and every need as it arises actually limit strategic and equitable systems reform?

When Responsiveness Inspires Confusion

During the UE implementation effort at Jefferson Elementary, responsiveness was given extra attention to help this new initiative take hold. The school had previously been staffed by an interventions team from the central office. This team frequently had vacant positions and teachers experienced long wait times in requests for support services for their students. As such, the newly formed coordination of services team (COST) prioritized responsiveness as a means to demonstrate that the school had taken on a new approach to supporting teachers and addressing students' varied needs. Further, organizational trauma had impacted teachers' expectations about the level of benevolence, support, and trust present in their relationships with others in the system. Given this backdrop, the team knew they had to intentionally overcome existing mindsets, disconfirming past experiences of abandonment. The team worked to build a culture of trust through intentional relationship building and responsiveness. In addition, the COST knew that teachers face numerous and unique challenges throughout each and every day. They have busy schedules, wear many hats, and often spend long stretches as the only adult among a sea of children who each demand their individual attention. As such, simple assistance—un-jamming the copy machine, stepping in to provide redirection to a boisterous lunch line, or managing a classroom disruption—can come as a welcome relief. Responsiveness demonstrated that COST members were noticing the pain points felt by classroom teachers and addressing them. Responsiveness conveyed mattering by delivering a message that "your need is my need." Done right, responsiveness builds relationship and fosters the engagement of teachers needed for long-term impact. Responsiveness is designed to quickly build trust where perhaps little has been built before.

At Jefferson, UE specialists bent over backward to respond to every student, every teacher, and every need that came up. A few specialists seemingly managed this feat and affectionately became known as "unicorns." The unicorns worked longer days than anyone else in the building. They managed to move the work forward significantly through careful planning and alignment to the model. They demonstrated their remarkable ability to be everywhere for everyone, to say "yes" to every request and to do so always with grace and a warm smile.

Alas, with time, it became apparent why unicorns are mythical creatures. These specialists may have mastered looking calm under pressure, but below the surface, many were fatigued and identified with clear symptoms of burnout (Hoglund,

Klingle, & Hosan, 2015). Trust is a funny thing. The first step relies on rapport building through benign offers of assistance. Keeping the trust of others, however, requires a quick integration between general responsiveness and real solutions to seemingly intractable problems (Forsyth, Adams, & Hoy, 2011; Tschannen-Moran, 2014). The quest to prioritize responsiveness pulled specialists away from the job of actually addressing the most critical needs of students. While specialists prioritized responsiveness over direct action, students rarely improved, and any trust built was quickly mislaid as teachers lost faith and came to see offers of support as just another set of empty promises. In addition, extreme responsiveness meant that specialists had little time left to document the processes they were using or even articulate clearly what they had done on any given day, leaving confusion in their wake.

Perhaps the most unexpected consequence experienced from Jefferson Elementary's quest to exhibit extreme responsiveness was the negative effect it had on some school staff. Where mistrust is common and betrayal expected, conspiracy theories abound; undefined roles and persisting questions about intentions and scope, over time, contributed to the dysfunctionality of adult relationships at the school (Vivian & Hormann, 2013). The lack of clarity regarding total in-the-moment responsiveness created a blurred understanding of specialists' specific roles. Without a clear sense of what they could or could not be expected to do, a level of uncertainty crept in for the rest of the school staff, leaving them to question: What exactly is the system for accessing help for a student? How are these decisions made? How are students prioritized? With further confusion these questions escalated: Is there a hidden agenda? What is this really all about? What are you not telling us?

Finding Balance: Structures That Promote Dialogue

Engagement and relationships without focused intervention and skill building fail to produce the desired outcomes for students, families, or schools. To balance responsiveness with strategic and sustained action, one important strategy is to create structures that allow for open dialogue among practitioners. By promoting conversation, school teams are able to continually assess where they are on the continuum from extreme flexibility to overt rigidity and make real-time adjustments as necessary. Examples of these structures exist in current implementation efforts and largely consist of a series of conversation checklists, leading teams through a set of guiding questions, rather than dictating a prescriptive solution.

One tool in particular has been useful in providing definition of specialists' roles while allowing for adaptation and flexibility. In conversation with the principal prior to the onset of UE implementation, specialists each create a pie chart that roughly corresponds to the amount of time they should be spending on different activities— from direct interventions with students, to consultation with school staff, to documentation time and planned collaboration periods. These charts are then shared explicitly, first among the coordination team and ultimately with the school staff as a whole so that all players know what to expect. As the year progresses, these charts are reviewed at regular intervals and strategically adjusted to address evolving needs. While the success of students requires that a school's team of specialists focus time and attention on the work they are uniquely skilled to do, specific time must also be set aside to address emerging needs. Within the chart a slice allocated for "responsiveness" enables skilled specialists to address the most pressing needs as they arise. Specialists on a high-needs campus will inevitably be pulled to this realm, and planning for some time in this role is an essential requirement for their own sustainability alongside that of the broader school system. In the pie chart exercise described, school leaders must decide just how much of this time will be optimal for their school.

EFFICIENCY WITHOUT STRATEGY

Questions of optimization arise in decisions about how intervention resources should be deployed across the school to maximize results, without wasting time or effort on tasks that have little to no impact on the lives of students. This book proposes that efficient systems are those that simultaneously consider the future functioning of the system itself, while working methodically to address the most pressing needs of its current members. Efforts that focus on Tier 1 approaches are a key lever for the development of an efficient system. These activities have the potential to multiply the impact of a specialist's expertise, by applying interventions to the larger systems that support students rather than to individual students themselves. But what if schools rely too heavily on systems-level intervention without consideration for the skills and capacities of their individual teachers? When, in the quest for inclusion, does an absolute focus on Tier 1 approaches stand in the way of a student's success?

When Capacity Building Looks More Like Abandonment

Amos was a middle school student who struggled to remain in class and follow any direction given to him by an adult. Amos's mom, a new resident of the country, knew little about accessing the services she needed to support herself and her son. While living in a neighborhood steeped in violence, she and Amos had experienced domestic abuse and on one particular morning had been threatened at gunpoint after witnessing a drive-by shooting on their way to school. Amos had been retained early in his school career and, now a seventh-grader, was older and bigger than most of his classmates. Like most middle school students, he was grappling with the challenges of identity formation that come along with adolescence.

After a few months at a new school, Amos' behavior began to escalate from small infractions to roaming the hallways during class time, and at times leaving the building and even school campus. Teachers became increasingly frustrated when

Amos blatantly refused their directions. He soon declined to even speak the string of providers meant to intervene on his behalf. He had ceased turning in any academic work whatsoever. Amos expressed a deep disinterest in engagement with adults. He did everything in his power to reject his exasperated team's attempts at relationship.

On the whole, the staff felt unsuccessful, lacking the tools and knowledge to make a difference for this student. In their frustration were the first signals of exclusion as various school staff began to wonder aloud if Amos even belonged at this school or whether he should have a one-on-one aide who would "make him" follow the school rules. At the heart of these requests was a sense of hopelessness and uncertainty in their own capacity. They had tried everything they knew how to do and had failed. These beliefs had cast a shadow over all of the interactions they had with Amos and he heard the message loud and clear: he was a problem, and preferably soon, he would be someone else's problem.

In an attempt to shield this student from the stigma and isolation of pull-out or one-on-one services in the classroom, the specialist team working to support Amos and his teachers advocated instead to employ a systems approach. The team believed in intervention approaches that prioritized the development of a strong and secure emotional connection between children and their primary adult caregivers. Rather than rely on direct interventions by outsiders, they eagerly set off to design interventions aimed at supporting the development and sustainability of Amos's connection with his classroom teachers. A behavior specialist initiated a functional behavioral assessment (FBA) and developed a carefully crafted behavior support plan, identifying specific interventions that adults could use that would match the function of his behavior and teach new, more appropriate behaviors. It was a beautiful plan. It was thorough, complete, and filled with interventions thought to help shape his behavior within his existing network of supports, promoting relationship building with essential school personnel.

The behavior specialist shared this plan with teachers and school leaders, carefully explained each of their roles in enacting it, and even planned sessions to model the interventions designed. Weeks went by and the team struggled to implement the plan. Still the specialist persisted, insistent on the ideal: that changes in whole-class structures and routines could be made and in doing so could enable Amos's success. But, they could not. The tension between Amos and his teachers continued to build. Frustration grew. Amos's time outside of the classroom only increased until, eventually, a change indeed came: Amos was moved to a non-public school. Intervention providers were frustrated that the classroom teachers had failed at implementing the designed behavior plans. One classroom teacher wondered why, despite her requests, help never came.

Teachers are at the heart of students' school experiences. However, the risk of relying too wholly on building teacher capacity as the primary means of intervention is a very real danger. Chapter 3 detailed the impact that stress from existing responsibilities, let alone new ones, can have on teachers' practice and overall wellness. There is also a reality that many teachers, particularly those most frequently assigned to our highest-needs communities and our highest-needs students, are new to the profession and lack the skills and knowledge to successfully execute in the face of this immense responsibility. Still other teachers simply have too many students to provide the intensity of support required for each to flourish in their care. As such, when emphasizing only teacher responsibility, well-intentioned actions aimed at "capacity building" often feel a lot more like "abandonment."

Perhaps it's not surprising that with an over-insistence on implementing Tier 1 solutions, Amos's plan failed. What Amos and his team demonstrated was that, in the end, it doesn't matter what the teacher should be able to do. When a teacher is not ready or able to learn these next skills, capacity building does not occur. Failing to consider the needs and capacities of the teacher alongside those of the student leads to teachers feeling isolated, unsuccessful, and, in turn, less likely to see themselves as capable of supporting students whose needs fall outside the norm.

Finding Balance: Assessing Readiness

An effective approach to capacity building within UE must place the teacher firmly at the center of a child's school experience, while providing the just-right amount and type of support from the specialist team. The just-right approach is not externally determined, however. It must take into account the experience and mindset of the particular teacher. Attachment theory informs us of the importance of meeting struggling young people "where they're at" and providing a caring stance capable of disconfirming their beliefs that adults cannot respond to them in their greatest moments of need. Combine this with learning theory's focus on identifying the ideal entry point by balancing the appropriate level of challenge and safety, and what arises is a call for careful data collection to determine the individual readiness of young people and their adult caregivers. Amos's teachers needed to be prepared for much more than simply learning how to implement new interventions effectively. They also needed to be flexibly supported throughout the process. In Amos's case, teachers would have benefited from a more gradual release of expectations.

CROSS-SECTOR RESPONSIBILITY
WITHOUT TEACHER AGENCY

A third implementation challenge arises in decisions around how to share responsibility for a unified system of student care. Throughout, this book has advocated that public systems beyond education take responsibility for the success of our most vulnerable students. It has promoted the notion that many students, particularly those with complex needs, benefit from the expertise of trained specialists and require an integrated system of supports to remove existing barriers to educational opportunity. Further, the book identifies that teachers are already asked to do jobs that are untenable, and that it is the role of specialists to provide a level of support such that classroom teachers are free to be the academic leaders in their classrooms. But what happens when specialists assume too much responsibility? When does the infusion of supports unintentionally limit accessibility?

When Specialized Support Looks More Like Exclusion

Javier was a third-grade student who demonstrated disruptive and at times explosive behaviors in the classroom. After several months of struggle, a counselor from a community-based organization was assigned to provide intervention for Javier throughout the school day. The highly skilled counselor arrived on campus ready to do whatever was necessary to support his assigned student. The school staff, who were feeling unsuccessful and weary after doing their best to quell these increasing escalations, were relieved that help had finally arrived. Within a few days, the counselor was assigned to be in proximity to Javier from the moment he arrived at school for early breakfast period to late in the afternoon when his grandmother could pick him up after her long work day. Javier's disruptive behaviors had only a slight reduction in frequency and duration, but now that someone was there to handle these outbursts, the school celebrated their success and considered their problem solved.

As the weeks went on, Javier continued to struggle and spent an increasing amount of time away from the classroom working solely with his one-on-one counselor. When they were in class, Javier and the counselor could frequently be observed working away from the rest of the group at a side table, and at the outset of any unexpected behavior, Javier was swiftly removed from the classroom so as to eliminate the risk of disrupting other students. During these escalations, the two went to the school's therapy space, a small room behind the cafeteria outfitted with comfortable couches, stuffed toys, and art supplies. Before long, Javier elected to start his day in this space and remain there for most of the day—in a setting where he experienced relative success—rather then enter the classroom where he knew sooner than later he would be told to leave.

The laudable intention was to promote inclusion within his home school while providing his teacher with the support she needed to teach both Javier and the rest of his classmates. However, by providing this level of intervention without focusing on transfer of skills or capacity building, Javier was isolated for most of the school day, resulting in a higher degree of exclusion than had he been placed in a separate classroom or school. By relieving the teacher of the stress and struggle required to intervene with a student with challenging behaviors, she had been freed up to focus on the other 24 students in her class. However, she had also unintentionally been relieved of something greater. Time and again, when student plans rely too heavily on specialists for deployment of interventions, teachers develop the belief that they are not capable of serving students whose needs fall outside the norm and that students who need something extra should be in other environments. When the success of students who receive supplemental supports becomes the responsibility of someone besides the classroom teacher, that teacher loses their primary relationship with the student, reducing the student's sense of belonging. This relationship, from the discussion of relational intervention in Chapter 3, is a critical element of a transformative school experience for students who have previously struggled. While intending to act as support, this intervention with a counselor created a dynamic that disempowered the classroom teacher, leading to additional levels of exclusion.

Finding Balance: Begin with the End in Mind

Focused planning from the onset of an intervention can help UE teams avoid unintentionally creating distance between students and their most appropriate champions at school. Some successful UE teams engage in an exercise at the start of their first planning meetings: they imagine a student's "graduation" from the new supports that are being put into place. They consider which adults should be sitting in the front row—for example, those who will have the longest connection with the young person, at school, at home, and in the community. From there, these UE teams plan backward, beginning by identifying the level of engagement each of these important student supporters will play throughout the intervention period, drilling in on the skill building necessary for them to do so effectively. This exercise and other intentional structures help clarify the roles of teachers and other natural support providers during a specialized intervention. On the one hand, such an approach honors the belief that teachers embrace every student, no matter how difficult that may seem. They are both instructors and case managers, all while adapting their approach to meet the unique and varied needs of each student who comes through their doors. On the other hand, the approach embraces cross-sector responsibility, knowing that often the needs of struggling students are too immense to be left to the teacher alone.

Imagining a graduation from services that are no longer necessary to sustain success is one thing, actually structuring a path to get there is another. Whether that work begins with a visualization exercise or a more simple conversation, in order to avoid the pitfalls experienced by Javier and his team, it is essential to have full transparency from the start. The goal for the assigned team is to serve as a bridge between the child's current needs and their existing team's current ability to meet those needs. This approach—planning the exit from the moment of engagement—helps protect against situations in which little progress is made because natural support providers are neither appropriately challenged nor appropriately supported to become active interventionists of their own.

LOCAL DECISION-MAKING WITHOUT ACCOUNTABILITY

A frequent misconception in initial discussions of UE is that its implementation relies on the reduction of services for students with special education in favor of allocating resources to schoolwide approaches. In actuality, the protection of the rights of students with disabilities is at the heart of the UE approach, and the provision of supports to the whole school should be a primary strategy in meeting the needs of students with disabilities in particular. Effective local decision-making must balance investment in whole systems with protections for those groups of students who have previously been excluded from the system, most notably students with disabilities. Just what happens when those responsible for decision-making don't uphold hard-won civil rights aimed at preserving student equity?

When an Underfunded System Helps Justify Inequity

By all accounts, Tasha was an amazing school principal. Having grown up in the same community Tasha now ran the school she and her siblings once attended as kids. She spoke passionately and convincingly about the school's promise and about her own path as a social justice educator. Every student at the school knew her story, too. And every morning when students arrived on campus, Ms. Tasha hugged them and told them she loved them. She spent the rest of her day planning for their success and well-being, and inevitably confronted on a daily basis the systems limitations and barriers in her path.

Tasha genuinely cared for each and every one of her students, but she was savvy enough to recognize that did not mean she knew how to serve them all well. She listened deeply to the voices of parents, students, and staff and harkened back to her own experience as a high-achieving student frustrated by the limitations of her high-needs school. And so when she would hear from her most active parents that a particular student was causing a disruption to the learning environment, Tasha often sprang into well-meaning action. She never acted from a desire to give up on any one student, but from time to time conceded that she just didn't have what was needed to serve every child. As much as she hated not having the answers for those particular students, she found pride and purpose in her role as a steward for the community, responsible for helping as many students as possible reach the shores that had been distant for too long, even if this meant a few would be lost.

As history has shown again and again, of course, there were predictable patterns in which students were deemed appropriate to be left behind. This utilitarian sorting exercise is nothing new to oppressed groups, including individuals with disabilities. As with all civil rights, the rights of individuals with disabilities have not been granted easily and would not have been granted at all were it not for the fierce advocacy of members of the disability community and their unwavering allies. Not until 1975 did federal legislation explicitly mandate the education of children with disabilities in American public schools. For the next 15 years, many students were served in unnecessarily segregated settings, until the passage of the Individuals with Disabilities Education Act (IDEA) cemented the practice of identifying the most appropriate, least restrictive environment for each child. It took over 10 additional years for No Child Left Behind to introduce the principles of accountability for special education, mandating, for the first time, that districts report on the outcomes of students with disabilities and to fill their classrooms with qualified staff. When we are talking about advocacy in the special education community, in other words, we are talking about advocacy for the basic rights and existential belongingness of young people facing disabilities.

Finding Balance: Local Decisions, Central Accountability

A discussion about where to best locate decision-making power around issues related to school governance is not a new one. For decades, schools and districts across the country have experimented with where to land decision-making responsibilities, and their answers have ranged from school staff and building principals to boards of education and superintendents. In California, for example, the Local Control Funding Formula (LCFF) has explicitly handed more control over funds to local districts and schools. Meanwhile, in some large urban districts, collective bargaining agreements spell out the need for all school staff, and predominantly teachers, to weigh in on decisions. In some of these districts, for example, school budgets cannot be approved until a super-majority of staff sign on to the plan.

Despite the frequency of the conversations, however, special education is seldom discussed. In districts large and small across the country, special education has continued to operate as a centralized function, even as multiple other aspects of school governance have been realigned to the site level. When considering the development of local control in relation to special education funding, equitable systems must protect the rights of students with disabilities, while simultaneously strengthening the whole system's ability to respond to diverse learners. When decisions are made at the district or network level about how and what individual student supports should look like and how they are accessed, perverse incentives exist and siloed implementation results. Similarly, when resource decisions are made without centralized oversight, reproducing historical patterns of inequity is a genuine risk.

School systems across the country are grappling with the best way to distribute decision-making control for special education funding, and a range of creative models have emerged that use weighted formulas to determine allocations of funding and, with it, levels of decision-making. Some bifurcate funding based on the type of disability with which a student qualifies; other are based on the amount of time a special education support is assigned. While any criteria related to funding will to some degree incentivize qualification, more nuanced systems for criteria can help to mitigate this challenge. These formulas have the potential to preserve a level of funding particularly for students with disabilities while relinquishing decisions about service design to the local level.

As some states and districts move to a decentralized approach in administering once centralized programs for other vulnerable groups of students, the question is raised as to whether similar measures of accountability could exist in the oversight of programs for students with disabilities. Federal guidelines under IDEA articulate the specific protections awarded to students with disabilities and their families, and a shift in decision-making control over funds would not, in and of itself, negate schools' responsibility to meet these mandates. No doubt, additional capacity building will be needed for school leaders to execute on this level of local control with a high degree of fidelity to ensure that explicit protections remain for students.

CONCLUSION

The implementation challenges described here are some of the many issues that force UE leaders to engage in a process of optimization to customize supports to their local context. There are no easy answers to the sticky dilemmas inherent in a complex change process. Leaders and practitioners must negotiate the nuanced balance on which successful implementation relies. For as long as students in our schools continue to confront the multifaceted challenges of poverty, racism, trauma, and disability, complexity in our approach will be required to understand and meet their needs. Only by acknowledging this complexity will we be prompted to work toward solutions ultimately capable of reshaping what we have come to expect of and accept from our public schools.

Glossary

Academic strand: One of three strands of the UE multi-tiered support model, focusing on the need for best practices in designing universal, targeted, and intensive academic interventions capable of meeting the academic needs of all students.

Acceleration of growth: The goal of a tiered intervention, the acceleration of a student's growth refers to a student's rate of growth from pre-assessment to post-assessment exceeding that of the typical learner during the same time frame; in other words, a below-grade level student making accelerated growth is one closing the gap between that student and grade-level peers.

Achievement gap: The persistent disparity in academic performance between subgroups of the student population, often defined by race/ethnicity or socioeconomic status.

Adaptive integration: A mindset of implementation that allows room for adaptation and modification of interventions as needed, so long as these modifications are consistent with the original design principles that undergird the intervention.

Adverse childhood experiences (ACEs): Stressful or traumatic events in a child's life, including abuse and neglect, which have been correlated with lifelong challenges to health and well-being.

Annual implementation plan (AIP): A UE staple, the AIP is a formally articulated set of schoolwide culture and climate goals and strategies for the academic year, often developed in the spring of the preceding year.

Attachment: A deep and enduring emotional bond that connects one person to another across time and space.

Attachment theory: A framework for examining the development and/or disruption of interpersonal emotional bonds, often between a child and caregiver, attachment theory holds that a child's first experiences with adult caregivers will shape their understanding and interactions with the world for years to come.

Baseline: The standard incidence of a given behavior prior to intervention, serving as a point of comparison for measuring progress toward reduction of a problematic behavior or increase of a positive behavior.

Behavioral learning theory: A framework concerned with the ways in which behaviors are developed or "learned."

Behavioral strand: One of three strands of the UE multi-tiered support model, concerned with the explicit teaching of replacement behaviors and the ways in which behavioral self-regulation techniques can be taught and learned.

Blended funding: The practice of joining together two or more funding streams to support a single program or initiative, with the allocation not necessarily separately tracked by source.

Braided funding: The intentional spiraling of discrete funding sources to fund a program or project, with the allocation of each funding stream tracked and reported on separately.

Burnout: A result of chronic stress, burnout is generally experienced as physical and emotional exhaustion and a sense of ineffectiveness; burnout may be accompanied by other signs of trauma.

Capacity building: Efforts focused on advancing the ability of school staff to implement strategies with fidelity, independent of outside support or guidance.

Case management: A process of individualized assessment, planning, and intervention coordination for students with particular areas of need, usually across different systems or providers.

Charter management organization: A nonprofit entity that manages two or more charter schools, providing back-office functions for charter schools to take advantage of economies of scale in much the same way that districts relate to non-charter public schools.

Child welfare: Collectively, state and federal systems which provide services to families for the care and protection of children, investigate reports of abuse and neglect, and oversee alternative placements for children who can no longer be cared for by biological parents.

Child welfare system: The system of supports for children and caregivers provided when parents are unable, unwilling, or unfit to care for their children.

Chronic stress: Constant or persistent stress over extended periods of time, sometimes resulting in health conditions such as anxiety and insomnia.

Community-based organizations (CBO): Nonprofit organizations that provide services, including education and mental health services, to members of the community and often partner with local schools to serve the needs of students and families.

Community schools framework: A school model incorporating a strategically aligned network of programs, partnerships, and strategies that connect students, their families, and the community to needed supports across various life domains, including but not limited to physical and mental health, leisure, parent training, employment assistance, and case management.

Community schools movement: The trend towards incorporating the community schools model of expanded curriculum, wraparound supports, and community involvement and engagement.

Complex change: Also known as second-order change, in which an entire system undergoes meaningful transformation.

Complex trauma: The compounded experience of multiple traumatic events, including neglect and abuse.

Continuum of care: Flexible, cross-sector services made available across time and place at all levels of need. As a client's setting and level of need shift, so do the services provided.

Coordination: The organization of a complex set of interrelated players in a manner that allows them to work together effectively.

Coordination of services: A key component of the UE model which includes the development of a transdisciplinary team responsible for reviewing data, assigning students to intervention, and monitoring their progress.

Coordination of services team (COST): An assembly of representative school service providers that meet regularly to collaborate on the development and monitoring of diverse supports and interventions across the school campus.

Co-regulation: The process by which a self-regulated adult assists a dysregulated child to stabilize the child's emotional state.

Co-teaching: The practice of two qualified educators with different areas of expertise, such as a general education teacher and a special education teacher, sharing joint responsibility for class management and instruction in a given classroom.

Cross-sector communication: Dialogue between service providers to coordinate services.

Cross-sector partnerships: Collaboration between organizations or entities representing multiple disciplines to implement a project or provide services.

Cross-sector responsibility: The shared responsibility of child- and family-serving professionals from different disciplines and sectors for the achievement of youth.

Cycles of inquiry: Regular and repeated cycles of assessment, planning, implementation, and evaluation for the purpose of affecting schoolwide improvements.

Cycles of intervention: 6- to 12-week-long intervention periods punctuated by several days of data analysis and decision-making as to the interventions to be used for the following cycle.

Data-based coordination of services: The use of student and schoolwide data to design and implement efficient and effective intervention strategies and services.

Decentralization (of funding): The process of reallocating special education and mental health dollars toward community school sites, giving school leaders the ability to make data-based decisions about what supports will best meet the needs of their students and families.

Dig-deep screener: A nuanced assessment conducted of students identified through a universal screener, clarifying specific areas of deficit to be targeted by additional support and intervention.

Disconfirming stance: An endeavor to reject and disprove negative aspects of a child's internal working model for the purposes of challenging and eventually overturning the child's harmful beliefs and expectations about themselves.

Discretionary funding: Uncategorized funds available to schools to meet the diverse needs of students, including through unrestricted state and federal funding, family or community fundraising, and competitive grants; the amount of discretionary funding a school receives from year to year is variable.

Dosage: The frequency or intensity of an assigned intervention, with the focus on identifying the "just right" amount.

Early Periodic Screening, Diagnostic and Treatment (EPSDT): A Medicaid program providing comprehensive preventative and treatment healthcare services to eligible children.

Efficiency: The strategic allocation of resources, including time, so as to maximize outputs or improve quality.

Emotional disability: A special education qualification category associated with mental health or severe behavior issues that adversely affect a student's educational performance.

English-language learner: A student whose primary language is not English and who has not yet achieved fluency in communication in English. English-language learners typically require modified instruction in order to learn effectively in an English-intensive learning environment.

Evidence-based curriculum: Educational programming which has been demonstrated through research to yield positive results for a given context or for a given demographic of students.

Exclusionary practices: Suspension, expulsion, and other school disciplinary actions that result in the removal of a student from their usual education setting.

Fail-first system: A cycle in which students must first fail in order to be identified as needing further supports and remedial services, in contrast to early intervention or preventative services.

Family stress model: A framework that describes the challenges faced by families experiencing financial strain, including undermined parent mental health, family relationships, and child adjustment.

Fidelity: Strict adherence to a model or strategy; accuracy and exactness.

First-order change: Change in which individual parameters shift but the system itself stays firmly in place; a term often associated with technical, non-threatening, simple change.

Formative assessment: Any assessment method that evaluates students' comprehension or growth in a given area for the purpose of adjusting future instruction or interventions to better meet students' needs.

Functional behavioral analysis: A formal assessment conducted by teachers and specialists that aims to determine the function of a child's problematic behaviors, often for the purpose of developing a behavior intervention plan or treatment plan to replace the problematic behaviors.

Function of behavior: The purpose or need served by a behavior, including past rewarding events or escape from negative events.

Funding: A supply of money for the implementation of a program or project.

Funding stream: A source of funding, such as local school levies, Medicaid funds, or grants.

Group therapy: The grouping of students of similar age and with similar needs for therapeutic counseling services.

Growth mindset: An approach to learning in which challenges are viewed as opportunities for growth rather than barriers, and in which performance on a given task is considered a measure of practice or investment rather than innate ability.

Gun-free Schools Act: An act passed by Congress in 1994 requiring the expulsion for at least 1 year of any student who brings a firearm to school.

High-poverty schools: Public schools in which more than 75% of students are eligible for free or reduced-price lunch. These schools are often located in high-poverty neighborhoods and lack sufficient resources.

Implementation fidelity: Strict adherence to a model or strategy when carrying out action steps.

Implicit bias: Attitudes or stereotypes that are activated unconsciously or involuntarily, affecting understanding, actions, and decisions.

Inclusive education: An educational model in which all students, including those with disabilities, learn side by side in the same settings.

Individual therapy: A one-on-one intervention in which a student receives services from a therapist, generally in a "clinic" setting effectively separate from the rest of the school experience.

Individuals with Disabilities Education Act (IDEA): Federal legislation that requires public schools to provide a free and appropriate public education to students with disabilities, regardless of the cost to the school or district.

Integration: A holistic, transdisciplinary approach capable of addressing multiple needs. Involves the removal of the artificial barriers between disciplines, allowing professionals and caregivers to work together in such a way that they begin to understand and learn from each person's expertise.

Intensive supports (Tier 3): One-to-one support to address considerable skill gaps in academic, behavioral, or social-emotional achievement, often for students with disabilities and those with intensive mental health needs.

Interdisciplinary: Referring to the analysis, synthesis, and harmonization of links between disciplines into a coordinated and coherent whole.

Internal working model: A concept describing the ways in which individuals internalize messages about their own sense of safety, self-worth, and capacity to engage in relationships with others.

Investment model: A framework that examines the long-term impact of a student's support network failing to respond swiftly and decisively to the earliest signs of the student's need for support. A delayed response can mean a much more difficult challenge to overcome.

Juvenile justice system: The system that processes youth under age 18 accused of committing a criminal act. In some cases, processing includes detainment and probation.

Learning theory: A model for describing the ways in which individuals acquire, retain, and recall knowledge. Generally broken into three categories: behavioral, cognitive, and constructivist.

Local decision-making: An approach to systems change that actively incorporates community members as experts on local challenges and needs.

Local Education Agency (LEA): A school district, charter school, or other entity operating public schools within a defined local area.

Locus of control: An individual's sense of causality and orientation toward personal responsibility. An internal locus of control translates to a more robust sense of personal agency.

Logical consequences: A response to misbehavior which directly addresses the consequences of the behavior itself rather than being generically punitive, such as a time-out or suspension. The use of logical consequences develops internal understanding, self-control, and a desire to follow schoolwide behavior expectations among students.

Mastery of skills: Fluency with a number of skills, including behavioral and social skills, to be used in various contexts and settings.

Mattering: Practices that disconfirm individuals' negative expectations for how interactions within formal systems generally flow; focusing on making staff, families, and students matter—taking time to understand and invest in what is important to them—conveys the message that their voices, and they themselves, matter, that they are valued and appreciated, and that they have something to offer.

Medicaid: A comprehensive entitlement program that makes individuals with disabilities, low-income families and children, and the elderly eligible for low- or no-cost healthcare.

Modular approach: Used to describe the UE model's 10 modules of service and the ability of school staff to design and implement interventions for a specific strand and tier of service (9 in total) and/or with regard to its data-driven coordination of services, the tenth module.

Multidisciplinary: Referring to the practice of drawing on knowledge from different disciplines but staying within their boundaries.

Multi-tiered systems of support: A service model that incorporates the response to intervention and positive behavioral intervention and supports frameworks. Support is provided at varying levels to meet students' individual needs.

National School Social Work Practice model: The framework guiding school social workers to provide evidence-based education, behavior, and mental health services; promote a school climate and culture conducive to student learning and teaching excellence; and maximize access to school-based and community-based resources.

Natural caregivers: Parents, kin, or adoptive family members who provide for a child's needs in the home setting, as opposed to professional caregivers such as social workers or medical personnel.

Natural supports: Natural caregivers and other members of a client's network that provide support and interventions outside of a specialized treatment setting (may include general education staff, general school personnel, community supporters, friends, mentors, and extended family members).

No Child Left Behind: An act signed into law in 2002 that significantly increased federal oversight of school performance and aimed to improve the achievement of certain populations of students, including English-language learners and students of color. In 2015, the act was replaced by the Every Student Succeeds Act.

Non-public school: A private, non-sectarian restrictive educational setting that serves exclusively students with disabilities whose needs are seen as too complex to meet on a comprehensive public school campus.

Outpatient model therapy: The most common form of mental health therapy available to schools, in which students have an hourly appointment with a therapist in a clinic setting but which involves little to no interaction, observation, or consultation outside of the formal weekly session.

Positive behavioral interventions and supports: Evidence-based behavioral interventions that utilize teaching-oriented, positive, and preventive strategies in interactions with all students.

Positive Behavioral Interventions and Supports (PBIS) Tiered Fidelity Index: A tool used to assess a school's use of or need for the PBIS model: the fidelity with which the model has been implemented in a school setting or to guide future implementation of the model.

Prevention and early intervention: An approach to the provision of services focused on identifying and responding to needs early and often. Service providers work to maintain children's well-being, rather than treating them only after they have experienced high levels of failure.

Professional development: Training and continuing education for staff to keep abreast of current best practice and generally improve professional knowledge and effectiveness.

Proximity seeking: Behaviors often exhibited by infants and children toward caregivers and other adults to elicit the adult's care and attention, driven by a need to feel safe, secure, and protected.

Psychology of success: An element which ideally permeates all aspects of school climate and culture that instills in students a growth mindset, sense of acceptance and belonging, and internal locus of control.

Realignment (of funding): The process by which schools or local education agencies move funds previously earmarked for some services or functions into other buckets in order to use them in new ways.

Reintegration protocol: The system by which teachers, administrators, and other staff formally welcome students back to school following an exclusionary discipline removal.

Relational intervention: An intervention in which the adult maintains a keen awareness of a child's internal working model in order to maintain a relationship, posture, and stance capable of disconfirming any unhealthy beliefs they child may have developed.

Relational trust: Mutual confidence shared between members of the school community, particularly parents, administrators, and staff.

Replacement skills/behaviors: Positive skills or behaviors to replace maladaptive or problematic behaviors which accomplish the function of the initial behavior.

Residential program: A service model in which youth temporarily reside full-time at a treatment facility and receive services, often for serious emotional and/or behavioral challenges.

Response to intervention (RtI): A multi-tier approach to the early identification and support of students with learning and behavior needs, integrating classroom instruction, student assessment and screening, and parent involvement.

Restorative discipline practices: A response to disruptive or harmful student behavior that focuses on the repairing of the relationships damaged by the behavior, rather than on punitive responses to the behavior.

Restricted funding sources: Dollars that may only be expended for express purposes and services, such as school district funds set aside for special education use.

Restrictive educational setting: An educational program for students receiving special education services in which they spend less than 100% of their school day in the general education setting.

School climate: Current conditions within a school that impact the student and staff experience, including teaching practices and interpersonal relationships among staff and administrators.

School Climate Assessment Instrument: A tool used to survey students, parents, and staff to evaluate the health of a school's culture and climate across eight dimensions.

School culture: A school's set of beliefs, values, and assumptions shared by all school stakeholders, including staff and students.

Schoolwide positive behavioral interventions and supports: A systems change process for an entire school or district with the theme of teaching behavioral expectations in the same manner as any core curriculum subject.

Second-order change: Change in which an entire system undergoes meaningful transformation.

Segregated setting: An educational setting for students receiving special education services that is separate from the general education setting.

Self-regulation: The ability to stabilize and regulate one's own emotional state and, by extension, behavior.

Sense of belonging and acceptance: A key component of the psychology of success, a sense of belonging and acceptance conveyed to students sends the message of mattering and helps to create an inclusive school environment.

Siloed services: Differentiated services, often the result of restricted funding sources, which each meet a student's needs to the extent that the accompanying funding source allows but offers no coordination of services to mitigate gaps or overlaps in service.

Social-emotional learning curriculum: Educational programming which builds the capacity of students to self-regulate their emotions, empathize with others, and build positive relationships.

Social-emotional screening: A system for identifying students with social-emotional needs at their earliest appearance.

Social-emotional strand: One of three strands of the UE multi-tiered support model, drawing on clinical expertise and trauma-informed practices to provide social-emotional support to students at all levels of need.

Social skills group: A small-group intervention facilitated by a special education teacher or specialist in which students practice interpersonal skills, including communication and problem-solving.

Specialized classroom: A self-contained classroom for interventions, support, and instruction of students with disabilities, separate from non-disabled peers.

Strengths and Difficulties Questionnaire: A survey used with students identified as needing additional behavioral and/or social emotional supports by universal screening measures. This questionnaire is completed by classroom teachers and provides more nuanced information on exactly what areas of student development should be supported.

Strengths-based assessment: A collaborative process incorporating input from the client in order to identify client areas of strength and meaningful goals for treatment that may draw on these strengths.

Student intervention teams: Problem-solving teams comprised of school staff and parents that recommend general-education interventions or accommodations for students needing academic, behavioral, or other support.

Student study teams: Teams comprised of a student's teacher, school administrator, specialists, and parents who collectively examine the student's school performance in order to recommend interventions or refer the student to special education services.

Summative assessment: An assessment that evaluates student achievement or progress as a measure of total learning or growth within a defined instructional period at the close of that period, such as an end-of-year final exam.

System efficiency: A key component of the UE model which looks at whether resources are aligned with the identified level of student need and whether schools are able to leverage braided funding, including general education, special education, and mental health dollars.

Systems of care: Youth- and family-serving systems which each provide for some component of the family's holistic needs, including food security, mental health, and education needs.

Systems theory: A framework for examining social systems and the way in which they influence human behavior and well-being.

Targeted and intensive supports: A key component of the UE model encompassing Tier 2 and Tier 3 supports, including the implementation of data-informed, high-quality interventions that are implemented with fidelity and monitored for effectiveness.

Targeted supports (Tier 2): Interventions and programs within a school that aim to provide direct assistance to students who are beginning to show signs of struggle.

Toxic stress: Traumatic experiences, particularly in childhood, that can affect brain architecture and brain chemistry.

Transdisciplinary approach: Efforts which draw on the expertise of multiple professional disciplines to achieve results transcending those of any one discipline.

Transdisciplinary team: A team of professionals representing multiple disciplines working toward a common goal.

Transfer of skills: The process by which skills that are learned given one set of conditions can be generalized across increasingly diverse contexts, increasing the independence of the individual.

Trauma Index: A tool utilized by UE practitioners to determine the existing level of trauma-informed practices within a school campus to aid the C3 in making strategic improvement plans.

Trauma-informed education: Curricula and behavioral interventions in schools which are shaped by an understanding of the ways in which trauma can impact student learning. Trauma-informed practices meet the needs of students who have experienced trauma while also generally benefiting all students.

Trauma-informed environments: Whole-school settings incorporating the principles of attachment theory and embracing trauma-informed practices when interacting with all students throughout the school day.

Traumatic stress/secondary or vicarious trauma: Symptoms that mental health professionals, teachers, and other service providers experience through contact with community violence and exposure to clients' and students' histories of trauma.

Treatment plan: A set of intervention strategies and goals informed by the functional behavioral analysis that is implemented by the client's treatment team.

Twofer: A solution to one student's needs that serendipitously translates to secondary benefits for the student's peers or school as a whole.

Unconditional care: Seneca's clinical treatment model that integrates attachment, learning, and systems theories to provide tools to assess and address youths' complex relational, behavioral, and ecological needs.

Unconditional education (UE): Seneca's multi-tiered systems of support education model, incorporating social-emotional supports that build the capacity of a whole school to implement trauma-informed practices while providing responsive behavioral, mental health, and academic interventions for students with identified needs.

Universal design for learning (UDL): An educational model used to develop curriculum that makes learning accessible to all learners, taking into account the diversity of learning styles, varying levels of need for support, and divergent interests of any given group of students.

Universal screener: An assessment tool used to assess all students' performance within a particular area for the purpose of early identification of students requiring intervention.

Universal supports: A key component of the UE model which includes all Tier 1 supports and interventions, such as the work of the culture and climate team and the schoolwide assessment and planning process. These schoolwide practices and policies that shape the experience of all students and families, fostering a sense of belonging and well-being.

Wraparound services: A defined service model that draws together a student's various support networks at home, at school, and within the community at large to foster a continuum of services in all contexts.

Zero tolerance: A school discipline policy requiring consistent and harsh disciplinary action in response to even minor infringements of certain rules.

References

American Psychological Association. (2008). *Children and trauma: An update for mental health professionals.* Washington D.C. Retrieved from https://www.apa.org/pi/families/resources/update.pdf

Anderson Moore, K., & Emig, C. (2014). *Integrated student supports: A summary of the evidence base for policymakers.* Bethesda, MD: Child Trends. Retrieved from www.childtrends.org/wp-content/ uploads/2014/02/2014-05ISSWhitePaper3.pdf

Baer, D. M., Wolf, M. M., & Risley, T. R. (1968). Some current dimensions of applied behavior analysis. *Journal of Applied Behavioral Analysis, 1*(1), 91–97.

Barnett, M. A. (2008). Economic disadvantage in complex family systems: Expansion of family stress models. *Clinical Child and Family Psychology Review, 11*(3), 145–161.

Barrat, V. X., & Berliner, B. (2013). *The invisible achievement gap, part 1: Education outcomes of students in foster care in California's public schools.* San Francisco: WestEd.

Barth, R. S. (2006). Improving relationships within the schoolhouse. *Educational Leadership, 63*(6), 8.

Blodgett, C., & Harrington, R (2012). *Research brief: Adverse childhood experience and developmental risk in elementary schoolchildren.* Retrieved from http://ext100.wsu.edu/cafru/wp-content/uploads/sites/65/2015/02/Adverse-Childhood-Experience-and-Developmental-Risk-in-Elementary-Schoolchildren-Research-Briefx.pdf

Bowlby, J. (1969). *Attachment and loss: Attachment. V.* New York: Basic Books.

Bowlby, J. (1988). *A secure base: Parent-child attachment and healthy human development.* New York: Basic Books.

Britt, D. W. (1998). Beyond elaborating the obvious: Context-dependent parental-involvement scenarios in a preschool program. *Applied Behavioral Science Review, 6*(2), 179–197.

Browning Wright, D., & Gurman, H. G. (2001). *Positive interventions for serious behavior problems* (2nd ed., revised). Sacramento, CA: California Department of Education Publications.

Bryk, A. S. (2016, March 17). Fidelity of implementation: Is it the right concept? [blog]. Retrieved from https://www.carnegiefoundation.org/blog/fidelity-of-implementation-is-it-the-right-concept/

Bryk, A. S., Gomez, L. M., Grunow, A., & LeMahieu, P. G. (2015). *Learning to improve: How America's schools can get better at getting better.* Cambridge, MA: Harvard Education Press.

Bryk, A. S., & Schneider, B. (2002). *Trust in schools: A core resource for improvement.* New York: Russell Sage Foundation.

Bryk, A. S., & Schneider, B. (2003). Trust in schools: A core resource for school reform. *Educational Leadership, 60*(6), 40–45.

Bryson, J. M., Crosby, B. C., & Stone, M. M. (2006). The design and implementation of cross-sector collaboration. *Public Administration Review, 68*(s1), 44–55.

California's Statewide Task Force on Special Education. (2015). *One system: Reforming education to serve all students.* Retrieved from http://www.smcoe.org/assets/files/about-smcoe/superintendents-office/statewide-special-education-task-force/Special_Ed_Task_Force_Report-reduced.pdf

Cassidy, J., & Shaver, P. R. (2016). *Handbook of attachment: Theory, research, and clinical applications* (3rd ed.). New York: Guilford Press.

Center for Mental Health in Schools. (2003). *Youngsters' mental health and psychosocial problems: What are the data?* Los Angeles, CA: Center for Mental Health in Schools, UCLA. Retrieved from http://smhp.psych.ucla.edu/pdfdocs/prevalence/youthMH.pdf

Centers for Medicare & Medicaid Services. (2014). *EPSDT—A guide for states: Coverage in the Medicaid benefit for children and adolescents.* Washington, DC: Author. Retrieved from https://www.medicaid.gov/medicaid/benefits/downloads/epsdt_coverage_guide.pdf

Child Trends. (2013). *Adverse experiences: Indicators on children and youth.* Retrieved from https://www.childtrends.org/wp-content/uploads/2013/07/124_Adverse_Experiences.pdf

Choi, B. C., & Pak, A. W. (2007). Multidisciplinarity, interdisciplinarity, and transdisciplinarity in health research, services, education and policy: Promotors, barriers, and strategies of enhancement. *Clinical & Investigative Medicine, 30*(6), 224–232.

Cole, S. F., O'Brien, J. G., Gadd, M. G., Ristuccia, J., Wallace, D. L., & Gregory, M. (2005). *Helping traumatized children learn: Supportive school environments for children traumatized by family violence.* Boston, MA: Massachusetts Advocates for Children.

Collier, L. (2014). Incarceration nation. *American Psychological Association, 45*(9), 56. Retrieved from http://www.apa.org/monitor/2014/10/incarceration.aspx/

Collins, K., Connors, K., Donohue, A., Gardner, S., Goldblatt, E., Hayward, A., . . . Thompson, E. (2010). *Understanding the impact of trauma and urban poverty on family systems: Risks, resilience, and interventions.* Baltimore, MD: Family Informed Trauma Treatment Center.

Committee on Education and Labor, U.S. House of Representatives. (2007). *Preparing teachers for the classroom: The role of the Higher Education Act and No Child Left Behind* (SN 110-39). Hearing before the Subcommittee on Higher Education, Lifelong Learning and Competitiveness, One Hundred Tenth Congress, First Session.

Conger, R. D., Conger, K. J., & Martin, M. J. (2010). Socioeconomic status, family processes, and individual development. *Journal of Marriage and Family, 72*(3), 685–704.

Connor, D. J., & Ferri, B. A. (2007). The conflict within: Resistance to inclusion and other paradoxes in special education. *Disability & Society, 22*(1), 63–77.

Cornman, S. Q. (2014). *Revenues and expenditures for public elementary and secondary school districts: School year 2011–12 (fiscal year 2012)* (NCES 2014-303). Washington, DC: National Center for Education Statistics, US Department of Education. Retrieved from https://nces.ed.gov/pubs2014/2014303.pdf

Cuban, L. (1990). Reforming again, again, and again. *Educational Researcher, 19*(1), 3–13.

Deninger, M., & O'Donnell, R. (2009). *Special education placements and costs in Massachusetts.* Commonwealth of Massachusetts, Department of Elementary and Secondary Education, Office of Strategic Planning, Research, and Evaluation.

Desforges, C., & Abouchaar, A. (2003). *The impact of parental involvement, parental support and family education on pupil achievement and adjustment: A literature review* (Research Report RR433). Nottingham, UK: Department of Education and Skills Publications. Retrieved from https://www.nationalnumeracy.org.uk/sites/default/files/the_impact_of_parental_involvement.pdf

Doll, B., Spies, R., & Champion, A. (2012). Contributions of ecological school mental health services to students' academic success. *Journal of Educational and Psychological Consultation, 22*(1), 44–61.

DuFour, R. (2002). What is a "professional learning community"? *Educational Leadership, 61*(8), 6–11.

Ed-Data. Fiscal, demographic, and performance data on California's K–12 schools. An education data partnership: CDE, EDSource, and FCMAT. Retrieved from http://www.ed-data.k12.ca.us

Editorial Projects in Education Research Center. (2004, August 13). Issues A–Z: Low- performing schools. *Education Week.* Retrieved from http://www.edweek.org/ew/issues/low-performing-schools/

Elmore, R. F. (2007). Local school districts and instructional improvement. In W. D. Hawley (Ed.), *The keys to effective schools: Educational reform as continuous improvement* (pp. 189–200). Thousand Oaks, CA: Sage Publications.

Felitti, V. J., Anda, R. F., Nordenberg, D., Williamson, D. F., Spitz, A. M., Edwards, V., & Marks, J. S. (1998). Relationship of childhood abuse and household dysfunction to many of the leading causes of death in adults: The Adverse Childhood Experiences (ACE) study. *American Journal of Preventive Medicine, 14*(4), 245–258.

Ferguson, A. (2000). *Bad boys: Public schools in the making of black masculinity.* Ann Arbor: University of Michigan Press.

Forsyth, P. B., Adams, C. M., & Hoy, W. K. (2011). *Collective trust: Why schools can't improve without it.* New York: Teachers College Press.

Gallup Education. (2014). *State of America's schools: The path to winning again in education.* Washington, DC: Author. Retrieved from https://www.gallup.com/services/178709/state-america-schools-report.aspx

Gilliam, W. S. (2005). *Prekindergarteners left behind: Expulsion rates in state prekindergarten systems.* New York: Foundation for Child Development.

Gilliam, W. S., Maupin, A. N., Reyes, C. R., Accavitti, M., & Shic, F. (2016). *Do early educators' implicit biases regarding sex and race relate to behavior expectations and recommendations of preschool expulsions and suspensions?* Research study brief. New Haven, CT: Yale University, Yale Child Study Center.

Gray, L., & Taie, S. (2015). *Public school teacher attrition and mobility in the first five years: Results from the first through fifth waves of the 2007–08 beginning Teacher Longitudinal Study. First look.* NCES 2015-337. Washington, DC: National Center for Education Statistics.

Greenberg, M. T., Brown, J. L., & Abenavoli, R. M. (2016). *Teacher stress and health effects on teachers, students, and schools.* Edna Bennett Pierce Prevention Research Center, Pennsylvania State University.

Greenberg, M. T., Cicchetti, D., & Cummings, E. M. (Eds.). (1993). *Attachment in the preschool years: Theory, research, and intervention.* Chicago: University of Chicago Press.

Greene, J. P., & Forster, G. (2002). *Effects of funding incentives on special education enrollment. Civic report.* Manhattan Institute, Center for Civic Innovation.

Griffith, M. (2015). *A look at funding for students with disabilities. The progress of education reform.* Volume 16, Number 1. Education Commission of the States.

Hammond, Z. (2014). *Culturally responsive teaching and the brain.* Thousand Oaks, CA: Corwin.

Hawley, W. D., & Valli, L. (1999). The essentials of effective professional development: A new consensus. In L. Darling-Hammond & G. Sykes (Eds.), *Teaching as the learning profession: Handbook of policy and practice.* San Francisco: Jossey Bass.

Hernandez, D. J. (2012). *Double jeopardy: How third-grade reading skills and poverty influence high school graduation.* The Annie E. Casey Foundation.

Hoffmann, J. P., Erickson, L. D., & Spence, K. R. (2013). Modeling the association between academic achievement and delinquency: An application of interactional theory. *Criminology, 51*(3), 629–660.

Hoglund, W. L., Klingle, K. E., & Hosan, N. E. (2015). Classroom risks and resources: Teacher burnout, classroom quality and children's adjustment in high needs elementary schools. *Journal of School Psychology, 53*(5), 337–357.

Jiang, Y., Ekono, M., & Skinner, C. (2016). *Basic facts about low-income children.* New York: National Center for Children in Poverty, Columbia University.

Kang-Brown, J., Trone, J., Fratello, J., & Daftary-Kapur, T. (2013). *A generation later: What we've learned about zero tolerance in schools.* Vera Institute of Justice, Center of Youth Justice.

Karen, R. (1994). *Becoming attached: First relationships and how they shape our capacity to love.* New York: Oxford University Press

Karnia, J., & Kramer, M. (2011). Collective impact. *Stanford Social Innovation Review, 9*(1), 36–41.

Kruse, S., Seashore Louis, K., & Bryk, A. (1994). *Building professional community in schools.* Madison, WI: Center on Organization and Restructuring of Schools, University of Wisconsin.

Lawson, H. A. (2004). The logic of collaboration in education and the human services. *Journal of Interprofessional Care, 18*(3), 225–237.

Leithwood, K., Day C., Sammons, P., Harris, A., & Hopkins, D. (2006). *Seven strong claims about successful school leadership.* Nottingtham, UK: National College for School Leadership.

Losen, D. J., & Martinez, T. E. (2013). *Out of school and off track: The overuse of suspensions in American middle and high schools.* The Civil Rights Project, UCLA.

Masarik, A. S., & Conger, R. D. (2017). Stress and child development: A review of the Family Stress Model. *Current Opinion in Psychology, 13*, 85–90.

Maslow, A. H. (1966). *The psychology of science.* New York: Harper & Row.

Masten, A. S. (2003). Commentary: Developmental psychopathology as a unifying context for mental health and education models, research, and practice in schools. *School Psychology Review, 32*(2), 169–173.

McCann, C. (2014). *Federal funding for students with disabilities: The evolution of federal special education finance in the United States. New America education policy brief.* New America Foundation.

McIntosh, K., & Goodman, S. (2016). *Integrated multi-tiered systems of support: Blending RTI and PBIS.* New York: Guilford Press.

McTighe, J., & Wiggins, G. (2007). *Schooling by design: Mission, action and achievement.* Alexandria, VA: ASCD.

Meier, D. (2002). *In schools we trust.* Boston, MA: Beacon Press.

Merikangas, K. R., He, J. P., Brody, D., Fisher, P. W., Bourdon, K., & Koretz, D. S. (2010). Prevalence and treatment of mental disorders among US children in the 2001–2004 NHANES. *Pediatrics, 125*(1), 75–81.

Millard, M., & Aragon, S. (2015). *State funding for students with disabilities: All states data.* Education Commission of the States.

Morris, M. W. (2016). *Pushout: The criminalization of black girls in schools.* New York: The New Press.

National Center for Education Statistics. (2015). *Public high school 4-year adjusted cohort graduation rate (ACGR), by race/ethnicity and selected demographics for the United*

States, the 50 states, and the District of Columbia: School year 2013–14. Retrieved from http://nces.ed.gov/ccd/tables/ACGR_RE_and_characteristics_2013-14.asp

National Child Traumatic Stress Network. (2014). *Complex trauma: Facts for educators.* Los Angeles, CA, & Durham, NC: National Center for Child Traumatic Stress.

National Equity Network. (2016). *Indicators: School poverty, United States.* PolicyLink and the USC Program for Environmental and Regional Equity. Retrieved from http://nationalequityatlas.org/indicators/School_poverty/By_race~ethnicity%3A35576/United_St ates/false/Year%28s%29%3A2014/School_type%3AAll_public_schools

Noltemeyer, A. L., & McLoughlin, C. S. (2012). *Disproportionality in education and special education: A guide to creating more equitable learning environments.* Springfield, IL: Charles C. Thomas.

Oberle, E., & Schonert-Reichl, K. A. (2016). Stress contagion in the classroom? The link between classroom teacher burnout and morning cortisol in elementary school students. *Social Science & Medicine, 159,* 30–37.

Oppenheim, D., & Goldsmith, D. F. (2007). *Attachment theory in clinical work with children: Bridging the gap between research and practice.* New York: Guilford Press.

Orfield, G., Kucsera, J., & Siegel-Hawley, G. (2012). *E pluribus... separation: Deepening double segregation for more students.* The Civil Rights Project, UCLA.

Osher, D., Woodruff, D., & Sims, A. E. (2002). Schools make a difference: The overrepresentation of African American youth in special education and the juvenile justice system. In D. J. Losen & G. Orfield (Eds.), *Racial inequity in special education* (pp. 93–116). Cambridge, MA: Harvard Education Publishing Group.

Poverty & Race Research Action Council. (2015). *Annotated bibliography: The impact of school-based poverty concentration on academic achievement and student outcomes.* Retrieved from http://www.prrac.org/pdf/annotated_bibliography_on_school_poverty_concentration.pdf

Power, T. J., Eiraldi, R. B., Clarke, A. T., Mazzuca, L. B., & Krain, A. L. (2005). Improving mental health service utilization for children and adolescents. *School Psychology Quarterly, 20*(2), 187.

Reinke, W. M., Stormont, M., Herman, K. C., Puri, R., & Goel, N. (2011). Supporting children's mental health in schools: Teacher perceptions of needs, roles, and barriers. *School Psychology Quarterly, 26*(1), 1–13.

Rice, J. K. (2003). *Teacher quality: Understanding the effectiveness of teacher attributes.* Washington, DC: Economic Policy Institute.

Robertson, J. (1953). Some responses of young children to loss of maternal care. *Nursing Times, 49,* 382–386.

Robinson, M., Atkinson, M., & Downing, D. (2008). *Integrated children's services-enablers, challenges and impact.* Slough, UK: National Foundation for Educational Research.

Rosenberg, M., & McCullough, B. C. (1981). Mattering: Inferred significance and mental health among adolescents. *Research in Community & Mental Health, 2,* 163–182.

Sacks, V., Murphey, D., & Moore, K. (2014). *Adverse childhood experiences: National and state-level prevalence.* Bethesda, MD: Child Trends.

Sadler, C., & Sugai, G. (2009). Effective behavior and instructional support. A district model for early identification and prevention of reading and behavior problems. *Journal of Positive Behavior Interventions, 11*(1), 35–46. doi:10.1177/1098300708322444

Schmoker, M. J. (1996). *Results: The key to continuous school improvement.* Alexandria, VA: ASCD.

Schmoker, M. J. (2004). Tipping point: From feckless reform to substantive instructional improvement. *Phi Delta Kappan, 85*(6), 424–432.

Schubel, J. (2017, April 18). *Medicaid helps schools help children.* Washington, DC: Center on Budget and Policy Priorities.

Shindler, J. V. (2009). *Transformative classroom management: Promoting a climate of community and responsibility.* New York: John Wiley and Sons.

Shindler, J., Jones, A., Williams, A., Taylor, C., & Cadenas, H. (2011). *Exploring the school climate—student achievement connection: And making sense of why the first precedes the second.* Los Angeles: Alliance for the Study of School Climate. Retrieved from http://www.calstatela.edu/centers/schoolclimate/research/School_Climate_Achievement_Connection_v4.pdf

Simmons-Reed, E. A., & Cartledge, G. (2014). School discipline disproportionality: Culturally competent interventions for African American males. *Interdisciplinary Journal of Teaching and Learning, 4*(2), 95–109.

Skiba, R. J., Simmons, A. B., Ritter, S., Gibb, A. C., Rausch, M. K., Cuadrado, J., & Chung, C. G. (2008). Achieving equity in special education: History, status, and current challenges. *Exceptional Children, 74*(3), 264–288.

Sosa, L. V., Cox, T., & Alvarez, M. (Eds.). (2017). *School social work: National perspectives on practice in schools.* New York: Oxford University Press.

Spitz, R. A., & Wolf, K. M. (1946). Anaclitic depression: An inquiry into the genesis of psychiatric conditions in early childhood, II. *Psychoanalytic Study of the Child, 2*(1), 313–342.

Sprinson, J. S., & Berrick, K. (2010). *Unconditional care: Relationship-based, behavioral intervention with vulnerable children and families.* New York: Oxford University Press.

Sprinthall, N. A., Sprinthall R. C., & Oja, S. N. (1994). *Educational psychology: A developmental approach* (6th ed.). New York: McGraw-Hill.

Stevens, J. E. (2013, May 13). *Nearly 35 million U.S. children have experienced one or more types of childhood trauma.* Retrieved from https://acestoohigh.com/2013/05/13/nearly-35-million-u-s-children-have-experienced-one-or-more-types-of-childhood-trauma/

Steward, R. J., Steward, A. D., Blair, J., Jo, H., & Hill, M. F. (2008). School attendance revisited: A study or urban African American Students' grade point averages and coping strategies. *Urban Education, 43,* 519–536.

Stiffman, A. R., Stelk, W., Horwitz, S. M., Evans, M. E., Outlaw, F. H., & Atkins, M. (2010). A public health approach to children's mental health services: Possible solutions to current service inadequacies. *Administration and Policy in Mental Health and Mental Health Services Research, 37*(1-2), 120–124.

Stormont, M., Reinke, W. M., & Herman, K. C. (2010). Introduction to the special issue: Using prevention science to address mental health issues in schools. *Psychology in the Schools, 49*(5), 399–401.

Sugai, G., & Horner, R. H. (2009). Responsiveness-to-intervention and school-wide positive behavior supports: Integration of multi-tiered system approaches. *Exceptionality, 17*(4), 223–237.

Sulzer-Azaroff, B., & Mayer, G. R. (1991). *Behavior analysis for lasting change.* New York: Holt, Rinehart & Winston.

Thapa, A., Cohen, J., Higgins-D'Alessandro, A., & Guffy, S. (2012). *School climate research summary* (Issue Brief No. 3). Bronx, NY: National School Climate Center.

The Education Trust–West. (2015). *Black minds matter: Supporting the educational success of Black children in California.* Retrieved from https://west.edtrust.org/resource/black-minds-matter-supporting-the-educational-success-of-black-children-in-california/

Treatment and Services Adaptation Center. (n.d.) *Secondary traumatic stress.* Retrieved from https://traumaawareschools.org/secondarystress

Tschannen-Moran, M. (2014). *Trust matters: Leadership for successful schools* (2nd ed.). San Francisco: Jossey Bass.

Tschannen-Moran, M., Hoy, A. W., & Hoy, W. K. (1998). Teacher efficacy: Its meaning and measure. *Review of Educational Research, 68*(2), 202–248.

US Department of Education. (2016). *A first look: Key data highlights on equity and opportunity gaps in our nation's public schools*. Retrieved from https://www2.ed.gov/about/offices/list/ocr/docs/2013-14-first-look.pdf

Van der Kolk, B. A. (2003). *Psychological trauma*. Washington, DC: American Psychiatric Publishing.

Verstegen, D. A. (2016). Policy perspectives on state elementary and secondary public education finance systems in the United States. *Educational Considerations, 43*(2), 4.

Vickers, M. H., & Kouzmin, A. (2001). "Resilience" in organizational actors and rearticulating "voice": Towards a humanistic critique of new public management. *Public Management Review, 3*(1), 95–119.

Vivian, P., & Hormann, S. L. (2013). *Organizational trauma and healing*. CreateSpace.

Vygotsky, L. S. (1962). *Thought and language*. Cambridge, MA: MIT Press.

Walker, D. C., & Cheney, D. (2004). *The SAPR-PBIS(TM) manual: A team-based approach to implementing effective school wide positive behavior interventions and supports*. Baltimore, MD: Brookes Publishing.

Warren-Little, J. (2006). *Professional development and professional development in a learning center school*. Washington, DC: NEA.

Waters, T., & Grubb, S. (2004). Leading *schools: Distinguishing the essential from the important*. Denver, CO: McRel.

Watzlawick, P. W., Weakland, J., & Fisch, R. (1974). *Change—Principles of problem formation and problem resolution*. New York: W. W. Norton.

Weist, M. D., Ambrose, M. G., & Lewis, C. P. (2006). Expanded school mental health: A collaborative community-school example. *Children & Schools, 28*(1), 45–50.

Weist, M. D., Mellin, E. A., Chambers, K. L., Lever, N. A., Haber, D., & Blaber, C. (2012). Challenges to collaboration in school mental health and strategies for overcoming them. *Journal of School Health, 82*(2), 97–105.

Index